JUMP
Into the Valley of the Shadow

JUMP

Into the Valley of the Shadow

THE WAR MEMORIES OF
DWAYNE BURNS
COMMUNICATIONS SERGEANT,
508TH PARACHUTE INFANTRY REGIMENT

BY
DWAYNE BURNS AND LELAND BURNS

CASEMATE
Philadelphia

Dedicated in loving memory of
Minerva Chastain Burns

Published by
CASEMATE

© 2006 Dwayne Burns & Leland Burns

ISBN: 1-932033-49-1

Cataloging-in-Publication Data is available from the
Library of Congress.

10 9 8 7 6 5 4 3 2 1

MANUFACTURED IN THE UNITED STATES OF AMERICA

JUMP
Contents

Prologue

Staring out the open door of the C-47, I see mostly nothing in the night sky of June 5th, 1944. On occasion the black silhouette of another plane on our starboard side slides into view and a bright blue flaming tongue flickers at the darkness from out of the engine exhaust. It is all very surreal and by now the time is probably after midnight so I even have the date wrong. It is actually D-Day.

Our ship is loaded and cramped, but these are solitary moments for the two rows of paratroopers lining each side of the fuselage. All talking had stopped at takeoff. Conversation is hard when you have to shout to be heard. We all shook hands and pressed our good lucks to one another before takeoff. Now each man sits wrapped up alone in a cocoon of noisy power.

We are too young to die, but we all know the odds of coming back aren't good. Many prayers have been said; before this night is over many more will be lifted. We are headed for the Cherbourg Peninsula with the hope of landing somewhere near the little town of Etienville. We are part of the 508th Regimental Combat Team attached to the 82nd Airborne Division, just one plane load of a massive airdrop behind Hitler's coastal defenses. We are the spearhead of one of the most crucial battles in history.

I wonder why I'm here but my Uncle Sam didn't give me much say in the matter. What made me think I wanted to be a paratrooper? Damned ego, I guess. If I had to be in this war then I wanted to serve with the best. With their shiny boots, silver wings and elite status among soldiers, the airborne seemed to reflect that. And now it was too late to join the motor pool or become a cook.

1

With another look out the window I make a last effort to see the
approaching coastline. Too dark, but then the red light goes on. It is
France. It is time to enter combat.

JUMP

One

"No one is to be off base for any reason."

"Woody, this is serious business," I said.

It was the 28th of May and the Red Devils of the 508th Parachute Infantry Regiment had just packed and left their camp at Nottingham, England. We were making a run by truck to Saltby Airfield. Woody Phelps rode beside me. Our truck drivers drove us right across the grass field taxi-ways and we couldn't help but notice there were curls of barbed wire all along the perimeter, with several guards stationed at the gate. Our C-47 troop carriers and the Waco gliders used by other airborne troops were having broad black and white stripes added to their otherwise drab olive coating.

"Yeah," Woody answered. "Look at the new paint jobs on all the planes and gliders!"

"War paint," came the voice of Ramon Prieto from somewhere behind me.

For months and months we had trained to be a fighting force. A year ago I had started training with the heavy machine gun and mortar. Then I joined the paratroopers. After earning my wings I was sent to communications school and my new specialty became radio operator and field telephone installer. There were hundreds of different training stories among the men but we all started a new job at Saltby Airfield. There our assignment was to wait. The junior officers and sergeants got the last minute checks underway and these we performed over and over. Early upon arriving, each company was introduced to a room where the top brass had set up sand tables with a mockup of the French countryside, all laid out with the division drop zones marked and displayed. German gun emplacements were pointed out

3

and anti-glider poles were plotted in from reconnaissance photos.

The more intelligence looked at the photos the more enemy positions they found, and each time we looked at the sand table there were more emplacements and plots. We would be facing the Germans' 243rd Division, their 709th and 352nd Divisions, and, as a latecomer, the 91st Air Landing Division. God alone knew what else they had waiting that our recon had failed to discover.

At first I was impressed with what army intelligence knew and the efforts they made to inform us. But as the next several days passed more items were added to the tables until, after a while, everyone started wishing army intelligence would just stop looking, or else keep it to themselves.

The waiting was a hard duty to pull. We knew what was coming; it was just a matter of when. Some called it Operation Overlord, most referred to it as D-Day. The one thing I was certain of was that "someday" had come. Before now it had always been, "but not today." I knew "someday" was out there. But when I was enjoying my last leave in Fort Worth, Texas and asking my girl Minerva to become my fiancée, it seemed a long way off. After reaching the Irish coast "someday" was still a distant date, and even after we settled into Nottingham and the regiment became attached to the 82nd Airborne Division, the troopers trained during the day, swung freely at night, and we didn't worry about "someday." Today, however, there were no more tomorrows to live, unless I counted war as living. I tried to stay busy and keep my mind on something else, to think of another time. Fort Worth, Texas was home but it seemed like another world now. It was a past life.

*   *   *

I remember on Induction Day sitting towards the back of the bus when John McGee got on. He looked around, saw me and sauntered my way. I soon learned that John never walked, but always had a Texas saunter, a stride like a slow, southern drawl in motion. He was a nice-looking kid with sandy brown hair and a prominent nose. He was slim as a rail and sported a mischievous grin.

Sticking out a strong, bony hand he introduced himself to me for the first time, "Hi, I'm John McGee. You headed for the draft board?"

I told him who I was and he was right, the draft board in Dallas was exactly where I was headed.

He then flopped down on my bench seat saying, "Well we may as well go together."

That started a tremendous friendship. It was May 11, 1943,[i] the day I began one of the biggest changes of my life.

John and I were on the bus early that morning. We waited while it filled up with a bunch of other inductees. Then we were taken to Dallas for our physicals.

When the physicals started we were both full of quips and smart aleck remarks, enjoying the camaraderie of our induction day. Late in the afternoon, after we were allowed to dress, our processing ended in a large lecture hall with many other guys.

An army sergeant came in and barked, "Congratulations! You men have just passed your physical. Now will you please raise your right hand and repeat after me."

Upon lowering our right hands, we were suddenly all in the U.S. Army. The sergeant then gave us seven days to settle our affairs before reporting back for active duty. If you preferred, you could have gone to camp that day. John and I took the seven days. There were a lot of guys there that afternoon, but fate had brought John and myself together, and for over a year now had kept us together. John too was a part of the 508th Airborne Regiment and we had really beaten the odds when we ended up together in F Company. He was in the 3rd Platoon. I was with company headquarters.

* * *

That was a good day but before long it led my thoughts right back to the coming invasion. Once there an image of a briefing officer kept haunting me.

"Sir," a trooper asked in humble respect, "what are our chances?"

The officer answered, "Some within General Eisenhower's staff are convinced the airborne troops will receive seventy to eighty percent casualties. That's a combined figure for the 82nd, the 101st and the British divisions."[ii]

This officer laid it on the line as if he were giving out the weather; just the facts and figures. Then he asked if there was another question.

After that last one we didn't want to ask any more.

I tried thinking of my fiancée, Minerva. She and I had met the same day I met John McGee.

* * *

It was after our induction. John and I had parted company at the bus stop and I returned home to break the news to my folks. I briefly shared some of my experiences in Dallas and discussed some final business with Dad. He knew what lay ahead. He had served in the first big war. Back then the army had set up Camp Bowie on the west side of Fort Worth. It was gone before I was born but Dad, a native of Missouri, was stationed there in the Engineering Corps. After his discharge, he returned to Fort Worth and made the community his permanent home.

After talking to my family, I told Mom I was going to drive over to see Ed Mize, my long-time school friend.

"I'll be home late," I explained, "because I've only got seven days of playing time."

The door slammed behind me as I stopped and took a moment to look at my car in the driveway. I'd had her for about six months. She was a thing of beauty: a Model A Ford two-door sedan with a new paint job, new upholstery and a rebuilt engine. Inside the house I had just told Dad to sell her, because I couldn't see my car sitting and rusting while I was away for years. After climbing into my car I just sat for a moment, running my hands over the steering wheel. Adjusting the rearview mirror and reaching down to shake the gearshift a time or two, I thought, "Lord I would miss her."

We drove together slowly, the car and I, over to Ed's house. It was going to be hard saying goodbye to Ed because he was the closest thing I'd ever had to a brother. We had been best friends since the fifth grade. We had fought with each other and for each other. Throughout most of high school we dated a lot of the same girls and even once dated sisters. He was a handsome sort, with an ever-ready line of bull and a head of wavy hair all the girls went ape over. It seemed funny going somewhere without him, but he sure wouldn't be joining the military right away. At seventeen, Ed was nearly a full year younger than I.

Inside Ed's house we sat and talked for a long time. He said he would go into the Navy, but with Ed you never could tell. He was always changing his mind. One day he planned to be a lawyer, the next he was joining the FBI. I had learned to wait and in another day or two he would pursue another dream. I told him about the examination, its poking and pushing, and about the swearing-in ceremony.

"Hey," I told him, "I met a guy who lives down in Brookside by the name of John McGee. He is going in the same time I am. Do you know him?"

Ed said. "Well yes, I know him when I see him, but we have never really met. He seems like an OK guy."

Then Ed said, "But listen, you're going into the army. This calls for some kind of celebration! Let's drive downtown and pick up my girl, Frances, when she gets off work. She can introduce you to one of the girls there and we'll go out for a night on the town."

Now, a night on the town for two men of the world like us was going to be a movie or a few games at the bowling alley. Later we might have a midnight snack at Tuck's Waffle Shop or a lime cooler at the Triple X. Those were two of the hot spots where all the high school kids could be found late at night.

Ed's girlfriend Frances worked at Martha Washington's Ice Cream Shop. We went there and sat down at a couple of counter stools. Frances saw us and came over, and we said hello. While she was getting our Cokes, I looked over the other girls who were on duty. There was a young woman at the far end of the counter with soft brown hair and big brown eyes and I thought, "So pretty! She's the one for me. I wonder if she'd like to go out."

When Frances came back with the Cokes Ed said, "Dwayne is joining the army and we thought we might all go out and celebrate, but his steady moved away so he needs a date. Can you fix him up with someone?"

Well, she turned to the other girls and thought for a moment. "How about Betty?" she said.

"Which one is she?" I asked.

"Betty is the brunette down at the other end. We're friends."

I said, "How about the little brown-haired gal beside her? What's her name?"

"Oh you mean Minerva," she answered.

"Yeah . . . she's the one," I said with a nod. "I'd like to meet her."

She grinned and chuckled. "OK soldier boy, let me see what I can do." ✓

Her name was Minerva Chastain, a beautiful girl as lovely inside as she was outside. I knew when I first met her she was something special, nothing like the other girls I had dated. My heart began doing handsprings right after our introduction, and before the night was over I found myself falling for her hard and fast.

Seven days I was given to settle, my affairs but after I met Minerva things became unsettled.

* * *

"Flash!"

A command broke into my daydream. It was John McGee. During the D-Day invasion briefing we learned to challenge with the word "Flash" and to countersign with "Thunder." We also were given a child's cricket snapper. One click of the snapper was to be answered by two clicks in return. John had walked up and challenged me with "Flash."

I slowly came back from my private reverie and answered with a half-hearted "Thunder."

"You better reply faster than that. I thought I might have to shoot ya." He tried to grin but I could see through him. He was tired, we had been there too long, and the place was becoming a prison.

"It will be dark soon," I said. There wasn't much to talk about.

"Yeah," he answered. "Do you think the town folk will miss us not coming out?"

I replied, "Well maybe. They'll miss us spending our money."

"Yes," he added, "and the girls will likely all miss ol' John."

"Sure they will, and should I bring up the last two girls you tried to introduce me to?"

* * *

One fine spring morning late in April, John came up the company street in Nottingham to see me. I figured something was up because we routinely didn't hook up together on a weekday, and never until after the days' training. But he wanted to tell me about two girls he had met the night before.

"I've made dates for the two of us tonight," John explained.

"Not if I can help it," I said.

He gave me a puzzled look. "What do you mean?"

I had to translate it for him. "McGee, there is no way I am going to join you on a blind date."

Now in the States John had been a champion at meeting girls. He still was, but in the States he was able to meet nice looking girls. Since moving to Nottingham he had met only one nice girl, by the name of Sheila Bull. Sheila, who John and I met early on, began to invite us into her home to meet her mother. Her father was away; he was an officer in the English Army. The Bulls' house became a place more suitable to call home than our tents and Sheila became a sort of English sister to me. We were always welcome there, we became very good friends, and they allowed us to show up whenever we wanted. Many a fine afternoon was spent in their home. I suspected Sheila had fallen in love with John, but I never did know what John felt for her. John might have had stronger feelings for Sheila than he showed; maybe he just didn't want her to get too attached.

"But Burns," John continued, "these are two really beautiful girls. We'll have a good time."

"Where did you meet these raving beauties?" I asked.

"In town, last night, and I told them I would bring a friend with me tonight."

I shook my head. "I'm still not going."

"C'mon Dwayne, you've got to help me out. I can't go out with both of them."

"Pick on somebody in your own platoon," I demanded, but the mulehead kept arguing with me. Finally it was agreed. I'd walk out the back gate with him and if I didn't like what I saw, then I'd just keep on walking and act like I wasn't even with him.

That night after we were dismissed, John and I got dressed to go out as planned. John said the girls had told him they would be waiting beside the rock wall across the street from the back gate. As we came past the guards these young ladies were waiting just as John had said, and just as I had expected they were ugly. Not normal ugly, but really bad, ugly English girls that you might feel sorry for.

John stopped as we came even with them but I kept on walking. He called, "Burns! Wait a minute!"

"Can't stop, I got a date in town and I'm running late now. See you later McGee," and I waved him off.

"Wait, I need to talk to you!"

I didn't say anything but just kept on walking. After about four blocks at a brisk pace John came running up, yelling for me to wait up. I stopped and looked around as he joined me.

"John, you told me they were attractive. They must be the ugliest girls in Nottingham," I had to lecture. "Now tell me again where you met them and how you managed to make a date for the two of us?"

He grinned and answered, "I couldn't help it. I met them in the dark and I never could get a good look at them."

"Why do you even bother?" I asked. "Go see Sheila, I think she loves you."

John looked kind of surprised but he answered, "Well, her daddy's an officer and I always feel like I have to be on my very best behavior. Look you don't really have a date tonight, do you?"

"Course not, but I had to say something. And if people are keeping score then leave me out. Remember I'm engaged and I don't need dates. Sure, they're fun, and I like girls. Some days I get lonely, but if I take a girl out I also like to look at them when we talk, and I'd feel creepy spending my evening looking at either one of those two."

John laughed and gave a quick glance over his shoulder. "I agree, let's get out of here before they come after us." He grabbed my arm and we left for our favorite dinner spot, the Paris Café.

* * *

Our regiment had moved in the early spring of 1944 from Ireland to Nottingham. England was more than we expected or could have possibly hoped for. The new camp was set up right next to the city in Wollaton Park, a gorgeous location with manicured greens and lots of trees. All the grounds were enclosed with miles and miles of red brick fence and black iron gates. In the center stood the great Wollaton home, which had been turned into a museum. The Wollaton home and grounds were the property of the King. On moving in, one Red Devil reportedly shot a deer grazing on the lawn for the venison. It wasn't a good start for the 508th P.I.R., as the King was not amused.

The house was a huge, four-story building with turrets and loads of ornamental work. By American standards it would have been called a castle. Behind the home and at the far end of the park were row upon row of eight-man tents.

Although we were living in tents, it wasn't primitive. All the floors were paved with concrete stepping-stones and each tent contained a very suitable heat-stove set in its center. Nottingham was a modern city with theaters, excellent restaurants and fine public buildings. The population was about 250,000. An abundant supply of fish and chips places and pubs were located all over town. Names over the pubs were some of the wildest you could imagine, like the Nag's Head Inn, Sir Admiral Rodney's Pub, and The Goose and Dungeon Inn. In addition to Wollaton Park, Nottingham had another large structure. Nearby stood a real castle made famous by the legendary Robin Hood. Street transportation in town proved to be convenient and the troopers never tired of riding on the top of those double-decker buses.

The American paratrooper loved the English people, and what really made the place special were those cute Nottingham girls with their sweet, English accents. Our American accents were probably having some effect on them as well, because the girls all seemed crazy about GIs, especially the ones with wings. It didn't take long for a sincere bonding to develop between Airborne and Nottingham residences and they soon began opening their homes to us.

There was plenty of free time that was mostly spent on nightlife in town. Most of the fellows had a favorite pub to go to, not just to drink but to play darts, talk, visit with girls and sing. Singing proved to be a favorite English pastime and the troopers got busy learning the words to the most popular songs. Living there became more comfortable every day but no one knew how long we would stay. Some of the 508th troopers wanted to "get on with the fightin'." Personally, I enjoyed life in Nottingham during this time and hated to think about it ending just to go off and do battle with someone I didn't know.

Most of us spent money like there was no tomorrow, and with 2,000 plus troopers in the 508th the Nottingham economy received a big boost. As usual, John and I found a great place to call our own, called the Paris Café. I could truly count the owner as a good friend. The café had a clean, homey atmosphere and tasty food. It was quite popular with the locals as well, but John and I never had to wait for a table. As soon as the owner saw us in line he would come and take us out of it.

*   *   *

"I could do with some fish and chips at the Paris Café," I told John while we sat and waited for the final go.

Our three days of waiting was tense. We would exercise as a unit in the mornings and then have long afternoons of "nothing." It was also a bit difficult dealing with the high concentration of soldiers—not unlike the ocean voyage that had me seasick for several days.

"The Café is a long way off but I bet we could find something else nearby," John thought.

"Sure, if they'll just grant us a quick two-hour pass."

"We'd get caught in a café," he said. "I'd rather go to the movies."

Caught? I thought. "What are you talking about?"

"Well you remember after we docked, we stayed at Clandibouy, right?" John was asking.

*   *   *

After spending twelve days at sea our troop ship had landed at Belfast, Ireland. The day was still early when we disembarked and trucks were waiting for us. The overland travel felt good even if it did take the remainder of the day. Maybe it was because I had seen nothing but water for nearly two weeks, but Ireland looked like the greenest land on God's green earth. Just before dark we reached Camp Clandibouy.

Our billeting put us in Quonset huts. The beds were low-cut sawhorses with three ten-inch planks laid across them and a mattress cover filled with straw.

"I wonder how often they change the straw?" asked a trooper.

"I'll be sure to ask the chambermaid when I see her; I may need an extra pillow."

One smart aleck popped off, "Burns told them he was from Texas so they thought they'd make him feel at home."

"Yeah right, very funny."

We were told we would not be there long and thus there'd be no passes into town. By the second night we figured we had been there long enough and it was time to see some action.

"It's time we checked out the local girls."

"Heck yeah!" someone agreed, "I haven't even seen a girl for two weeks. Let's get out of here."

"And if the brass don't like it they can just ship us back home."

We all got dressed in our Class A uniforms, shined up our boots and took off for town. Of course there were guards on all the gates, but paratroopers are trained to be resourceful. We discovered we could go through the obstacle course to the far end and scale a rock wall to freedom. Heck, the rock wall looked easier than some of the obstacles we routinely trained on. Once over the wall it was just a short walk into town. Judging from the number of guys going over the wall, camp was going to be real quiet. A blackout was in effect and knowing where to go got confusing. What we could see of the town didn't look like much. For a price, some of the local kids agreed to act as guides and take us where we wanted.

We made for a pub, but I didn't like the beer; it was very dark and very heavy. Then we decided to find something to eat. This night was our first encounter with English money and questions arose when it came time to pay.

The barmaid said, "That will be six and twenty."

We replied, "Six and twenty what?"

Finally we ended up trusting her and held out our money, letting her take what she needed.

If there were any local beauties around, the town had them locked up at home. Out of boredom we soon headed back to camp.

As we approached the gate one trooper hollered out to the security guards, "Real swinging place you keep back there buddy."

No replies, but one guard took a couple of steps toward us.

"Let me see your passes, everyone get them out."

That stopped us dead in our tracks.

"Uh, what if we don't have a pass?" we asked.

He shook his head and said, "If you ain't got a pass you ain't getting through."

"Say, Sir?" came a voice from the rear, "If I left my pass on my bunk, can I go into camp and get it and then I'll come right back here to the gate and . . ."

"No!" The guard thundered.

Another trooper asked, "How do you think we got out of camp if we didn't have a pass? We must have all lost them."

The guard was getting mad. "You didn't get out of camp because you didn't have a pass and therefore you don't belong here. So I recommend you guys leave on the double."

Even though his tone was serious, some troopers are rather thick skulled and some started giving out a lot of lip.

"Now look buddy, we just got here yesterday and they've got us sleeping in a cow trough and we're getting awfully sick and tired of..."

But somebody else jumped in, "Come on guys let's go."

So the lot of us walked back down the road. At the edge of camp we turned, followed the rock wall a short way then went back over it the same way we had left camp in the first place.

* * *

"I remember that," I told John, "and I like where you're headed. You want to jump the fence."

"Do you think we can?" he asked.

I was sure of it. "Heck yeah, its' worth a try even if we fail!"

So the bright idea to slip out of camp was born. When evening came we nonchalantly walked away from the hanger and over to the razor wire fence. By methodically walking along the stretched coils we found a place where we could get through. Then we just strolled along the road like we owned it and were making good time towards town. It seemed we were doing okay, but then a jeep with a raised canopy pulled up beside us.

An officer seated in the back asked, "Which one of you troopers would like to explain what you're doing off base?"

John started to answer. His speech was slow as he searched for words to make our explanation.

"Well, Sir. We are, or rather we have, he and I, we're to, uh, to go into town, and we need rations."

"To the show, sir!" I jumped in, blurting out the truth. "We're going into town to the show."

"That's it, the show." John confessed.

This officer wasn't going to accept any of our guff, but in a diplomatic voice he asked, "What company are you from?"

"F Company, Sir!" John replied with a snap. We were both at perfect attention but also trying and see into the jeep.

"Will you two do me a favor?" the officer asked.

"Yes, Sir!" we answered smartly.

"You go back to the field right now and tell Captain Flanders no one is to be off base for any reason."

"Sure will, Sir!"

We saluted and watched as he drove away.

Before the tail light even began to dim John asked, "Burns, do you know who that was?"

"No, I couldn't see him." But I didn't think I wanted to know.

"Well that was 'Jumpin' Jim' Gavin—he's like second in command of the whole stinking 82nd." John's voice contained a mixture of fear and awe.

I shuddered. I knew I didn't want to know. So the two of us walked back the way we came.

"John, I know this is a stupid question but we're not really going to tell Flanders anything are we?"

"Gosh no!" he relied. "Hell no! I'd rather jump into a nest of Jerrys than go to Flanders."

"Well I think you'll get your chance," I sort of chuckled despite the serious future we faced.

Then he asked back, "How long do you think before we go?"

"I believe we are real close buddy," I told him, "and if that was General Gavin back there, well he isn't out here for any false exercise."

We walked a ways in silence reflecting on the possible future.

"We're lucky to have Captain Flanders," I shared.

"Indeed," John agreed. "He's a good one. I'm not anywhere ready to leave God's Earth but he'd be a good one to go out with. Lieutenants Goodale and Gillespie are also good officers; I would follow them into the worst of battles."

* * *

It was a day or two after the troopers had successfully jumped the wall at Camp Clandibouy, Ireland, that our makeshift company hit the road again. During this time we learned that our company was not staying together but would be splitting up to strengthen the units already there. We were scheduled to travel by train to our permanent units. They said some of us would be going into the 82nd as replacements and the rest to fill out the 101st. Last time I saw John we worked out the chances of pulling assignments together. The odds were 13 to 1 against us and I didn't see him on the train.

Thinking ahead, I knew that I could find a home wherever my destination was, but ever since seeing the movie *Sergeant York* as a kid I thought the 82nd was the only outfit around. In my opinion York would approve of the division's new role as a strictly airborne unit. It had a good nickname, "All American." York gave it fame and now paratroopers made it elite.[iii] So while sitting on the train I convinced myself the 82nd was for me and my hopes were centered on getting there.

The train stopped at Port Stewart in County Antrim where a number of other troopers and I were told to unload. Stepping down to the platform I noticed there were men coming out of the rail cars on my left and right. All we could see was a bunch of Quonset huts back in the trees. A sergeant there to meet the train quickly got our attention and filled us in.

He said, "Fellows, this is the home of the 508th Parachute Infantry Regiment, the Red Devils."

We had never heard of the Red Devils, or the 508th, but the name had an exciting ring. Guys started whispering.

One voice rang louder. "I knew we had the devil in us."

"Pipe the hell down!" yelled the sergeant. Now right at the moment we're a bastard unit, but we're going to be attached to the 82nd Airborne.

The 82nd! *I had made it,* and for the next minute this sergeant was like Sergeant York, so I better not miss a word he said.

"Now we're going to move over to the front of Regimental Headquarters. A lot of brass is waiting, so I want you to fall in quickly when we get there. You'll be presented to the commander, Lt. Colonel Lindquist, and the rest of our Regimental Command. Then we'll start calling off your names. All the company commanders are there and you'll each be assigned to a company. Grab your things and report to your CO. Your company will take it from there. Alright, let's move it, keep it quiet and remember, fall in quickly."

He said to keep quiet but I could hear a few excited whispers around me. To the front of Regimental Headquarters we went and then silence ruled. After establishing our formation the officers came out to meet us. There was a bunch of them and they spread out to face us like chessmen. Little time was spent with formalities and the roll call got started.

"Adams, Richard."

"Sir!"

Charlie Company, Adams. Captain Stokes, Commander."

"Yes Sir."

"Atkins, Mark..."

As each man's name was called I mentally checked whether I knew him and what company he was in. Then I knew my name was close.

"Burns, Dwayne."

"Here!"

"Fox Company, Captain Flanders."

I picked up my duffel and moved to the ranks, getting started for F Company.

My new commander shook my hand and said, "Glad to have you with us, Burns. What kind of training have you had?"

"I'm a radio operator, Sir." I didn't breathe a word about being trained as a machine gunner. I had my reasons.

"The company has a radio operator," the captain said. A hollow feeling started within me until he added, "I'll put you in Company Headquarters as an assistant radio operator."

"Yes Sir, that sounds good." I nodded to my new First Sergeant and then stood waiting for the rest to be assigned. As I thought about it, "assistant" sounded even better. I wouldn't have to carry the radio, only know how to use it. I had once carried a homing pigeon on a training mission in the States and those memories returned. I'll carry the bird, I thought. But to my knowledge no pigeons were ever used by paratroopers in WWII. I daydreamed a little about the future until I heard a familiar name shouted out.

"McGee, John."

My attention returned to the roll call and assignments.

"Here, Sir."

Then I knew John was also to be a Red Devil.

"Fox Company, Captain Flanders."

John made his distinctive saunter our way, a little peppier than usual. He stopped to meet our new CO. I couldn't believe that we had beaten the odds. Us ol' Texas boys were now back in the same company.

John came past me and gave a wink.

"Third platoon," he whispered.

The officers dismissed us and everyone assigned to F Company walked with our new First Sergeant to find our quarters. He pointed out a small hut. This housed members of Company Headquarters so I took leave of John and the others. Upon entering I stopped and gave a look at all the new faces as they turned and looked at me. Then I met John Hurst, Woody Phelps, Eddie Alexik, Wilbur Scanlon, Ed Chatoian, Ramon Prieto, Ralph Burrus and all the rest of the guys. It was Chatoian who served as company radio operator.

While shaking Ed's hand I told him, "I'm a radio operator too. Captain says I'll be your assistant."

"Oh good," he said with an evil smile as he lightly rubbed his hands together. "You're exactly what I've been waiting for."

But he didn't mean anything by it, just his way of making me feel like one of the guys. An empty bunk was shown to me—"home" they called it. One trooper, Ramon Prieto, came over with an O.D. neck scarf.

"Here, put this with your things."

"What's this for?" I asked

"I have two of them," he explained. "It's been nice lately but it gets damn cold around here so I want to give you one. You'll need it."

"Well thanks," I said. "Thanks a lot."

I thought it was a real cordial welcome to a new man. Then the realization came to me that these men were the ones I would be jumping into combat with and my very life might depend on what they did or didn't do. I stopped my unpacking and gave them another looking over. At every stop I had made in my army career thus far I knew that the guys around me and I would one day split up. Now I was with my final regiment and these were to be my battle buddies.

None of them had the appearance of a super hero or wonder boy. They looked more like the average teenager back home. Just like me. What would they be like when the time came to fight? Would they lead the charge or creep at the rear? How would they die if such were to be their fate?

In pondering this I realized that some of the faces before me might not make a return trip to the States. Such a fact had always been there, even at the draft board in Dallas and during processing in Mineral Wells. You expected some of those around you would be killed in action. This was one of those reflective "someday, but not this day" occasions one tried to put out of mind.

✳ ✳ ✳

After our encounter with General Gavin, John and I reentered the air-base the same way we got out, fearful we'd be shot for desertion if we tried the airfield gate. We hadn't made it to town, but we had given it our best shot. It gave us something else to think and talk about and some of the others asked us to tell the story over and over. It was a mental escape that helped for a while.

There was a photo I was really missing. In the mail only two or three days before our lock-in I had received a new picture from Minerva. What a lift it gave me. My thoughts had been heavy with the death of the young trooper on our last practice jump and that accident left my mind when I viewed this fresh image. I felt good again, and believed nothing could stop me from returning home. But the photo was in my tent in camp and I sure wanted to see it again. Another photo was with me of course. Minerva had to be the most beautiful girl in the world and she had signed the new picture, "Darling, I love you!" They said the lucky ones would go home. Could anyone be luckier than me?

One of the last nights of this forced incarceration I found myself wanting to memorize the 23rd Psalm. I almost had it anyway. The prose had a special meaning between Minerva and I.

One of the letters from Minerva while I was training for the paratroopers was actually a card, on which she had written on three of the

four sides. On the front was printed the 23rd Psalm. After reading the
letter I spent some time reading the verse. I read it more than once—
slowly. My reading almost became a study. Sure, I had read it before.
Now, however, it seemed to lock in a lot more meaning for me.

For the first time I had felt this scripture move deep within me. It
came on like a warm blanket and my bones gave a quiver of comfort.
After reading the card several times I took out my new jump knife and
cut the heavy paper into two pieces. Pulling some Scotch tape out of
my footlocker I taped the verse to the inside of my helmet. The card
fit perfectly and looked good as well. I was getting all the help I could.
From that day forward the card was with me every day, and a part of
Minerva was with me as well. It was the previous Thanksgiving, however, when this verse helped to bond the love Minerva and I shared.

*   *   *

My two weeks of leave following paratrooper training had fallen at a
wonderful time. I was home during Thanksgiving. Minerva and I had
our Thanksgiving meal with Dad, Mom and my youngest sister. The
dinner was great; Mom cooked all the things I liked and I really put
away the food. After eating, everyone had a nice visit around the table.
Minerva and I held hands through most of it and when the family discussions slowed down I asked her, "Honey, how about a walk?"

"Fine," she answered, and we started a stroll along the roads
around Lake Worth.

It was one great day in Texas. The air was a bit cool but it was
nice, nearly warm, out in the sun. The trees had turned in color and
the leaves were starting to fall. I began kicking leaves as we walked.
Minerva teased me.

"What are you doing?" she asked.

"Well you should know I happened to be an ol' leaf kicker from
way back. In fact I come from a long line of leaf kickers, and our leaf
kicking is only exceeded by our handsome looks and our extreme
humility."

"Oh please spare me the details," she laughed. Then she said,
"Well I'm a leaf preserver. Don't kick that!"

She playfully tried to shove me away from a small pile of collected
leaves. Our walk turned into a silly drunken weave down the road. I

would steer her towards the fallen leaves; she would push or pull in another direction. At times we wandered to the other side of the street. When the game played out I gave her a squeeze.

"What?" she asked softly.

"Nothing, I just have to squeeze you every once in a while to make sure you are really, truly here."

She said, "I'm here Dwayne. I will always be here."

After we walked another two or three steps I stopped her. Taking her face in my hands I kissed her lightly on the lips.

"Will you marry me?" I asked her.

"Yes," she replied, and her eyes looked deep into mine. "When?"

A small feeling of fear rushed inside me. I didn't fear the marriage commitment; life with her wasn't a scary thought at all. It was just a fear of the future. I didn't know where I would be or what I'd be getting into. Hitler had just given the British Isles one horrific banging, yet the Brits had thankfully held on. I might go there. Our forces in the Pacific were beginning to hold their own against the Japanese attacks. I might be sent there. War in Africa might be over, but troops were still there. War in Italy continued, and there was war in the Philippines and in China. The only places where there wasn't a war were the only places I knew I wouldn't be going. A slim chance remained that a soldier could pull duty in the States but there was no such chance for a paratrooper. We weren't trained to jump into friendly territory. We were lead combat troops and anywhere the war raged was where my future laid.

So I told Minerva, "I wish it could be right now, today, or before I leave, but I don't think it's the smart thing to do. If something goes wrong I don't want you to be a young widow." I paused to read her reaction but saw none. I suggested, "How about as soon as I'm discharged from the army?"

"OK," she said, "whatever you think is best."

I kissed her again. We took a long embrace standing in the middle of the road in the middle of a lakeside neighborhood in the middle of Fort Worth, Texas.

"Dwayne," Minerva said as we turned back to the house, "God watches over us, He and His angels. I'm sure He has a plan and I believe He means for us to be together. If you will also believe our marriage is meant to be, then nothing will go wrong."

I once again squeezed her, not playfully but in acknowledgement to her that I understood.

I then quoted a part of the 23rd Psalm, which came to mind. "Yea, though I walk through the valley of the shadow of death, I will fear no evil, for thou art with me. Thy rod and thy staff they comfort me."

It was all I could recall and we took a couple of steps in silence. Then Minerva finished where I could not.

"Thou preparest a table before me in the presence of my enemies, thou anointest my head with oil, my cup runneth over. Surely goodness and mercy shall follow me all the days of my life and I will dwell in the house of the Lord forever."

Forever, I repeated, because I felt my cup was truly running over.

Hearing her tender voice reciting the song's final words caused my eyes to tear up. I tried to fight them down because I thought a man shouldn't show any softness. The heart of my spirit had been suddenly touched like never before, and a kind of conviction overcame me. I quickly tried to think of a happier moment to dry my eyes, but at no moment in my life had I ever been happier than now. I decided I would believe in us as she did, and that I would fear no evil.

*   *   *

Sitting on my assigned bunk at the airfield I read this Bible verse and then reread it again and again. Where it was written, "I walk through the valley of the shadow" I took my fountain pen and crossed out "walk through" and inserted "jump into." This was now my prayer for battle. I wanted God there with me and I needed to feel Minerva's love as well. If I could feel this, then I could do anything, even die if necessary.

Around the bunks there was more waiting by the men, playing cards and looking at that blasted sand table. Cleaning our equipment and repacking our field bags continued. Then, on June 5th, about midday, the word came down. This was it! "Someday" had arrived!

JUMP
TWO

The ship was bouncing like some wild bronco.

I repacked one last time but everything I had or wanted to take wouldn't fit into my bag. The Red Cross had a mobile doughnut and coffee stand in the hanger. It was their job to hand out sinkers and coffee and cheer us up with good old-fashioned American girl smiles. I walked down and handed one of the girls a big jar of hard candy I had received from Minerva in yesterday's mail.

"Would you care to have this?" I asked her. "It's good candy and it just arrived from my fiancée in the States."

She sort of cocked her head in response. "Well don't you want it?"

"Darling," I explained. "I've got no place to put it."

Her eyes began to water and when she answered there was a definite quiver in her voice. "Why yes, I guess so. Thank you very much."

Then the tears in her eyes grew too large to hold and great big streams ran down both her cheeks. She was doing some job of cheering us up. Surely I could do my job better than she did hers.

There were also handouts of gum and cigarettes, and most soldiers took both even if they were non-smokers. I preferred smoking a pipe myself, but a pack of real American smokes made for great trading material.

During the last couple of hours, before moving to the planes, I wrote two more letters, first one to Mom, and then one to Minerva. I wasn't allowed to tell them where we were or what we were about to do, but long before my letters arrived they would know I was fighting the Germans in France. I didn't intend them to be my last letters but, just in case, I wanted them to be positive.

Using a burnt cork I joined the other guys and blackened my face.

"War paint," said Ramon with a big ear-to-ear smile. "We're going to match the planes."

Ramon was a crazy sort and always good for a laugh.

* * *

One late Saturday morning about the first weekend of May, Ramon, Woody, John and I headed out for a walk in the country. After several miles we came to a little café, and having worked up a little appetite we went in for a serving of tea and halfpenny buns. Over our first cup of tea we visited with the owner and she told us she had an apple pie cooling in the kitchen and would we like some? We couldn't help but chuckle.

Ramon darn near laughed himself to tears.

"Excuse me ma'am," he asked, "but are you talking about a real apple pie?"

She grinned real big and replied, "Yes deary, just like they make in the States."

I caught Ramon's eye and those of the others. We weren't too sure about the quality of English pie, but I returned her smile and spoke up, "Well bring it out here!"

We each ate two pieces and from that time on we started walking in the country on our days off. It was a good contrast from all the wild nightlife in Nottingham.

* * *

To become battle ready, several of the guys cut their hair Mohawk-style. It might have had something to do with our jump cry of Geronimo. Some shaved it all off. Each trooper was going into combat in whatever style suited him best. I left mine in a crew cut. In briefing they told us we would be back in a month, so I wanted to come back looking like myself.

John McGee and I found each other. There wasn't much to say but a quick "Good luck and see you in France."

Gathering our equipment we moved out to the planes just before dark. The chutes were laid out in rows beside the ships; each of us selected a main and a reserve. I found two chutes and carried them to one side of the airplane to look them over carefully.

Lying in the grass, waiting for someone to tell us to saddle up, we took turns talking about our homes, wives and kids or sweethearts, and the good times we had in school. I was surprised to learn a lot of guys had brothers getting ready for this same mission but were in some other outfit.

"There ain't no other outfits," one of them boasted. "There's only Airborne." Most agreed, until we realized we'd be surrounded by Germans until the leg troops fought their way to us.

"Sisters," I had to tell them when I was prodded about who else might be serving in my family. "I've got two of them."

Then I told them how protective my mom was, and how since I was a soldier now I didn't know who would have the rougher time, me fighting the war or her worrying about it.

"Two things I grew up with: a mom who worried about everything I did and a dad who popped me with his walking cane any time I got out of line."

The question came, "Why does he have a cane?"

"Motorcycle accident," I explained, "Dad helped start the Fort Worth Motorcycle Club and rode a big Indian bike. While riding to a Club event he and Mom were hit by a car. Dad's foot got pretty cracked up."

"Are you saying that your Mom, the protective one, was riding?" they asked.

They made me laugh. "Yeah, but she wasn't hurt. It was at least ten years ago. The cane doesn't slow Dad down much."

I continued, "It seems Dad is always into cars, planes or boats. He enjoys anything resembling transportation. Dad once owned the Castleberry Bus Line before selling out to the City of Fort Worth. I used to have a free bus ride any time I wanted to go somewhere."

"What about airplanes? What'd he do?" someone wanted to know.

"Well, I was pretty young then but I know he worked for Bowen Air Lines. He was in charge of maintaining the fleet and I got my first ride in an airplane when he worked there. They had a bunch of early Lockheeds, Vegas and Orions. Right now he owns the Lake Worth Boat Club where he rents out slips and repairs old wooden boats for folks, or else builds them a new boat to order. Nobody can lay down a paint job like my dad."

Then I had to add another telling story. "Let me tell you, Dad isn't afraid to try new things or experience something firsthand. Dad is missing most of one thumb and parts of two fingers. This was from an accident he had as a boy. He was using a hammer to try to get a blasting cap to explode. Well . . . it did."

They laughed, "Gee Dwayne, now we know where you got your brains."

I smiled but snapped my reply back, "Yeah well, he still had the nerve and drive to become an engineer in the Army. He was a part of the first fight with the Germans."

One of the troopers asked, "How do you think they'll take the news back home, all our kin, when it's learned we jumped into France?"

"The old men will be excited and all the women will worry."

Another added, "I imagine it will make quite a headline in the paper."

Our conversation continued until the last rays of the sun expired and the darkness took over. For many of the Red Devils this was their last sunset. It came and faded away and no one seemed to notice. It was solid dark when we finally received the signal to get on board. Our jump stick came together like a football huddle and everyone took time to shake hands with everyone else.

"I'll see you on the ground," we all said to one another.

We chuted up and pulled the adjustment straps down good and tight. With the specialized equipment and supplies for three days, every trooper weighed between 300 and 400 pounds. We had been advised that pilots, who didn't mind slowing down for training jumps, seldom flew at anything less than full throttle during actual combat jumps.[iv] They didn't want to be coasting around up there while some Kraut took potshots at them. So between their higher expected airspeed and the fact we were so loaded down with combat extras we knew we were in for one hell of an opening shock.

Every item must have a place to go. When completely loaded and ready I had the main chute on my back and the reserve across my chest. Below the reserve chute was the musette bag and in it were a land mine, four grenades, rations, toothbrush, and a change of socks and underwear. On my belt were the first aid kit, shovel, canteen kit and bayonet. The trench knife was tied to my right ankle and the jump knife was in a zippered compartment in my jump jacket. I wore a bandoleer over each shoulder. The gas mask was over the left shoulder while the M-1 carbine was over the right shoulder with the muzzle pointed down. All the odds and ends: New Testament, message book, the last letters from home and other small items were in my six pants pockets and four jacket pockets. Being the assistant radio operator I knew I wouldn't have to carry the radio, but then neither did Ed. It was placed in an equipment bundle and strapped to the belly of the ship. When we landed Ed would find it and carry it.

Once we were chuted up, we had to stay on our feet because it was impossible to get back up without help. To get on board the airplane every trooper helped push and pull one another to get up the steps of the ship. An Army Air Force ground crew member had to help the last man on. When I moved to my seat there was a flak vest on it.

"Hey guys," I said. "Look what I got!" I folded it in the seat and sat down on it. "This is great; I'll take all the protection I can get."

After the last man was seated our pilot came back and looked around. He seemed to be giving the ship one last inspection before take-off. Then he suddenly barked, "Which one of you troopers is sitting on my flak vest?"

A few eyes drifted my way. Darn the luck.

"This aircraft is not taking off until I get that vest," he yelled.

Reluctantly, I began tugging it out from under me, having to squirm around a bit due to my increased weight. Upon presenting it to the pilot I received a dirty look. He turned around in silence and went back to the front.

At 22:30 the engines of our plane, and those of aircraft all over England, were started and the Airborne was ready to go. In the lead plane was "Jumpin' Jim" Gavin, who John and I had encountered during our ill-fated attempt to reach town. He would be jumping with the 508th. He had already seen action in both Sicily and Italy, where he served as commander of the 505th P.I.R. Now, as the newly appointed and recently promoted Exec. of the 82nd Airborne Division, he led not just our 508th regiment, but also our sister regiment the 507th, and the battle-proven 505th to Normandy.

General Gavin was popular with the troopers, not just because he conducted his command from the lead position but because he was also a jump school student from Fort Benning. He earned his wings like the rest of us and had full rights to be called a paratrooper. We didn't call him "Jumpin' Jim" for nothing.[v]

In another plane close behind the General's was our own regimental commander, Lt. Colonel Roy E. Lindquist. He was as green as the rest of us when it came to combat experience, but he had the 508th honed to a fine edge. The regiment was as trained and ready as any could ever hope to be. Although we didn't know just what was ahead, many troopers were tired of waiting and ready for the next step, even if it was a giant one, out the door and into France.

The planes started to taxi in what looked like a never-ending procession toward the end of the runway. This was much bigger than a practice jump. I listened as planeload after planeload of troopers took off, one right after another, and I watched what I could out the window. The throttles of the plane I rode in were advanced and then pulled back several times. It seemed we only inched forward. Our aircrew waited for their turn, but I believed the waiting was worse for us jumpers. We longed for the air. Once in the air we were committed; there was no turning back and we could only look forward.

Finally the ship rolled out and lined up with the runway. The engines roared to full power and the plane started to rattle and shake down the grassy strip. All talking stopped. Well beyond the point of a normal takeoff the ship was still rolling on the ground. Troopers started exchanging glances because it was something new. The heavier aircraft needed an extended roll, as was expected, but it was a different feeling, and the men didn't like change. The tail of the ship finally began to lift and I crossed my fingers. Sweat beaded up across my forehead. It seemed like a long time had passed, but at last the smoother sound and free feeling of flight began as we went airborne, and I breathed a little easier.

We were all bunched up, but each man in the surrounding darkness sat deep in his own thoughts and fears. These friends around me were the best I could ever know. Four months is a long time when you live, work and play together all day and night. I wondered how many we'd lose before sunrise tomorrow.

I prayed silently, "Lord, help me do everything right. Don't let me get somebody killed and don't let me get killed either! You know we're too young for this."

As I sat looking out the door of the C-47, I could see the black silhouette of a plane on our left. The exhaust from its port engine was a bright blue tongue of flame licking the night sky. A wing lifted a little, then it dipped back, weaving a pattern through the air as small night thermals and down drafts moved it around. It was a warm night and our flight was smooth, and that was good, for it wasn't a time to be airsick. This night, of all nights, everyone wanted a clear head. As we crossed over the English Channel, heading south toward France, I found it too dark to make out anything below, and inside the plane it grew darker still. I found myself longing for daylight so I could again watch one of the jump instructors standing in the doorway and gather strength from their calm demeanor. I longed for someone with a vast amount of experience to tell me I could do this because they had done it.

* * *

On my very first training flight, the jumpmaster was standing at the door looking out and holding onto the anchor line. The sleeves and pants legs of his fatigues had a constant and heavy rolling snap to them as the air stream rushed past. It was as if wild animals were all about nipping at this master of the parachute. I remember wondering how many hundreds of takeoffs and landings he had made. How many troopers had he watched go through that jump door? Thousands? I wondered also if there was any count to the number of times he might of planted his boot onto somebody's backside to help him out the door.

He wore a parachute, a natural part of him not unlike the shell on a tortoise. The only protection he needed. Without it he was only a step away from certain death. With it, even with the wind howling about him like mad dogs, he maintained an easy calm. Today was just an average day, another day on the job. Just behind him sat twenty excited young men who felt they were partaking in the experience of a lifetime. This was our golden opportunity; this was the big number one jump.

When the jumpmaster turned to face us he shouted, "Today we have a six-mile-an-hour wind out of the west at twelve hundred feet and a three-mile-per-hour wind on the ground out of the southwest. Skies are clear." He spoke with all of the thrill and excitement of a farm report—dry and to the point.

The plane started a banking turn and our jumpmaster looked back out the door. Beyond him I watched as the city of Columbus, Georgia and the Chattahoochee River moved into view. At times I thought I could see the vortex of wind slightly distort his face. He didn't mention our airspeed; maybe it was something they didn't want us to know.

"First stick, stand up and hook up," he suddenly shouted.

All the guys across from me got to their feet and coupled their static line hooks to the anchor cable.

"Check your equipment. Sound off."

The last man in the stick yelled, "Ten OK," and he slapped the next man on the back.

"Nine OK," and the count continued on down the line.

My packing partner Joe was in the first stick. I looked at him and told myself if this little Yankee could do it then so could I. Looking forward through the windows and over the wing I saw the field just ahead and also noticed Cactus Hill, the one place you didn't want to land.

"Stand in the door," came an order. "Move up tight."

The first man pivoted into position, hands on either side of the door, left foot forward, just like in mock-up. I was glad to be in the middle of our stick and not the one who had to stand there first, looking down, waiting for the word to go. Suddenly the aircraft engines throttled down. There was a pause in the action then I saw the jumpmaster's eyes sparkle.

"Is everybody happy?"

"Yeah!" the stick yelled back.

"Is everybody going to jump?"

"Yeah!" they answered again.

"Go!" shouted the jumpmaster, and he slapped man number one on the leg.

Then, as they say in the paratroopers, the first man went out like a big-ass bird with the other nine right behind him. I watched them shuffle up the aisle and go out the door leaving only their static lines flapping out the door to show that they had been there. Not one man in the stick had hesitated.

The jumpmaster turned to us with a big smile and gave the thumbs up sign. I looked across the aisle at all the empty seats. It suddenly looked to be the most vacant place above God's green earth.

The ship made a slow banking turn to the left and for a brief moment we could look out the door and see a row of white canopies. We kept banking into the turn with a giant arc and I knew the pilot was making another immediate pass. Our jumpmaster shot us a quick glance.

"Stand up and hook up," came the yell. "Check equipment."

This is it, I realized. You can't stop now. Besides, Joe made it and by this time is touching down.

Quickly I looked at the back of the man in front of me checking for anything wrong, not much to see. I looked at my reserve chute and at the release handle. My static line hook was still in my hand and I gave it a couple of good pulls against the anchor cable.

"Sound off," the jumpmaster commanded, and a count started from the back of the stick. I felt a hit and yelled "Three OK," as I reached to slap the man ahead of me.

"Stand in the door. Close up tight."

Man number one pivoted into the doorway and the number two man moved into position. I moved up close enough to put my hand on the doorframe.

"Is everybody happy?"

"Yeah!" we shouted.

"Is everybody going to jump?"

"Yeah!" we shouted again.

God, one thing about parachute jumping is that you must do it right every time or you may not get another shot at it. God, even if I've done something wrong you can make it right. Good Lord, don't desert me now when I need you.

"Go!"

The first man went out the door. The rest of us all began to move up the aisle doing the parachute shuffle, always keeping the left foot forward. I didn't feel any slap on the leg from the jumpmaster. When the number two man went I stepped up and went right behind him.

Outside the door I was trying to keep my eyes on the horizon as I turned to face the tail of the plane. Everything looked like it was happening in slow motion; my adrenaline was really pumping! The wind on my back was giving me a huge shove and the left-hand aircraft elevator went sailing by overhead. In front of me I saw number two man's chute start to open and extend.

Another shove of wind started to slowly rotate me face down. *One thousand, two thousand . . .* and the opening shock jerked me back to an upright position. I took a look around at the rest of the stick. All seemed to be OK and not too close. Everyone had a full canopy of air.

I looked down. I still had a long way to go. *Oh yeah, supposed to look up and check my own canopy for blown panels or a Mae West.*

A Mae West occurred whenever a suspension line went over the canopy and divided it into two parts. Looking up I saw the most beautiful sight in the world. A great big fully blossomed span of white nylon, all the panels intact and risers in their proper places. *Looks like everything is right. An A+ in parachute packing.*

I looked back down; all I had to do now was enjoy the ride. Below me I spotted an ambulance and a jeep. An officer with a bullhorn was talking to guys who were having trouble. I looked around, no problems; we were all coming down together at a normal rate of descent. The joke was to pack a rock with you; if you let loose of the rock and it dropped you were ok, if the rock floated beside you or went up then you pulled the reserve.

The bullhorn came on again and I heard its operator say, "Just take your time trooper. You have lots of time, just reach up and get a hold of that line and pull it off."

There is someone in trouble! I twisted about to see. Sure enough, one fellow had a suspension line wrapped around one foot and there he was floating down with his foot over his head. If he hit in that position he was bound to break something. I watched as he reached up. The officer on the ground kept telling him to just take it easy. The trooper was really in a struggle to get loose. Finally, the suspension line slipped free and his foot dropped.

"Good work soldier," the officer called over the bullhorn.

We all gave a cheer and continued our descent. I could see some bushes on my left so I reached up, pulled on my left-hand risers and slipped towards them. I pulled on my right-hand risers and slid away from them. Everything was working just as they said it would. Then, with the ride just about over, I took up the landing position. My head was down at a forty-five degree angle, knees slightly bent, feet together and toes pointing down and I knew it would be perfect. I hit the ground and rolled forward as my chute collapsed beside me. I got up and got out of my harness quickly.

The field was in complete commotion. Everyone tried to talk at the same time and I just nodded at all the comments with a big silly grin on my face.

"Boy am I good!" one soldier bragged.

"Geronimo, man, Geronimo," said another.

"What a swell ride."

Nothing feels so good as jumping. It's like when you kiss your new girlfriend for the first time. You knew it was going to be good and couldn't wait to do it, and then it proves to be a whole lot better than you ever thought, and now you can't wait to do it again.

I rolled up my chute and headed for the truck that would take us all back to Lawson Field. I couldn't help singing as I went. I was ready to go right back up and do it again. I threw my chute in the back and jumped in after it. Everyone kept talking and laughing and recounting their jump to anyone who would listen.

The trucks dropped us off at the airfield near the parachute loft where we went to hang up our chutes and shake them out. Then it was back to the packing shed with them so we could repack for the next day's jump.

"Ain't life beautiful," someone said, and everyone else agreed. We were all still talking and there was laughter. Never before had the packing shed atmosphere been so lighthearted.

After we stowed our chutes, we walked back to the barracks. By this time every man had individually become something new; we were no longer the same men. Sometime between landing from the first jump and stowing chutes for the next one we all knew it. We had joined a fraternity, a military one. From now on the world was divided, and it didn't matter whether your rank was PFC or general; you were either going to be a jumper or a non-jumper. We had joined the jumpers. That day we had put our hide on the line and then we made it happen. Each man had found the right stuff inside of him, be it bravery, coolness, or plain old moxie. We had what it took to be paratroopers and we now stood in the ranks of Uncle Sam's best.

* * *

Such lighthearted joking felt far away as we continued our flight to France. By this time it was past midnight, the date turning to June 6th, 1944—D-Day. Although we were packed in tight, the trip was a solitary experience. It could have been a silent one, but the twin engines continued to pound their deep throbbing sounds deeper through flesh and skull. Each man sat wrapped in a cocoon of noise, speaking only to his own fears and reliving the last good memories of home, family and sweetheart.

"Minerva." I whispered her name softly. I gained strength by doing so. Would I ever see her again, and would I ever get to reach out with my arms and hold her and tell her I loved her? Minerva Chastain, her name was like the lyrics to a song, her spirit was the melody, and I could sing about her all day.

I questioned if we hadn't made a mistake. When I was home on furlough maybe we should have gotten married. Two weeks together wouldn't have been much, but it might have been better than nothing. I didn't want to leave her a young widow, but right now I sure wished I had taken the chance.

Death was foremost on everyone's mind. The odds given us for making it back alive kept droning through my thoughts, kept in place there by the thrum of the engines. The odds weren't just bad; they were terrible.

Lord, must we die before given a chance to really live?

Many other prayers were going up around me as well and I knew God would be working late into the night and for the next several days. Most prayed simply to live, but later I knew that with the battle engaged, some that were badly wounded might pray to hurry up and die.

I mentally repeated the 23rd Psalm. My card was placed in my helmet and I reached up and touched it every once and awhile.

The LORD is my shepherd I shall not want. Yet I do want, I want to live, why do I want to live so bad?

He maketh me to lie down in green pastures. He leadeth me beside the still waters. He restoreth my soul.

As I glanced towards the front of the ship, here and there, I found the glow of cigarette tips as some of the troopers had a last smoke. There were twenty-two of us on board, yet only I seemed to have noticed the head count; two more than a practice jump. All the others continued in their thoughts.

He leadeth me in the paths of righteousness for His name's sake. Lord this not a righteous path, this is a war. Our destination, we hoped, lay near the little town of Etienville. We were just one plane-load, however.

Yea though I JUMP INTO the valley of the shadow of death, I will fear no evil. Surely King David never expected that. Was it even natural?

The objective of Etienville, on the Cherbourg peninsula, belonged to the entire 2nd Battalion.[vi] We wouldn't be the first to land there, though, because our pathfinder group was already on the ground. Their task was to mark our drop zone with lights and some may already have died this night.[vii]

For thou art with me; thy rod and thy staff comfort me. Thou preparest a table before me in the presence of mine enemies. Wouldn't that be grand, a feast awaiting us when we touched down. The pathfinders lit the marker lights and then lit the dinner candles. The Germans had all surrendered.

Thou anointest my head with oil; my cup runneth over. Surely goodness and mercy shall follow me all the days of my life, and I will dwell in the house of the Lord forever.

As I remember it, each company sent two men to work as pathfinders. I'd had pathfinder training but Ralph Burrus, also with company headquarters, got the job. I started another little prayer. "Dear God, please give swift action and success for our pathfinders, keep them safe during their mission. Anoint their heads with oil, and God, it would be nice to see our assembly point from the air." But I knew at that point the fate of our pathfinders had already been decided. Either the markers were going up by now or else they never would.

Then I thought about some of the guys who were going to charge across the beach. Running across the naked sand with no cover didn't seem any smarter an assignment than jumping out of a perfectly good airplane. However the leg units had to successfully fight their way in or else all us airborne troops would be cut off to fend for ourselves. I prayed again, this time for the ground troops coming in over the beaches.

I wondered about John McGee, my hometown buddy, and if I would ever see him again. His ship was flying somewhere behind me. The chances were slim both of us could make it through this. We had beaten the odds before by getting into the same company, but how much longer could we do that? I sure didn't want the job of going to see John's family when the war was over and telling them how sorry I felt. His visiting my family wouldn't be something I'd wish on him either. He had only briefly met Minerva and I didn't know how he could possibly console her.

I felt the ship bank slowly left. If on schedule, it meant we were approaching the islands of Guernsey and Jersey that sat off the western coastline of France next to the Cherbourg peninsula. Our troop carriers entered French airspace in a roundabout fashion, but after delivering us paratroopers they had a straight shot for England with little resistance. Only a few moments remained to reflect on the better times.

Once more I thought of Minerva, our first meeting, our first kiss.

The morning after Ed and I had met Minerva, as my family was having breakfast, I told my mother, "Mom, last night I met the girl I'm going to marry."

She smiled and asked, "Are you sure?"

"Yes, I am. Don't ask me how I know, but she is without a doubt the one."

But it all depended on this duty to country I had to go through first.

Minerva, I love you. Pray for me.

The red warning light came on and the stick stood and hooked up together. Duty to country would start now. In practice the light meant four minutes to drop zone, but this time troopers were told to hook up as we neared the coastline and the red light would reflect this. That way if our plane took a hit we'd be in position to jump. Number one man was hanging out the door, trying to see how far we were from land, when our airships entered a cloud cover and the pilots started to spread out. Most pulled up and tried going over the top. It was going to be bad for jumpers because we would be widely dispersed at landing, but the aircrew needed to avoid possible collisions. No one wanted to be taken out of action that way. The air remained quiet, so I figured we were still over water.

It seems we stood in position for a long time before our flight began picking up flak. It was light at the beginning. At least I knew we were finally over the coastline. Then our waiting for the green light really started.

The flak grew quickly and became really heavy while we tried to wait it out. The ship was getting pinged from all sides. The noise became awesome, an indeterminate mix of twin engines, flak hitting the wings and fuselage, and men yelling, "Let's go!" But still the green light did not come on.

The ship was bouncing like some wild bronco. A ticking sound danced across the bottom side of the plane as machine-gun rounds found us. It became hard to stand up while the pilots tried to maneuver and troopers lost their footing and fell down. They fought to get back up. Other jumpers had to help them but they could hardly remain standing themselves. Some were getting sick, I know, because the stench of vomit drifted my way from somewhere else. It was one hell of a ride. With all the training we'd had, there was still nothing that could have prepared a soldier for this event. I wondered if anyone of us would get out of the plane alive. As bad as I wanted out, I knew we had to wait for the green light. Yet if we waited too long we would be across the peninsula, past the beaches of Normandy and back over water again. Tracers swept by in a graceful, slow-motion arc. Flak continued knocking holes in the wings. I expected it to come up through the bottom of our plane but I kept praying for it not to. Then the red light went off and the green snapped on. We started a fast shuffle out the door and into the darkness.

I don't even recall the opening shock. What I sensed and saw was fresh air and how quiet it was outside. We were to jump at 600 feet but it seemed much higher. The sound of our aircraft faded away, leaving the sound of distant gunfire to softly fill the night. We appeared to be far south and east of our drop zone[viii] and our assigned objective, 'Etienville. It looked like I was on the outer edge of all the action. To the south everything was quiet, but north there were tracers arcing across the sky and in spite of it all I felt impressed by their beauty.

The sound of an airplane, seemingly out of control, diverted my attention. Looking back over my shoulder I saw one of our C-47s in the far north going down. The left-hand engine was trailing fire all the way back to the empennage. The engine, revved to full power, seemed to scream in protest as I watched it dive into the trees. I hoped the troopers and aircrew had gotten out; I doubted all could have.

With another long look around I felt as though I was just hanging in the sky all by myself and not even descending.

Here I hang—one mighty large target for some crummy Kraut to take a pop at. How will I ever live through all this? I can't even see my stick. But I knew the men were out there somewhere, drifting down in the darkness with me. I looked down and all was still and the rows of trees could barely be made out. Just feet off the ground I realized, "This is for real. This is France, and I'm in combat."

JUMP
Three

"There are no options. We'll hold our ground right here."

On D-Day, I landed in a long, narrow field that had two anti-glider poles in it. I hit hard on solid ground, rolled over on my back and became tangled in my parachute shroud lines. I found myself alone; no one else had landed in the field with me. It was very quiet. One chute went down behind the trees on the far side of the field; it was a good feeling to know I had another trooper there. Lying in the grass I fought to get out of the harness.

In my mind's eye I saw visions of Germans running out of the shadows with fixed bayonets, eager to kill, and here I was having trouble with the harness buckles. To call me scared was an understatement. Reaching down to my right ankle, I pulled out the trench knife and stuck it in the ground beside me. The knife was better than no weapon at all and if any bayonet-charging Germans tried to stick me I was going to try and stick them back.

With that thought I took my time unsnapping the harness, untangling myself from the shroud lines and finally getting on my feet. Without hesitation I ran for the hedgerow where the only other chute I had seen went down. I forgot my trench knife back in the field but I didn't dare retrieve it.

"Flash" was our code word and the countersign was "Thunder." Unable to find my voice I pulled out my cricket snapper. One snap was to be answered by two . . . or was it the other way around?[ix]

Oh hell, just snap the damn thing a few times.

In reply to the clicking a voice yelled, "Look out I'm coming over."

It sounded like good ol' American English to me so I replied, "Come on!"

39

Recrossing a corner of the field where I landed, we found other troopers prowling along another hedgerow. I didn't know who they were but right then it made no difference, just as long as I joined up with someone. After stalking about one hundred yards we stopped and I decided to chance a look over the hedgerow to see what was there. After a short climb up and cautiously looking over the top, I saw another figure on the other side rise up and look at me—my first German! Was it a German? I couldn't make out his features; he was just a silhouette in the night but that helmet shape couldn't be anything else. Each of us stood frozen, looking at the other, and then, almost on cue, we slowly lowered ourselves back down. I sat a moment and wondered what to do with him. Perhaps he couldn't see me because of the light angles. I could toss over a grenade but wondered if the blast would come through the hedgerow. I might kill more troopers than Germans. *I should rise up and try to shoot him. Why didn't I have my weapon in position to kill the first time?* It was a stupid greenie mistake; one that could get me killed. I needed to be ready.

Someone in the group then motioned to move again so I left him sitting on his side of the hedgerow, maybe wondering what to do about me.

It is hard to recall everything that happened the night we invaded. It was very scary with a lot of careful lurking and no sleep. We prowled from field to field and quietly climbed half a dozen or more hedgerows. At the first road we crossed it seemed we were terribly exposed. I tried always to have my weapon prepared should more of the enemy appear. At times everyone stopped and we would discuss which direction to go. Some of the others seemed sure of themselves so I acted as more of a lookout while a hushed debate went on beside me. Then it was easy to just follow their lead. In short order one man seemed to gain everyone's' confidence and we viewed him as a leader. He was part of the 505th Regiment and a veteran of combat in Italy, and maybe Sicily, so we were more than willing to do whatever he said. When dawn started to break I noticed this guy wore three stripes on his sleeve. We had no officers with us. At the sound of an engine we hid ourselves off the road and a flatbed truck went by. On the back I saw my first dead trooper. The Germans had thrown him in feet first and face up. His bare head was nearly hanging out the rear. It was Lt.

Gillespie, who I really only knew as one of the platoon officers, but someone McGee thought well of. Someone McGee may have been jumping with.

"Damn," I grumbled.

We stayed hidden but it proved to be a lone truck and we could have taken it easy. The flatbed passed from sight and we continued on. In hindsight we must have moved through the night in a northeast direction as we had moved towards what we thought was Picauville. This town, one of the many small towns in the area, was east of 'Etienville. It belonged to another part of the 508th but it sounded good enough to me. With luck the town had been taken, or if not we could help those fighting within.

We somehow knew we were close to Picauville,[x] if it were not some other town, and sure enough, around the next curve a Jerry roadblock appeared. It became our introduction to the enemy. With no other preset plan we rushed toward the few German guards, opening fire as we ran. Perhaps the idea was to surprise them and get a quick upper hand, but the Germans were ready for us. We discovered they were alert and on the lookout and they immediately began shooting back; their small arms fire was overwhelming. More Germans were hidden or sitting out of view who quickly rose to fight. We continued our firing but started hitting the road ditch for cover all in the same motion.

The ditch we were in, however, didn't offer our group much protection. Unable to make any advance, we tried shooting it out from our precarious position. Additional enemy soldiers moved into positions at the roadblock, then even more appeared on either side. The lack of cover finally forced us to pull back, but we continued firing while making a retreat down the road. I didn't see any of our guys get hit but it seemed like we were missing at least one. We backed up alongside a rock wall and as the Germans started moving up we decided the best place to be was on the other side.

After going over I realized the wall lined an orchard. I thought we were going to stand and fight at the wall but the noncom motioned us to make a disappearance through the trees. This action started a long string of events best described as evasion and survival.

At the far end of the orchard we came onto a deep gully and everyone jumped in and scrambled into defensive positions. They weren't far behind and it wouldn't take them long to reach us. When they did, we'd have a little reception for them.

I leaned against the bank; the dirt felt cool pressed against my back. It was loose to the touch and my hand dug in easily. I brought up a handful and watched the soil escape slowly through my grip. *French farmland, where American and German soldiers meet to kill each other. It doesn't make sense.*

I complained out loud, "Lord I feel sick." But no one listened.

Taking off my helmet I looked at the card of the 23rd Psalm from Minerva. I took the time to read it slowly so each word would be absorbed and give all the strength and comfort possible. My reading was cut short.

There was the noise of footsteps at my side and I hurried into my helmet. Several Germans were coming from a new direction and I thought they must have us pinned in. Instead they were another small group of our own troopers; there were five, maybe six of them. They came up the ravine and joined us. Now there were roughly twenty of us.

I thought: *good, now when the Germans catch up we're only outnumbered by ten to one.*

We didn't have to wait another minute. We could hear them coming. They did a lot of yelling while firing a few shots.

"Get ready!" came an excited voice.

I climbed back up the gully and looked over the top where I saw some of them moving in the trees about 100 yards off. A few of our guys began to return fire. I took aim at one and squeezed off a round and now everyone else opened up. My shot missed. It didn't seem to do anything but make the guy run for cover. I must have made someone mad, however, because a machine gun answered me somewhere over to my right. I ducked down and heard the rounds hitting the leaves above my head with a snapping sound.

Someone yelled, "Hell, they're gonna kill us if they keep this up!"

Those were my thoughts exactly. It may even have been me yelling but I was too scared to notice.

I pulled back up and emptied my clip into the trees on the right. The German fire became heavier as they closed in on our position.

There were so many of them we just couldn't hold them back. I slipped in a new clip and looked to our assumed leader, the sergeant from the 505th. I believed he could help us stay alive, or at least keep us from stupid mistakes. But jumping the roadblock may have been a mistake. Looking back, we should have done some recon and formed a plan. At least learn who held the town.

"OK! That's enough," yelled the sergeant. "It's time we pull back and find another position."

"Yeah buddy! Let's go!" hollered several agreeing troopers.

The noncom shouted out orders. "You and you! Lay down a round of cover and then pull out behind us. Everyone else make for those trees. Then we'll get these two men out. Ready? Go! Let's go!"

We sprang out of the gully like supermen and hit the trees for cover. The sergeant turned and fired several rounds as the other two joined in our run. We continued this action all day. Fight until the enemy came close, then pull back again. With every move we headed east. There was no real reason for heading in that direction other than it was away from the Germans.

Our pace of travel each time was tremendous. We ran harder and faster than we ever had before. Our boots took a pounding through streams and the surrounding mud and moved us through skinny rabbit trails and supported our jumps over countless hedgerows. I became very thankful for the extreme amount of running we had done as paratroopers.

*　　*　　*

Training in California, John McGee and I had been assigned to the 88th Infantry Battalion, where we dealt with heavy weapons. Boot camp started with calisthenics and close-order drill. Drills were boring because I'd had four years of R.O.T.C. in high school. It was two weeks before some of the boys learned their left from their right. Running was a big part of our conditioning, more so here than I had in football.

Before long our soldiering started, working in teams on both the water-cooled 30-caliber machine gun and the 61mm mortars. The heavy weapons broke down into parts and we began hiking mile upon mile with these weapons.

There was not a lightweight part to be had. In addition to lugging about a part of a gun or mortar we also had to carry our own small arms weapon. During our seventeen weeks of training, we must have carried those machine guns and mortars over every one of those 47,000 acres and learned well why they were called "heavy weapons." When it came to the firing range and learning how to aim and shoot, I felt I did my best work on the machine gun, but I didn't relish carrying it.

I felt as if we hiked half a million miles with those weapons, but we ran another half-million and a lot of that running was on the obstacle course. Made up of wall barricades, rope swings, rope bridges, monkey bars and other assorted sneaky items, and it sometimes looked much easier than it really was. In time we learned many of the obstacles had a trick to them. It often depended on how you attacked them, where you planted your foot or how you balanced yourself. The obstacle course was always taken in double time—running. But long hard running was best defined at the Frying Pan.

The "Frying Pan" was so nicknamed by the 501 Parachute Infantry Battalion because life there was tough, but once you left the "Pan" is was into the tougher "fire" of war. On arrival, the duty sergeant said they would make it hard on us. They didn't want anyone who might have volunteered for the wrong reasons or with improper expectations; therefore rough training lay ahead.

The very next morning came early, so early the sun hadn't come up. We fell in for a five-mile run. We had a nice easy pace; I liked it. Then I learned that some guys had had only two weeks of training before starting paratrooper school; those were the guys who really struggled. Having done our share of calisthenics, those of us from California were far ahead.

The next morning started just as early. They all started this way. We fell in for a five-mile run. Down the road each day toward Lawson Field we would go. On most mornings fog was lying in the low spots and the morning dew was clinging to the grass. The dew reflected back a stunning shine. All we could hear on these runs was the thump, thump, thump of boots hitting the black top road leading to the airfield. We ran around the field before turning back to the barracks.

On or about the third day we all went down to supply and they issued us our jump boots. About the same time, we received the news we would have to wait a month before we were allowed to start the jump training, but while waiting the cadre would keep us entertained at the rifle range, doing calisthenics and even work in some extra chances for running. On the morning following we woke with instructions to put on our new jump boots. They said we were going to break them in; it was important for jump school.

"Oh boy," we thought, and then we were led out for our five-mile run. Our feet broke long before the boots did. Everyone had blisters all over the tops of their feet where the bootlaces went across. Two guys dropped out of the run that morning. After breakfast they were gone, shipped off. The cadre only told us they weren't fit to be Airborne and they didn't show any sympathy for any of us with bleeding feet either.

Knowing we could be dropped out of the program so quickly, John and I made a pact that evening. We were going to make it no matter how hard it got or how rough they made it. There would be no turning back or giving up. We were going to be there when jump school started and we were going to be paratroopers.

Back at Camp Roberts, California, everyone thought the superiors had tried to run our tails off. Now we were glad, for it really was paying off. Whenever the paratrooper cadre led us anywhere as a company or platoon, it was a double-time march. Running became so much a part of our life some of us started running in our free time.

* * *

Our foot travel across France required the endurance to go further and longer than we had ever run before. Yet somehow we seemed OK. Maybe fear drove us, or it could have been the fact that we stopped every half-mile to fight back. But we kept going, and by late morning it helped build our confidence. At the pace we were setting here, if we couldn't shoot them all, we might run a few to death. Early on we had started shedding our extra equipment. The gas mask was first to go and some medical kits followed. My musette bag was lost somewhere; it seems I took it off at one of our brief encounters and failed to pick it back up. The extra gear meant extra weight but I think the way it flopped around as we ran was a bigger issue. I noticed more than one soldier wearing a flak vest; I knew firsthand they were heavy but the guys kept those.

With every other move we picked up another stray American trooper or two, or three, including at least one medic, but on some stops we lost a few also. Late in the afternoon we came up to a river. This was a dead end, and some guys got nervous because running had been working so well. Our non-com didn't seem to like it either but he didn't hesitate.

"OK, this is it, let's spread out over here, these two hedgerows," he bellowed in a smooth voice but you could certainly hear some desperation. "And I want two guys to check out that little house. If anybody is in there then make 'em leave. There are no options. We'll hold our ground right here."

Our area of control was a thinly wooded area lodged between several open fields. Here we made our final defense, the last stand. The Germans came and gathered on three sides of us, water behind us. Knowing we were trapped I guess the Jerrys decided to take their time and figure out how best to attack us. Their first efforts were minimal in intensity. Then we watched and waited for more. Before very long we noticed how tired from the running we really were, but it felt strangely good because we were alive. We had been sly foxes all day and the German hounds had failed to catch us.

There were approximately four acres of French earth and a little two-room farmhouse to fight for. Our number had increased to about forty but some were hit and hurting. Maybe thirty-two men were in full fighting form and we were spread rather thin.

There was no way of knowing how the bigger fight around us was going. For all we knew the beach landing had failed and we might be the last ones alive. Additional gliders were expected in on D-Day, but none had been seen overhead and we heard no other firing except our own. The future seemed less than bright, but we were not about to give up. Not yet.

Everyone started a foxhole. Hedgerows that separated us from the fields surrounded most of our location. One side was swampy; it seemed the river sat at a flood level. The sparse woods helped give some cover but the whole area was mostly viewable through the trees.

As darkness came we began to settle down for the night. I brought out a K ration and ate my first meal of the day. We had been too busy entertaining the Germans to take time out to eat. Never in my life had I been so tired, and I realized that without the hard training given to us as paratroopers we would all be dead or captured.

I was glad to be among the living but wondered, was it luck, was I better than most, or was I just more careful? I couldn't sleep, few of us did. Everyone kept to his foxhole and tried to rest a little.

I visited with the trooper next to me some; he was with the 507th, and if fate had made him a Red Devil I felt we could have been good buddies. It was his first action as well, and the two of us maintained a close watch during the night waiting, for the Germans to hit us again. The German troops kept quiet, however, and seemed content to keep us bottled up while they slept.

With the rise of the morning sun on D-Day plus one, the enemy tried again, although they didn't show too much enthusiasm. The attack soon ended and we waited again. After several hours another attack came from a different position but we fought it off, too. Our enemy couldn't get at us, or else refused to pay the price, but we in turn couldn't get out. This was a stand-off for certain.

I worked on my foxhole most of the day and paced myself with my last remaining rations. A report came around to look out for sniper fire. Someone had taken a hit. On the positive side, a dozen or more paratroopers had joined us by sneaking past the Germans through the swamp. It was encouraging to keep gaining strength.

On the third day, the Germans again tested us. They failed to find a soft spot and we held out. When there was no attack underway, snipers tried picking us off. When the snipers stopped trying to scope in on us, the Germans tossed in a few artillery shells. Another trooper would be lost with each attack, but sometime during each night, and at different times of the day, additional small clusters of troopers found us and worked their way to our position. Despite our casualties we continually grew stronger.

But our strength lay only in our numbers, because that day the food ran out and first aid supplies were low. We now had two medics within our makeshift company and they established a first aid station and mortuary in the small farmhouse. The sniper fire and occasional artillery shells took out as many guys as all the ground attacks. One round of artillery hit a tree on the hedgerow between my foxhole and the one next to me. After letting the dust settle I looked about and found the 507th trooper was hit badly. He was alive but he didn't look good at all. I grabbed some help and we moved him to the medic's station at the farmhouse.

When I returned, the guys reminded me again to keep clear of snipers, but some of the boys were working out a system to deal with them.

"Look we've got about a half dozen of these air force flak vests scattered about," said one trooper. "One guy puts about three of them on and walks out into the field. When the sniper fires on him we'll pinpoint his location. Then everyone else opens up and lets him have it."

Another trooper asked, "Just who is going to walk out into the field?"

"I am!" said the first. "Then somebody else can go next."

The plan worked well. Our man walked out toward the Germans and dropped when the sniper fired on him. Everyone watched the trees and whoever saw the shot pointed out the location. We'd shoot until we saw the Kraut drop, then yell for our trooper to come back. Late in the day a new German sniper took over and we started the little game again.

Toward evening a message, at last, came in from Regiment. I didn't know if it came by runner or if there was a radio somewhere but it was sure a nice feeling to know friends were out there. Regiment said they knew our location, and we'd be resupplied by air. Our spirits soared—the beach landing had worked. There were other troopers east of the river and food was on the way.

My fourth morning in France began like the one before, with a half-spirited attack from the Germans, a shell or two from their artillery guns, and a new sniper in position for us to shoot at. Then at mid-morning a flight of C-47s came over the horizon and we gave a great shout of joy. We were sure looking forward to the supplies. There had been no food to eat yesterday, medical supplies were down to nothing, and ammo had also made the endangered list.

The planes veered left toward us and it was encouraging to realize that the pilots knew our exact location. Parachute bundles started dropping right over the top of us and with the opening snap of each chute I felt closer to home.

Then everyone watched the bundles drift down and land where only the swamp and the Germans could enjoy them. We did get a few landing close to our side of the lines but they had to be retrieved under fire. Upon opening them, our 505th sergeant found enough food to send to the farmhouse and some ammo for the rest to pass around. We could feed our wounded; the rest of us had to tighten our belts.

Morale stood pretty high despite the missed drop. We had friends out there trying to help us, and we figured they would try again soon. Not near as disappointing as the airdrop was the Germans wising up to the sniper game. We knocked off at least three, perhaps four, before they finally quit picking on us.

Late that afternoon I decided to make a visit to the farmhouse. I could check on my 507th friend, and it occurred to me there was an outside chance of finding a leftover K ration. It was quiet outside as I reached the porch. I don't know why but it shocked me a bit when I stepped inside and found it lined wall to wall with wounded soldiers. More troopers had found their way to us than I remembered.

The two medics worked in the center of the bloody scene, examining a trooper on the table. There was just enough space to make my way across the small room to them. I got the attention of one of the medics and asked him about the 507th trooper who had dug a foxhole next to me.

"Oh him," the medic answered. "He died. He went fast, but there wasn't any pain once the morphine sank in. Sorry if he was your buddy."

He gave me a half wave toward the back room door. I made my way over, apologizing to someone different about every third step, and moved into the only other room in the house. The carnage of that back room overwhelmed me. It was pure butchery.

The dead were in four or five stacks, one on top of the other, three and four high. Several bodies had been there all four days, and the warm June sun had brought a very foul smell to the room. I didn't bother looking for my friend. I just closed the door wishing I'd never opened it.

My rattled nerves needed some fresh air. Once outside I started to shake it off. I gave a long look around and tried to find the beauty of

France underneath the current battle zone. If God wasn't looking out for me, I'd have been laid out in that back room myself.

"The Lord is my shepherd," I verbalized softly and then I walked back to my foxhole. Regardless of the bloody mess I had just witnessed I was still hungry. I thought of Ireland. I thought of Ireland because there I knew where to find some food.

* * *

Ireland was a beautiful little well kept country, far from the war. It was green but also had rolling rocky hills, which produced a kind of rough contrasting edge. At the coastline the North Channel was wild and pounding. We enjoyed the scenery and getting to know the people. There wasn't entertainment offered in Port Stewart except for a few pubs and a skating rink. Skating was one of John's favorite activities and he could have found this rink if it had been in the middle of London. They only provided the old clamp-on style of skate, but that didn't slow us down. We had the rink all to ourselves because town folk stopped showing up whenever we were there. Our favorite time was forming a line and playing a game we called Pop-The-Whip. It got pretty rough, as guys on the end would get slammed hard into the wall. Everyone took his turn on the tail end. Some of us better skaters learned to put out one foot. This way we skated with one foot on the floor and one on the wall.

If we had a weekend pass, John and I would head for Port Push. We found a lady there who had rooms for rent and we always stayed over for a night. She was a large woman with a winning personality. On Sunday afternoon she ran a penny ante poker game in her living room that always drew a crowd. Even if you didn't play it was great fun to watch. Several troopers began to stay with her and we all looked upon her as a kind of mother figure. She gave troopers high-class treatment and always made everyone feel at home.

The downside of Ireland was the food in our camp. I had eaten a lot of army chow but this proved even worse than training at the Frying Pan. Those of us in headquarters, and I believe most of the platoons, were sending out two-man raiding parties to steal food from the kitchen. Each evening we would cook up a little dinner for anyone who stayed in camp that night. Soon headquarters built up a fair size food supply. When we learned that we were going to Nottingham to join the 82nd orders also came to pack up everything.

"Hey guys, what about the food?" questioned Ramon Prieto.

Hurst answered, "Hell I don't know. We can't take it with us."

"We've got to take it back." That was Eddie.

But nobody could come up with a plan to sneak it back to the kitchen.

"We could just get honest and take it back," Eddie continued his argument.

"Great Eddie, you do it," Woody chimed in.

"Why me? Why not cut cards or draw sticks?" But Eddie's plan fizzled out.

Then it was Wilbur Scanlon who recommended a bright master plan. "Look," he said, "there are rocks all over this place. Let's take the food outside, dump it into a low spot and bury it under a pile of rocks."

So we all went to work; rocks were plentiful and it didn't take long. A few guys stomped on top of the rocks to set them in place. It seemed we were safe until someone found one more can. He tossed it behind one of the tents into a rubbish pile and Colonel Lindquist happened by and found it. He called us all together and gave us a real chewing out for throwing food away.

"If you have any food, take it back to the kitchen."

"I told ya!" shouted Eddie in a stage whisper.

Several men tried to choke back a big laugh and were ready to burst under the pressure. Others grew really nervous, scared the laughter would defeat us all. The colonel gave his lecture while standing on the only high ground he could find—the pile of rocks that hid our discarded food supply.

* * *

During those first days in Normandy, what I wouldn't give for a can or two of all that food we had buried in Ireland. I'd have happily eaten a couple of the camp meals as well.

Between the periods of fighting I spent time working on my foxhole. Not only did I put a roof over most of it, but also after digging down a ways, I turned my shovel and dug back into the hedgerow making it L shaped. It may have been the best-built foxhole in the area, but there was no bother checking. It wasn't a contest, it was just survival. Maybe building was in my blood. Dad was home building boats and I had the good fortune of working as a draftsman with Consolidated Aircraft. When my draft notice arrived I spent the next summer in California where foxhole building was a part of every soldier's education. But as good as this French foxhole was I hoped it didn't prove to be my life's work.

My efforts on the foxhole were rewarded on D-Day plus five. That morning our sergeant came by to spread the word to keep our heads down. Another message came in from Regiment; they were going to lay down an artillery barrage all around us.

"Then they'll come in and get us out," he explained.

"Tell 'em to bring in lots of rations when they come, Sarg," a soldier cried out. Everyone agreed.

A short time passed and we heard the first thin whistle of our shelling begin. The skinny whine grew stronger and heavier and it sounded like it was coming in on our positions. It seemed odd that I could tell the difference between our artillery and the German stuff by the sound. Everyone popped down into their hole. Deep inside there it was nice to know the incoming belonged to us, but it scared the dog out of me anyway.

The explosions were so close the trees around our position were blown away. The air filled with noise and dirt, and the shells just kept on coming. Before long the dust hung in the air so thick you had to beat your way through it. It drifted into my foxhole and I started to choke. Some explosions came so close I swore the next one was planning to land right down in the hole with me. With every striking round I pushed into the back of the L-shaped trench, wishing my truly fine foxhole was a little deeper. More artillery from our lines came over in two minutes than the Germans had thrown at us in five full days. After several more minutes of nonstop explosions it all ended abruptly.

I waited a bit after the barrage had lifted. With no more shells and no sound from the German lines, I grabbed my weapon and shimmied out to see what was going on. The area around the hedgerows was a wreck; all the trees in our area were stripped of their leaves. But no trooper was harmed.

Around the German positions only a few trees were left standing, most were blasted into firewood. A few American leg soldiers were crossing the fields. Down the line I spied a lieutenant coming toward me. The 90th Infantry Division had come through and this officer had a huge armload of K rations. He handed them out to troopers as he walked among our foxholes. His voice rang out with high praise but what he carried was a lot more important to us.

He commented to each man as he handed out packages, "Good going soldier. Here you are. Nice job. That was really good work. Here, have something to eat. You guys put up one heck of a fight."

He handed me a K ration package and I started in without hesitation. I ate all the meat and crackers right down to the last crumb. I tossed some wood pieces together and started a fire to make a cup of bouillon. Drank it down as if it was really good soup. Then I started in on the fruit bar. That was the first time in my life I had ever been truly hungry.

At midday we received an order to pull out. Trucks came in for our dead, and our inter-regimental band of fighters was sent in different directions. I wondered if our paths would cross again but I knew I'd never forget the days we fought together. The 505th sergeant should have earned a medal or a battlefield commission and been given his own platoon; he saved a lot of men and showed outstanding leadership. I never did learn how he communicated with regiment or even which regiment it was. It is possible we may have been near the larger group of defendants on Hill 30. We were maybe close enough that some troopers made the risk of acting as messengers between them and us. I would guess that the party I fought with was somewhat north of that but I will never know.

By early evening I found myself back with F Company of the 508th. It sure felt good to look around and see familiar faces again, though there were not as many as I'd hoped to see.

I got settled, received a place to sleep on the line, another foxhole, and then started taking a good second look at our position. When I realized how many were missing the news was nothing but bad. I couldn't come up with names right off, but several faces of F Company were gone, including Captain Flanders and my best buddy, John McGee. As one of the last to rejoin the company I was told, "This is it," but I hoped that maybe more troopers would still come in. Captain Flanders was known to be captured and John McGee was officially listed as missing in action.

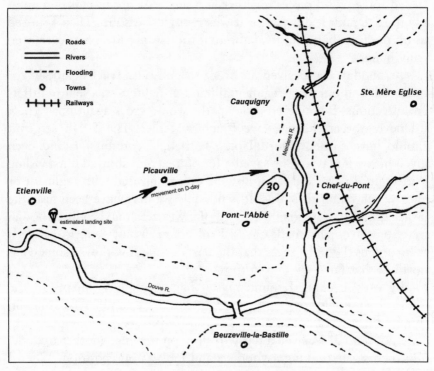

The 508th's area of operations in the triangle between the Douve and Merderet Rivers in Normandy.

JUMP
Four

"He didn't make it. He's dead."

I had a hole in my chest. My buddy could be lying out there dead somewhere and no one had found him. News of the capture of Captain Flanders, our commander, was at first considered a tragedy for the company. Lieutenant Goodale was now our acting Company Commander, I could live with that. We also had a new acting First Sergeant, Wilbur Scanlon, and I couldn't think of a darn thing wrong with that move either.

Before walking out to the planes for the invasion on D-day, Captain Flanders had given us a pep talk. I tried to recall some of his words but the talk that came to mind was more of an ass chewing from a month earlier.

* * *

There was a song that every paratrooper learned while training at Fort Benning. It could be heard most anytime of the day coming from almost any direction. The melody was lifted from "The Battle Hymn of The Republic" and the song was called "Blood Upon The Risers." These are the words to the first verse and chorus.

"Is everybody happy?" Cried the sergeant looking up.
Our hero feebly answered, "Yes," and then they stood him up.
He jumped into an icy blast, his static line unhooked.
And he ain't gonna jump no more!
Chorus:
Gory, gory, what a helluva way to die!
Gory, gory, what a helluva way to die!

55

Gory, gory, what a helluva way to die!
And he ain't gonna jump no more!

The song continues with an almost second-by-second account of the doomed soldier's drop from the sky and a detailed description of his bloody landing with his comrades exclaiming over and over that its "a helluva way to die."

Three practice jumps were made in England. The first one in March was a complete mess and the weather was completely unfavorable. After flying around for an hour looking for the other planes and experiencing a near in-flight collision, the pilots turned back to the airfield for a landing.

An April jump was smooth and the pilots were much improved. On May 17th it was back to the airfield for the third time, this one a night jump. This time the regiment wasn't so lucky. A trooper in one of the other companies just plain disappeared. At bed check his buddies covered up for him thinking he was getting lucky in town.

When he still didn't show they covered for him again. Two nights later they realized no one had seen him since the jump and they finally came forward to their CO. A detail was promptly sent to the drop zone to look for him.

At the DZ they found what they came for, lying silently in a field. The poor guy's chute had failed and he had harnessed his reserve on upside down. That put the release handle on the left side. In the dark the guy hadn't found it but the men in the detail said they determined he had clawed at the right-hand end of the chute, trying for the handle before he hit the ground. As news reached us in headquarters, we learned the brass was plenty upset about it. Captain Flanders rounded up the company and he had a reserve chute with him.

"Anyone want to volunteer to tell me which is the top and which is the bottom of this chute?"

Everyone was silent.

"Well? Don't I have at least one of you who knows the difference?"

It was the junior officer, Lt. Cook, who provided the information everyone in the room already knew. "This is the top, Sir; it's worn with the handle on the right."

"Thank you, Lieutenant. I don't want to have to remind everyone again, so get it right! And if I catch any of you doing it wrong I'll either kill you myself or take your stripes away, whatever seems appropriate. F Company is too good for this to ever be a problem. Any questions?"

There was silence again briefly until some smart aleck shouted out, "It was a helluva way to die."

Suddenly "Blood On The Risers" brought out a whole different set of emotions. The tune echoed through my mind like a funeral dirge. What jerk had said that? Now it might have been the guy's way of shaking it off because it could have happened to any of us; nor was it something we could afford to sit around and dwell on. Everyone had to put it behind them and press on.

* * *

Those were the words I remembered from Captain Flanders. One and a half weeks after that last jump was when everything changed. We ended the girl chasing, there were no more fish and chips dinners, and no more drinking or dart games. The 508th was moved to Saltby Airfield to standby for the invasion.

The loss of our Captain and First Sergeant was another thing that F Company had to put behind us and move past. John McGee's MIA status was something I had to try and keep out of my mind if I wanted to keep going and keep living. Members of company headquarters seemed to fare very well and those who made it back included John Hurst, Woody Phelps and radio operator Ed Chatoian. Rejoining the company at the same time as me was Ralph Burrus who had been on Hill 30. My friend Ramon Prieto did not make it.

Ramon either died at the battle for the bridge at La Fiere or fighting west of the river somewhere north of my own action. I never learned for certain but that was common. Stories flowed in abundance but they were also in occasional conflict. Someone would claim that a certain soldier had died at a certain town, then you'd hear he had jumped somewhere else. Lt. Gillespie, who I'd seen dead on the German flatbed, had died from machine-gun fire. Eddie Alexik didn't jump; he had the designation of being our company clerk, which meant he stayed behind and tended to company business. He collected

our mail and kept the shop open, so to speak. It was a good job if you
could get it.

Acting First Sergeant Scanlon took pity on me. I wasn't scheduled
for any duties during my first full day back; I got fed a large meal for
supper and that night I slept well, my best sleep since leaving my tent
and traveling to the airfield to go on alert for D-Day.

Next day, after my night of peaceful sleep, I knocked off a solid
breakfast and felt almost new. I had no duties other than to get my
personal and issued items cleaned and ready to move again. By now
supplies were coming in through the beachhead at Normandy. Most
troopers spent the morning putting a finishing touch on the company
to bring it back up to full preparedness. Others maintained the ever-
constant guard duty. Stories continued getting passed around nonstop
about all the different jumps made during the invasion. Some landed
in towns that were occupied by German soldiers. One trooper went
through the roof of a greenhouse and another went down a well. Two
men landed on a church, with one of them getting stuck with his chute
wrapped around the steeple. Others died when they hit burning buildings.

There were several reports of troopers who landed in trees and
were shot while they hung helpless, unable to move. Many were shot
and killed while still in the air but others died from flak and never left
the plane.

The English Channel claimed the lives of at least one planeload,
which jumped too late. Some others who jumped late found themselves on the beachheads due to be attacked the next morning. My
landing in a solid field was what I had expected but it wasn't exactly
the norm. There were countless troopers who proved to be less than
lucky.

The Germans had purposely flooded the fields in many low lying
areas and several sticks of men had drowned there. With that news I
thought of John again. A man could go into the river, drown, and not
be found for weeks or months.

*   *   *

Our last practice jump in Georgia had been a night jump. I remembered the weather was great as we took off that night; cool, not cold,

no wind, no clouds, lots of stars out, but we had no moon. We were going to have trouble seeing the ground. Outside the plane a few lights twinkled here and there from the ground. A short view of town became visible and I hoped the pilot knew where he was going. I sure didn't want us to land in the Chattahoochee River. A picture of us hitting the water came to mind that night. Dozens of men, weighed down with heavy boots, fully clothed, and wearing extra equipment, fighting to remain afloat. Even if you could lose your helmet and boots you were harnessed to a sinking parachute. There seemed no way you could quickly remove enough equipment to keep from sinking like a boat anchor. In my case it wouldn't have mattered anyway. I never had learned to swim.

* * *

Any trooper hitting the river was in trouble. We were taught to roll on impact. Training would have these men roll under the water before they realized it and they might not ever recover. Some troopers drowned in areas only a couple of feet deep.

I heard of one trooper who did not jump. Exploding flak ripped open his main chute and shredded it, just before the green light. Several of his jump mates died from the flak but someone was alive and had the good sense to inform this guy his chute was ruined, so he better ride the airplane back to England. He did.

The jump accuracy of the 508th and our sister regiment, the 507th, were graded the worst of the D-Day airborne missions. Most of the 508th landed east of the Merderet River, including our commander, Lt. Colonel Linguist, and General Gavin, who jumped with the Red Devils. Our mission from D-Day, June 6th, until June 11th had been to keep the enemy from reinforcing their troops at the beach. Although our forces west of the Merderet never properly organized and most of the 508th's objectives were abandoned, the overall main task was still accomplished with small groups fighting independently of each other. I know my own makeshift bunch on the west side sure tied up a lot of Krauts at the time. Our battalion commander, Lt. Colonel Thomas J. B. Shanley, was the ranking officer west of the Merderet; he managed to gather some 200 men from a mixture of regiments. This was the party of soldiers making the stand on Hill 30, not far from where I fought. Their account is well documented in war history. Soldiers under Shanley's command formed the largest number fighting together west of the Merderet.[xi]

Lt. Colonel Lindquist, on the eastern side, found himself without a regiment. Starting with fewer than a hundred men, he attempted to march to the 508th's main objective and enroute he gathered a battalion-size number of troopers though most were from the 505th and the 507th P.I.R.s. With this force he fought for, captured and held the bridge at La Fiere. The expense in lives lost was high on both sides. Since Lindquist was in command, history gives credit for this victory to the Red Devils.

A moment was taken at midmorning to formally brief us that all within the 82nd Airborne had received a Presidential Citation for gallantry in action during the first two days of fighting. We all cheered and patted each other on the backside, but we were not going home yet.

"Burns?" It was a trooper from the 3rd platoon running to catch up to me.

"Yes?" I answered. "What is it?"

"You and McGee are good pals, right?"

I grew a little nervous, and then told him, "Yeah. John comes from the same hometown and we took all our training together, that kind of stuff. I heard he was missing."

"Look, I'm sorry to have to tell you this but I'm pretty sure he's been captured. Some of us who jumped with him saw the Germans take several of our guys prisoner. We all think John was taken. He must have hurt his foot though, this prisoner was limping."

"Oh. Where 'bouts were you?"

"We were hiding in Picauville, slipped out right after that. We passed the information forward about John but they haven't changed his status yet."

"Well thanks for letting me know; it's better than being dead I guess."

Over a year had passed since meeting John on the way to the draft board. It seemed a lot longer. We went though a lot of experiences together. It was going to be strange not having him around and I would miss him terribly. I tried putting stock in the account that he was captured and maybe I'd see him after the war. The story about him limping made sense to me because John had hurt a foot once before and I had wondered on occasion if it had correctly healed or if it was a break waiting to happen again.

* * *

Training jump number five, the night jump, was also our last one before graduation. With four jumps made our training was all behind us now. We were all in excellent shape but we figured if anything were going to go wrong, it would happen that night.

There was no moon to aid us but the weather, at least, was perfect. Outside the plane only a few lights twinkled here and there on the ground. I thought maybe we wouldn't jump at night during wartime, just this once for training. Get through this and tomorrow we could get our wings. Then we would be off for two weeks and that time span would cover Thanksgiving Day. What a great thought. Home with Minerva for two weeks. Like a kid waiting for Christmas, I just couldn't wait.

After the jumpmaster yelled for us to stand up and hook up we went out the door like a well-greased machine, hitting the silk right over the drop zone. As I floated down I strained to see the rest of my stick. They were there drifting with me but I couldn't make anyone out. By the lights on the edge of the field I could tell the ground was coming closer so I looked for it instead. Then I could see the ground and got ready. But it wasn't there and I just kept on drifting. I tried looking again, then all of a sudden, wham! The ground hit me hard. I hadn't seen it at all. I lay there with my wind knocked out but with no real damage done.

John's trouble was much greater. He fractured an ankle during his landing. He required help in getting his chute rolled up and limped badly to the truck. He said it hurt like hell, but shook off any suggestion of going to the dispensary.

"No way," he said. "There is no way. That's our last jump and tomorrow we get our wings. I'm a paratrooper now and just like the rest of you s.o.b.'s I'm going to be there to get mine."

The trucks took us back to the packing shed and we had to tend to our chutes before our night was over. We had to help John because he couldn't get it done. Despite the advancing hour I knew on the walk back to the barracks there wouldn't be much sleep that night. We were all worked up and ready to celebrate, and anyone who might have wanted to sleep didn't.

The next morning John's ankle looked awful. It was swollen to about twice its normal size and had turned black, blue, green and yellow.

I told him, "John, you don't want to hear this, but you need to go to the hospital and let them look at this. It's no sprain, it has to be broken. I don't know how you can walk on it."

"Hell, Dwayne, we're going to graduate in just a few hours! I'm not going over there."

"Well then go after graduation," I tried to reason.

"No, no, no," he said and shook his head. "There's two weeks of leave waiting for me. Now help me with my boot." He had loosened all the laces and the tongue stuck out past the toe. He gave it to me.

"You're lucky there's no running on graduation day," I joked as I gingerly slipped the boot on his foot.

"I know what you're saying," he replied, "but tomorrow, good buddy, with your help, when you get on that train, I'll be there too. Pull those laces up as tight as you can because I need all the support I can get."

"OK," I said. "I just hope you don't expect me to play nursemaid for you all the way to Fort Worth," and I jerked hard on the bootlaces.

"Ouch! No. Of course not," he said through his pain. Then he sort of chuckled, "What I expect is for you to find me a nurse."

* * *

During that first day, following my return to the regiment, I learned that not everyone missing was killed or captured. We had just as many wounded in action who'd been shipped back to England. That was a positive thought. Some of the other wounded were still with us, the "walking wounded," and this included John Hurst.

After some lunch on that first full day back with the company the filling meal under my belt helped me believe I was ready for anything. This was about the time we got updated word on Captain Flanders. He was dead. He had been among several GIs taken captive and

German trucks were transporting the lot of them to a prisoner of war camp. Allied planes spotted the column of trucks. Our planes of course didn't know who or what was in those trucks, so they strafed them several times, doing as much damage as possible. Several of our guys died in the attack. When I learned the truth about the Captain, I couldn't help but think about John once again and wonder what had happened to him. Prisoner was bad enough, but this news nearly shattered my hope.

The rest of the day remained quiet and that evening we were able to enjoy a great dinner. I figured there must have been a butcher's son or hunter among us, because someone slaughtered a cow and fresh juicy steaks were passed around. I helped build a broad fire and then prepared myself a forked green limb of wood to cook with. Everyone found a spot at the fire and we settled down, grilling our great looking cuts of beef over the campfire.

A runner came up to us.

"F Company?" he asked.

Half of us ignored him, but we sort of eyed each other.

"Is this F Company?" he asked again.

Someone finally answered, "Yeah, close enough, so what do you want?"

The runner explained, "I've just come from Regimental Headquarters."

Our interest in him picked up a little and our self appointed spokesman jumped in, "So whadda ya want?"

"Colonel Lindquist sent me. It seems there's a farmer complaining that someone shot his cow."

We started to squirm a bit; the runner really had our attention now.

The runner continued, "The Colonel immediately needs four one-inch steaks for evidence."

One of the troopers recruited the man next to him to watch his steak and he started leading the runner away. They were still in sight when Woody started chuckling. The rest of us gave him a glance and joined in, and then it suddenly became roaring laughter. It was funny, yes, but we kept laughing because it felt so good. For the first time in weeks we finally remembered how to laugh.

On June 12th, about mid-morning, Ed Chatoian singlehandedly developed the worst idea of the war: a spare battery for the radio.

"Why do we need that?" I asked him.

"In case the one in the radio plays out or takes a hit."

He took off for Regiment and returned with the battery in his arms. This was a heavy, awkward piece of equipment.

"How you gonna carry it?" I asked. Ed however had that figured out too.

With some suspension lines cut off a parachute, he fashioned a carrying handle for it. Ed stayed busy cutting and wrapping and tying knots until he was happy. Then he handed it over to me. ✔

"Here Burns, you're the assistant radio operator, you have to carry it."

"Oh boy, lucky me," I harped. "Just what I need, something else to carry!"

"Be glad you don't have to carry the radio."

"This isn't going to work Ed," I complained. "The suspension line cuts into my shoulder."

"Well try it out and see," he said, ending our conversation.

* * *

On the evening of June 12th our rest time ended. Acting F Company Commander Goodale led us down to the Douve River. The 508th was going to attack the bridge, which crossed to the town of Beuzeville-la-Bastille. Moving hours before the main body, F Company had orders to cross over in boats and attack the bridge from behind—from within the town while the other Red Devils charge across.

We carried the boats with us. They had flat metal bottoms and wooden sides. I didn't much trust them. None of us had ever seen an assault boat before, much less gone into action with one. They didn't look a whole lot like any boats I'd ever been in before and I had spent plenty of time in boats around Lake Worth. Also traveling with us was a reporter from *Life* magazine. While waiting on the bank for two hours, the reporter asked each of us our name and where we were from. There was a certain thrill at the thought of getting our names in ✔ *Life*.[xii] Overshadowing any excitement, however, was concern about F Company's mission.

Around midnight we quietly loaded up and began the river crossing. We started for the south side of Beuzeville-la Bastille's riverbank.[xiii]

We paddled silently and all seemed to go well. The boats were not
built for any speed records, however, and the crossing took considerable time. I grew quite nervous. On my best days I was still a poor
swimmer, and being loaded down with combat gear didn't enhance my
chances should the Germans catch us out in the middle. Dipping my
hand into the river I found the water surprisingly warm, just right for
a Saturday bath.

*When was my last bath? Good Lord! We haven't bathed in twelve
days. If the wind is right the Germans will smell us coming.*

Our raiding party paddled well over halfway, but a hundred yards
still remained before our boats reached the far bank when the
Lieutenant gave a signal to stop rowing and we slipped over the sides
of the boat. The water was only four feet deep. Not even I could
drown in it, and actually I was glad to be out of the clumsy craft. We
wadded the rest of the way through the river.

Shortly after we came out of the water, three light German tanks
drove up the river road. I don't think they knew we were in the area.
One of the platoon leaders, 2nd Lieutenant Lloyd Polette, called for
our bazooka team. Some of the guys had bragged earlier about
Polette's bravado under fighting conditions and his keen sense of
awareness. Polette took charge of the gun himself, but according to
Emery Van Every, the bazooka man had been too nervous to handle
it. At some point the bazooka failed and Polette had to rely on hand-
delivering the shell into one of the tank's tracks. Two tanks were
knocked out before the third turned tail and left. Then Lieutenant
Goodale had Ed radio back for artillery.

The incoming must have been heavier than anything we had ever
used before, because I heard it from a long way back. It sounded like
we were throwing boxcars at the Germans. Everyone stayed low on
the riverbank as the town exploded deep within. With the lifting of the
artillery we attacked the town. By five o'clock in the morning the rest
of the Regiment had fought across the bridge and the sweep of the
town was quick. Fighting was light and by late morning all the Red
Devils moved on to tackle other objectives.[xiv]

* * *

F Company didn't linger about. The town of Baupte was assigned to the 2nd Battalion, and F Company rejoined the larger unit. A mile outside the town we ran into heavy fire. The battalion commander, Lt. Colonel Shanley, ordered an artillery barrage and then we were on our way again. Shanley split the battalion, and ordered Companies D and E to attack the north end of town, and good ol' F Company to start fighting in the south. As the company worked its way to the town's edge I found myself in a graveyard.

This seemed to be great luck. The fire was light, and I could make my way forward slipping from the shelter of one tombstone to the next. Maybe three or four guys followed my path. Suddenly the firing increased ten-fold and a machine gun opened up. The rounds began ricocheting off the tombstones all around me and the bullets were coming from all directions. I was pinned in crossfire.

I couldn't see where the others crouched. Hopefully everyone was behind a stone. Then I realized: if anyone gets killed they'd need a cemetery, we were in a cemetery, and today is the 13th. Too much bad karma was going on here and I felt the need to get out quick.

Using whatever cover I could find, I started over to the graveyard's border until I reached a fence. Here was a spot well shielded by the headstones and I could wait until the fight became a little quieter. I slipped a quick glimpse at the 23rd Psalm. *I will fear no evil. I will fear no evil.* When the firing eased off, I came up and went over the fence all in a single motion and then made a strong dash across the street into an open doorway. The others made it as well and someone must have found the German machine-gun crew because it went quiet for good shortly after.

We continued working through the southern half of Baupte, a typical French village with narrow streets and houses set side by side. The real heavy fighting lasted over an hour, with skirmishes occuring at almost every street. In the north end of town Companies D and E captured a German motor pool of four-dozen vehicles plus a large supply of gasoline and support equipment.

* * *

During our weapons training between jumps we'd been introduced to a new invention called the Gammon grenade. One end of this device looked like the top of a black sock into which plastic explosives were packed to form a ball. At the other end, there was a cap we were to unscrew before using the grenade. Under the cap was a lanyard with a lead weight. The grenade was thrown like a football and, as it spiraled through the air, the lanyard unwound and pulled the safety pin. From then on it was a deadly weapon and the slightest jar would set it off. It was easy enough to carry and a highly effective weapon against light tanks and trucks. I figured right away it would prove handy.

At midday of the 13th, after pushing and fighting all night and morning, a few of us were getting a quick meal and short rest behind some of the houses when we heard the sound of a tank coming down the main street. Sergeant Red Thomas and I reacted at the same time. Each of us grabbed a Gammon grenade and our M-1s. I made a run around the left side of the house; Red raced through the house itself and got there first.

As I stepped past the corner I saw the sergeant release his grenade. It spun as if in slow motion, the lanyard unwound, the pin jerked free. It clanged upon hitting the metal and then, ka-boom!

The tank made a sudden side-sliding turn and crashed to a stop, demolishing the front of a house. The top hatch was already open and we both took positions at each end of the house with our weapons ready. It suddenly seemed quiet. I could hear my heart beat. Nobody moved in the tank.

Sergeant Thomas yelled out, "Cover me Burns."

"You got it," I said. I took a short look down the street from which the tank had come.

Red moved to the tank, climbed the tracks to the turret, and popped a quick glance down the hatch. Then he took another, longer look.

"Burns, come here, you ought to see this." He motioned for me.

It was a small French tank with German markings. I clambered to where he stood and looked inside to see the crew. Both of them died from broken necks. We closed the hatch on them as if it were a coffin lid and went back behind the house to resume our rest. Scratch off another enemy tank.

The fighting lasted all day. Baupte proved to be a lot harder to take than Beuzeville-la-Bastille, and as a united Regiment it was the first fierce action we had seen.

After going for nearly forty hours, a good night's rest was needed by all, but first we had to dig a slit trench.

Rex Spivey down the line asked, "Where is Kulwicki?"

"He didn't make it. He's dead."

I stopped digging.

Then Rex asked, "How did he get it?"

"He and Polette walked right past this German who they didn't see. The German stood up and shot Kulwicki, who fell on top of Giegold. Seale was following behind them so he shot the German."

Everyone went back to work on the trench but conversations continued.

Don Yoon was thinking aloud, "Why would a lone German stand up to shoot in the middle of several enemy soldiers? That is pretty stupid."

"Maybe he panicked," Hurst replied.

"I overheard Joe Harold tell about two Germans who were hiding in a truck. He set his weapon down to look in the truck for food. He wasn't even armed and these two had the drop on him but they just gave up. That's pretty stupid too."

Sergeant Joseph Harold was a squad leader. We revisited the day street by street and bullet by bullet until the digging was deep enough for protection. Then we raided a nearby barn and hauled a few bundles of hay to our slit trench. After lining the trench we used the remaining hay as cover for the top. It would offer as much comfort as we could get and I slept well that night.

JUMP
Five

"Strap on the radio and stay close."

The next morning I awoke hungry; most active soldiers stay that way. Yesterday's fighting had left little time for a decent meal and now I was hopeful a field kitchen would serve us breakfast. I visited a moment with the guard on duty. All was quiet, he told me.

A machine gun was set up in a nest and I took time to study how the gun crew had arranged things. During my initial training they'd been fun to shoot at the practice ranges. I could have been a good gunner; heck, I *was* a good gunner prior to becoming a paratrooper, but then they thought I should handle a radio instead. Remembering the gun's weight, I gave thanks I didn't have to carry it all day. I enjoyed being as light as possible and as Ed's backup I didn't have to carry the radio either. It was a good scenario. I returned to my part of the slit trench with a fresh issue of morning K Rations.

While I ate, Ed walked by, having just finished his own box of breakfast. He gave me a nod and headed my way. I threw him a joking and ugly left-handed salute.

Right away he asked, "Burns, where's the spare battery?"

"Sorry Ed, I lost that thing in the fighting yesterday." I didn't tell him that at the first shots of the attack in Beuzeville-la-Bastille the thing got tossed as far as it would go. Damned brick was lucky to have made it across the river.

"Oh, well I'll see about getting another," Ed said and he started back to Regiment.

Later in the morning he produced another battery for me to carry. This time he found some webbing to tie around it.

"With this webbing it won't cut into your shoulder," he said with

69

a look of inventors' pride.

It was indeed better, but I couldn't get very excited about his creativity. "Big deal," I grumbled. "I still have to drag it around. I don't think we need a spare."

"We need it just in case."

"OK then, I'll carry it." But I told myself that at the next firefight this particular burden was again going missing.

* * *

We had taken Baupte, and over the next couple of days we held a defensive line. On the 16th we went into Division Reserve status west of Etienville. Etienville was a primary objective for the 508th on D-Day and the objective I should have been fighting for upon jumping into France, but this was the first I had seen of it.

After a day we moved west to relieve the 505th at St. Sauveur-le-Vicomte, and we stayed there until the 20th of June, seing no action. We returned to Etienville for another stay. During this second stop in Etienville, we started sending out patrols deep into German territory.

A platoon of us went behind German lines to do some recon work. It was quiet for us and our travel remained undetected. We learned a few things stalking about and believed we had done a decent job of recon. Our path back to our lines would be easy.

We traveled single file alongside a road that tended to be clear. The French people stayed out of the way near the lines of fighting, so anyone on the roads could be taken for friend or foe. Word came from the head of our file to spread quickly.

"There's a bicycle coming, everyone down."

"Where? Where is it?" Donald Yoon asked from behind me.

"Over there, idiot, get down." Woody said in an excited but hushed voice.

"Say, do we know if it's even a German or not?" I questioned.

"He's German, look where he's coming from."

Yoon had another question. "Why are we all hiding from one single Jerry on a bicycle?" It was a very good question.

"I don't know, they said get down."

"Well let's shoot him."

The sole German soldier started pedaling past our position. We remained squatted behind the road hedge and the trees, discussing his fate.

"Man, what a sitting duck."

"Too easy," I commented.

"Well somebody ought to shoot him."

A few troopers looked at one another.

"Ah, just let him go."

He was no threat to us and no one in the group could bring themselves to make the kill. We should have captured him, since he may have been a messenger, but we didn't think of it until later.

* * *

Back in Etienville, some of us decided to cook a pot of dehydrated beans that came in a ten-in-one ration kit. First thing, we needed something to cook them in. We scrounged around, but all we could find was a large crock bowl. This would have to do.

We scrubbed it good, both inside and out, filled it with water and sat it on our campfire. Beans were poured in and we sat back to watch them cook for a while. We spiced them up with what we had but that wasn't much.

"We need some cut up spam," Ed thought. But we didn't have any. John Hurst asked for pineapple chunks which we also didn't have. Everyone had something different they wanted to add, but basic salt and pepper was about all there was. After a couple of hours on the fire, however, those beans smelled just like Mom would have cooked 'em back home. Outside of some fresh beefsteaks, they qualified as the best-looking things we had seen in a month.

Watching the simmering and bubbling action really made our mouths water. We finally decided they had cooked long enough and we took to moving the crock off the fire so we could cook the rest of our dinner.

Woody said, "Burns grab the other side of the rim there and help me."

"Where do you want to put it?"

"Right here beside the fire. They'll stay hot that way."

"OK, just lift the pot straight up and then we'll set it down there."

"Alright, let's go."

Woody and I each got hold of the rim and lifted. We heard a muted snap, followed by a rush of sizzling sounds. We stood holding only the sides; the bottom of the bowl and the beans had stayed with the fire.

With no restraints the beans spread quickly into the burning coals and ashes. It was a sudden shock to both of us and I saw Woody's face go pale. The other guys looked at us with widening eyes. For a second I wanted to crawl under the beans and hide, but then everyone started laughing together. If it hadn't been so darn funny I'm sure we would have all blubbered like babies.

*   *   *

On June 29th we took up positions in Bois De Limors, near Pretot. In this area laid the famous 88 Junction, a crossroad intersection so well covered by German artillery fire that a detour had to be constructed around it.

Very early on the morning of July 3rd we received orders to attack against Hill 131. Elements of the 2nd and 3rd Battalions formed the assault wave and F Company headed up the attack. Dawn was just over as we moved toward the hill, and one of the lead platoon sergeants called a halt. I remember the day as being dull gray, the air full of drizzle. The area had recently been harvested for lumber. The trees were all fallen but giant trimmed logs remained where they fell.

While we waited for word to move up, we heard the startup of mortar fire. We dived between the logs as the first round hit the ground. Two troopers on my right were both killed by a tree burst, and there I was, just twelve inches away. One of the fatalities was Don Yoon and I think the other one's name was David Miller. Ralph Burrus took one in the knee and also hurt his back after the blast tossed him a good nine or ten feet.

Before we got orders to resume our advance, a heavy rain started. Things didn't look like they were going our way. We all got muddy in short order, and then we stood up to assault the hill. Turned out the rain actually helped us because the Germans were trying to stay dry and were not nearly as alert as they should have been. Thanks to the Krauts' own artillery and mortar fire, their communications were briefly disrupted and we got in before they knew we were coming.

As we drove deeper into the enemy territory, their resistance weakened and large numbers of prisoners were taken. By mid-morning the rain ceased and we had Hill 131. We had reached one objective but this was just a prelude to the big fight. Amazingly I still had the spare radio battery.

F Company had captured a machine-gun emplacement on the way, which yielded four prisoners. Lieutenant Goodale, who had taken a minor wound in the battle, came to Woody and me and assigned us the job of taking them back to the rear. We marched the four down the road until we ran into the reserve unit and they said they would take the prisoners off our hands. We were glad to get rid of them.

As we returned to our company area, we dropped into the first empty trench. It was about waist deep, and we set down to rest. Our bodies felt completely worn out.

I stretched out in one end of the trench that had some tree limbs over it and quickly fell into a sound sleep. A bit later I awoke when cold water started running down the back of my neck. It was raining again. I looked over at Woody sleeping on the other end of the trench and he was still out of it, deeply asleep. He had his mouth wide open.

Woody, you son of a gun, if you're lucky, you'll drown and get out of this mess the easy way.

Just prior to noon I had to go back to the rear area again on a company errand for Lieutenant Goodale and I took the same road traveled earlier. Just outside the rear area, in a ditch alongside the road, I found the same four Germans that Woody and I had escorted. They were quite dead. Someone had used a machete on their heads and I thought I was going to be sick.

Why was this done and why like this? Those poor slobs were low men on the totem pole, just pawns in the game of war. Like me they had dreams, desires, ambitions, and maybe a wife or sweetheart back home. But there they were stretched out in a muddy hole, with their brains oozing and mixing with the rain. How long would it be before it was my turn to be lying in some dirty, weed-choked ditch?

Oh Lord, how does a man get used to looking at such things? I hope whatever war does to cause men to treat other human beings with such disrespect misses me, passas me over, since it is nothing that I want.

I asked some of the reserve unit guys when I saw them why they had killed the German prisoners. They claimed it was the same machine-gun crew who had shot down their medic while he was trying to help the wounded. They had demanded an eye for an eye.

* * *

I had asked Minerva to marry me on Thanksgiving Day, she had accepted. Returning home we shared the news with my family and sat around dreaming of the possibilities awaiting us.

The next day Minerva and I went to pick out her ring. A few words and a promise wouldn't do this time. I wanted it official before I left town and I wanted all the good ol' boys out there to know this girl was spoken for.

She and I were engaged and it was a good feeling to be so. Life dealt the cards: my Army job, although extremely hazardous, was one I liked and now there was a beautiful girl who would be waiting to become my wife when I returned from duty. How any guy could be luckier I didn't know. We had shared the 23rd Psalms with each other on our walk and it was as we had spoken of, surely, the LORD had indeed set a table for me in the face of my enemies. This is what we had to believe in.

There has never been a soldier serving in the U.S. Army who could have experienced a shorter two-week leave in their military career than I. Days spent with Minerva sped by too quick, quicker than the week when we met, and before I realized it I was at the station ready to find John and board the Georgia bound train heading for camp. It was a painful goodbye; I was holding Minerva tight.

"I love you," I told her. Our eyes penetrated each other, seeking out one another's soul.

"I love you," she responded.

"Don't worry about me." I tried to give a forceful order. She laid her head on my shoulder.

"I can't help it."

I lifted her head gently and captured her gaze again. I said to her, "God watches over us. We were meant to be, I believe!"

She showed a soft smile but there were tears in her eyes. "I believe," she said and we had a last kiss when the announcement came.

"All aboard."

John and I were on the train heading back to Columbus.

"Damn! I can't believe you're engaged." John's voice was a near shout.

"Believe it John. It's a great thing," I said.

He grumbled back, "You're not going to be any fun now."

"I'll still be fun, but from now on I'll just let you have the girl."

"Oh, right; like you're the one doing all the talking and jiving when we hit town." He gave me a friendly shove.

John had me there, but of course I wouldn't let on. I wasn't shy but I didn't enter into an encounter with the female sex like a wild bronco either. John was always quicker to speak and faster to open up whether we were at a camp dance or in town at the roller rink.

"Damn I can't believe you're engaged," he swore.

"Hey, how's that foot?" I asked him, hoping to move him beyond the subject and accept my engagement as fact.

"Oh, it's great. Would you believe it? I even went skating the other night! It's still a little sore, but it's coming along real well," and he raised his dukes like a boxer to indicate a kind of victory.

"Good," I said. "I don't want to carry you on to camp like I carried you off."

The train ride continued. Another mile went by and another mile and soon we were nearly out of Texas. My thoughts however remained at the station holding on to a certain young lady.

*   *   *

We didn't rest any longer at Hill 131 but received orders to move on to the main objective, south to Hill 95.[xv] 1st and 3rd Battalions moved out, but soon suffered heavy losses. F and D Companies were sent to support them. In this action, Goodale took on other duties with D Company, and Lieutenant Lloyd Polette acted as F Company commander. This lieutenant who had made the river crossing with us was gaining a reputation.

We all liked Polette. He'd been hit in an earlier battle and was walking around with a hunk of enemy steel in one hip.[xvi] He'd skipped treatment for the wound and was still going. If not for his refusal to go back to the hospital, I guess the company would have been left short of officers. Polette was popular with the enlisted men. He was daring but not necessarily reckless; he was a soldier's soldier with a knack for correctly sizing up the situation.

Lieutenant Goodale was the same way. Later on we learned that on his side of Hill 95 at one point he went running across a field just so everyone else could figure out where a German machine gun was located. After pinpointing the gun they all attacked; Goodale from his location and the rest of D Company from theirs.

Facing our own objective, Polette started working F Company on its way around the north side of Hill 95's base. D Company swung around on the southern side. Our northern side of the hill attracted a lot of artillery fire so we quickly dug in. Polette then formed several patrols that he sent to the top so he could get a feel for what we faced. While working my way to the top with the others, word came that the radio operator had been hit. The lieutenant wanted me to report back to him.

*   *   *

After my two-week leave over the Thanksgiving holiday, as soon as I returned to camp, the cadre informed me I had been selected for Communications School. How I got this honor or why, I will never know. Luck of the draw, I guess. At first I wasn't so sure about it, but it turned out to be a good deal and I came to enjoy it. All the troopers who were attending Communications School moved into one barracks so they would be together.

The communications building mostly consisted of one large room where we all sat at long u-shaped tables. Each station had a telegraph key and a set of earphones where we sat and listened to dots and dashes on a record. In the beginning it all sounded alike, but after hours of sitting and listening, the meaning of it slowly came through. When we got to a point where we could take down the receiving signal, they sped up the delivery. Each man progressed at his own speed.

I asked another student what he thought of this special training.

"Man this is great," he said. "Think about it, some duties will put you right up front and get you killed. I mean the machine gunners are always going to get hit first. Right? At least that's what we would do to them."

He had a point.

We went to school five days a week learning both to send and receive until we could dream about it in our sleep. We also sat around the barracks and tapped out messages to each other in Morse code. We ran field problems with radios and strung field telephone wire by the mile and followed that by splicing a thousand splices. We also worked with flags and lights. Our field problems were the best because we could be out in the sunlight and fresh air, so much better than sitting in that comm. room learning a dot from a dash.

To end our schooling we made a jump into Alabama on December 15th and ran problems in the field. The drop zone was across the Chattahoochee River from the main part of the camp in Georgia. Just one plane and one stick including our instructor went up there.

The air was smooth and our flight moved us over the field just after sunset at one thousand feet; the time was 6:45. We had nice, cool weather and there was only a hint of winter when we filled our lungs with the fresh sky air. Personally, it was my best jump ever and that was important because this was the jump when I carried a passenger with me. Strapped in a case under my left armpit I had a beautiful black and white homing pigeon. As we descended, the little fellow made light cooing sounds. The pigeon had to have special care because in the morning it would be his job to take a message back to Fort Benning.

After I reached the ground and dropped my harness I took a collapsible cage out of my backpack to set up for my new little friend. I then took him from his straight jacket and put him in the cage. He fluttered his wings with commotion but then settled down just like a real trooper as I tied him to the top of my pack.

Our first problem was to act as a pathfinder group and guide in another C-47 that was jumping 20 more troopers. We were behind schedule and would have to hurry to set up on time. It was getting dark fast. White lights were set at each end of the field and a green one off to the side where it would be facing the door of the approaching ship.

Our lights were barely in place when we heard the plane off in the distance. We turned on the white lights and waited. Then we saw it: a black silhouette, heading straight for the field. We were at the side of the field and as the ship came even with us we turned on the green light, aimed right at the trooper standing in the jump door. Immediately there were troopers spilling into the dark sky. It was a pretty sight to see them drifting down out of the night. Then they were down and out of view as the darkness swallowed them up.

At daybreak the next morning we wrote a message. I slipped this message into a little container fastened to the pigeon's leg and I released him on the ground. He took a strut walk around and then took off flying in circles with each circle becoming bigger than the one before. After three of these he took to a straight line and flew out of sight on an invisible path back to camp. I sure hoped the pigeon knew its way back and he didn't run into a hawk, as part of our message back to Comm. School was where to drop chow.

Only an hour later we heard an aircraft engine. The sound seemed different and we watched as a Grasshopper, an Army J-3 Piper Cub, came overhead and circled. I thought surely they wouldn't drop chow from such a small aircraft! About that time it made a diving turn straight at us.

The instructor yelled, "Enemy aircraft!"

Momentarily stunned we watched something drop from the plane while we tried to move our feet.

"Take cover, take cover!"

But it was too late. We were only beginning to jump for safety when a sack of flour splattered right in the middle of us. If it had been a real bomb we would have been wiped out from its blast. Boy did we ever feel like there was mud on our face.

"Lucky shot," came a cry from somebody who tried to shake it off.

A little later we saw a C-47 lined up on our field. A bundle dropped, its chute blossoming out. There was a shout of "Here comes chow!" and the bundle touched down.

"Open that honey up!" one trooper cried.

"What the hell do you think I'm trying to do?"

When the bundle came open we found sack lunches for twenty men. We all took two. This was a surprise, but not near the surprise we figured, as the one awaiting the other twenty troopers out there if there were only ten sacks in their bundle.

Field training that day went well; we practiced the roll-out and set-up of field telephones, and many of the other things we had learned in camp. I felt good about the training and believed I was ready to take this work into real-life action, a/k/a war, something nobody is really ready for.

* * *

After moving back down Hill 95 I found Polette. He was in deep discussion with platoon leader Lieutenant Cook—another good young officer. Our eyes met and just that single glance told me what to do. "Strap on the radio and stay close." Under battle conditions I became the acting Communications Sergeant. I unloaded the latest battery sling from around my neck. Sergeant Joe Harold and several others were also there.

"How's Chatoian?" I asked the guys.

"He's not good at all," one said.

"He's not dead," said another. "He got it in the head."

"He already get moved back?" I asked.

"Yeah," they answered, "but we've moved over a little since then." They gestured back to some far away trees clustered together. "The Krauts are really tearing us up."

I dropped my line of questions and moved near Polette. It sure was a sorry thing for Ed. He was a buddy, but I couldn't help thinking it put a stop to anyone having to carry a spare battery.

As darkness fell I left my radio in the trench and fell in with all the other 508th north-side troopers. We made a full assault to the top of the hill. Some accounts credit the Red Devils with killing more than 150 Germans and taking 80 prisoners, but the Germans still didn't yield. We took some licks from them as well, and the fighting carried over to the next day. On July 4th the real fireworks began.

We still didn't control the hill. Patrols from D and H Companies operating to the south ran into constant enemy fire and lost several men in the action. Artillery was landing on and off just about everywhere so nobody knew where it was safe. The command post for 2nd Battalion was hit more than once and Lt. Colonel Shanley and then his replacement, Mark Alexander, were both hurt and had to be pulled out. Captain Chester Graham took command. On day two it was decided once more that F Company would attack and destroy the resistance at the front of the hill. Several units had already tried and failed. This time, however, the attackers would receive support from tanks. With those big beastly machines in place and firing at select targets, we made our run.

Resistance was stiff and we were bone tired. On the run up I saw a good buddy, Rex Spivey, go down, but I knew he'd live as we went on. The losses were mounting up; Woody was wounded on the hill, but we finally got the job done. Overall, the action at Hill 95 was the 508th's bloodiest day of the Normandy campaign. F Company alone had four more troopers killed, including Lieutenant Cook and his squad sergeant, Joe Harold. More than twenty others were wounded and Lieutenants Goodale and Polette both made the list. However, neither was hurt badly. The company was now down to a mere 28 able-bodied men, and that included a few walking wounded.[xvii]

* * *

Woody's injury allowed him to continue in the field, and after the fighting had died down, he and I decided we would have a first-class foxhole for the night. We worked for hours making it four feet wide, six feet long and three feet deep. We planned to sleep in the horizontal position!

We cut down three- and four-inch diameter trees. The smaller branches with leaves were put inside and covered over with a blanket. We placed the large stalks over the top, side by side, and sealed them together with cakes of dirt. Not only were we going to be sleeping in comfort, we were going to be safe and secure. It was by far the best foxhole I was ever a part of building and it was going to pay off in quality sleep.

I said to Woody, "Boy, it does look good."

"We got a real work of art here."

"I don't know what else we can do to it."

He responded, "Well, outside of a rug and indoor plumbing, I don't think there's anything else to do. We've got a good night's rest ahead of us."

A shout came from behind, "Hey Burns, Phelps!"

We turned to face one of the guys, Larry Nelson.

"Grab your stuff and get ready. The Lieutenant just got word, we're moving out." ✓

Things like that could make a grown man want to cry. We broke contact with the enemy and started a long march to the northern coast.[xviii]

* * *

On the 13th of July we were able to load onto LSTs at Utah beach. An LST was a large landing craft that could come right up on the beach. They weren't used for launching troops but for trucks and tanks and larger loads.

I took my place on the deck of the ship where I could stand and get a good view of the beach. All kinds of equipment stood stacked up and ready to move to the front, anything a soldier needed, from ammo to rations to gasoline and spare tires. Scattered here and there were wrecked out vehicles, destroyed during the invasion.

In the sea behind us I saw several more of the LSTs waiting their turn to come in and unload more supplies. Despite the activity around us, an unmistakable peace filled the air. Yet I heard it had been something else on D-Day; I heard it had been one living hell.

An hour later we sailed north for England and the guys were feeling good. This wasn't celebration time, but it felt like a Christmas afternoon, when you feel good just because it's the holidays.

The guys said, "We're going home to Nottingham." But it seemed funny to think of Nottingham as home. Maybe it was because things would be quiet and safe there. As we pulled deeper into the English Channel I watched the French coast. I reflected long moments over the last 37 days. So much had happened; would it change us as men? So many soldiers lost, too many were not returning with us.

John McGee wouldn't be going back, and neither would Captain Flanders. Ed was badly wounded, his exact status unknown, and Ramon was killed. Several other quality soldiers were going to be sorely missed. A poem came to mind. I had read it in the *Stars and Stripes*, liked it, committed it to memory, and it has stayed with me all my life. Written by another soldier, it said all that I was thinking at this moment.

This is but a simple field
so long, so hot and wide,
where shamelessly I shed the tears
I do not try to hide.
This bit of ground is hollow now,
some friends of mine are here.
They sleep the sleep they have earned so well.
They'll wake without a care.
My friends they were and will remain,
as yours they should be too,
for men like these are worth so much,
they gave their lives for you.
So, earnestly I beg of you,
retain this single thought.
This pile of dust was once a man
and must not be forgot.

I didn't know if the writer was alive or dead. Did he make it or was he buried somewhere on a bit of ground now hallowed. The poem applied well to Utah Beach, which was why I couldn't help but feel a distinctive calm there. It was hallowed ground and those men busy upon its sand understood. With sudden insight I turned my eyes from France. I turned away from the valley where the Shadow of Death roamed, and stood instead facing England. I was going "home," to Nottingham.

JUMP

Six

"Make me a sergeant."

Going "home" sounded good, but it should have meant returning to Fort Worth, Texas, as it had when John and I completed our training at paratroop school.

* * *

Graduation was conducted on another gorgeous Georgia day at Fort Benning. The temperature was just right, the sun shone through the pines, birds sang from the branches. A fresh smell drifted in the air. But to anyone waiting for silver wings it would have been a great day even if it meant standing in the rain.

John with his busted ankle walked better than I expected. He had a look on his face that told me it hurt but I had already said my piece. I laced his boot so tight he couldn't move his foot, but the boot also offered a lot of support and he managed to walk without limping too badly. As we fell into formation that morning the feeling swept over me that everything was as it should be. The facts of a world gone mad with war had been pushed so far back in my mind that on this day I didn't remember or even realize the goal of our training.

We marched to the parade field and took up a company formation. The colonel made a stirring speech, he talked about the few who could ever make it to this point, and how most never tried. We were told how good we were, and he told us to know how proud of us he was.

"And remember," he concluded, "that outside of the army there are also many others who are going to be proud of you. Your mama's going to be proud of you. Your daddy's going to be proud of you. All your old high school teachers are going to be proud too. But the one who's going to be proudest of all is your luscious lassie with the classy chassis!"

After his speech the colonel walked down each line and handed us our wings. Time was taken to shake hands with each of us and he said, "Good luck, trooper!" That word "trooper" said it all. It had a good ringing sound and brought forth connotations of all the hard work we had put in. In those war years "paratrooper" had a status all its own and I was so proud I was ready to pop my buttons.

On November 20th we pinned on our wings. We were all now officially Airborne, and our wages went up 50 bucks a month for jump pay. With those new silver wings shining on our chest, we strutted just a little bit on our walk back to the barracks. I found that anytime I crossed paths with someone I wanted them to see my "good side," an angle where the paratrooper wings would flash in the sunlight. I knew those who were still in training must have been just a little envious. I had been.

We had a big company dinner and party that night. Finally, the cooks managed a really good meal. I dare say their only good meal at all. After dinner there were a few short speeches. Members of the cadre had to tell us what sorry soldiers we were when we first came into camp and what an excellent job they'd done in turning us around and making decent troopers out of us. We booed and hissed at them, laughed and told them we got through training in spite of them. It was a lot of fun, harmless horseplay with much binding camaraderie. When the company party broke up, each of the barracks then started its own party. And it was some evening!

Special bottles, only to be opened after earning wings, came out and got passed around. Everyone relived certain parts of the training. Things that were serious before got joked about. As more bottles made it around, the bigger and funnier the stories became. I could see there were going to be some bloodshot eyes in the morning. Some troopers stayed up all night. This was their night to howl and they were going to make the most of it.

The next morning there were furlough papers for all who wanted them, and we all wanted them. Several trucks were lined up ready to take us to the train station. John's ankle was still badly swollen and black. It had gotten tender overnight but by using me as a crutch we got him on. It was a crowded train ride, but at each station they held all the people back in order to let soldiers board the train first. We always had a seat.

The civilians all wanted to talk to us because we were in the service. A fair number of girls who were traveling alone seemed attracted to us. Since we were first in line to get on the train a young lady could insure herself a seat if a trooper invited her into line with him. Normally I enjoyed a female visit but today I had too much on my mind. There was only one pretty girl I wanted to see and her name was Minerva. John and I traveled alone.

The hours dragged by slowly. Still, having some friendly folks around helped the time pass.

"You fellows headed home?" someone asked.

"Yes sir!"

"Where is home?"

"Fort Worth, Texas. I've got two weeks to spend with my girl."

"Has the Army given you any overseas orders yet?"

"No sir," I told him, "We just finished training, but we'll get them soon enough. That's what this is all about, putting the Germans and Japanese in their place. We'll be reporting back to Fort Benning afterwards."

"What are those badges you're wearing?" Sooner or later everyone asked about our wings. The paratroopers' wings were a recent addition in the army. Of course we never tired of telling everyone about them.

"We're Airborne," we said and explained what that meant.

Some people would look at us like we weren't playing with a full deck when they found out what a paratrooper did. Often they wandered away in a daze and at a loss for words. They just couldn't believe someone would want to jump out of an airplane. That was the kind of recklessness reserved for airshow stuntmen.

We arrived in Fort Worth late at night, past ten. Both John and I saw our families waiting at the station when we pulled in, but I couldn't locate Minerva. Mom gave me a hug as big as her small frame could manage as I came off the last step from the train.

"Dwayne, it's good to see you!" she said.

Dad shook my hand. "You're looking fit, son. How was the trip?"

I smiled but I knew my expression showed I was disappointed.

"It was fine, Dad. Where's Minerva? She wrote she would be here."

Mom explained, "Dear, I'm afraid she's home sick with a cold. She wanted to be here but with the train coming in so late, and this night air, she needed to stay home in bed. You can see her early tomorrow."

I was heartbroken; I had so looked forward to her being there. Christmas had come but my package was missing.

"Let's go by and see her!" I suddenly blurted out.

Mom's eyes rolled. "Dwayne, she's sleeping! Wait until morning, she'll feel stronger and you'll have a better visit."

I sighed. I wasn't sure I could get any sleep but I finally agreed she was right.

John and I quickly introduced our families to one another and then went our separate ways. We had exchanged phone numbers but I wasn't sure if I would see him again until our furlough was over. There were tentative plans to meet at his high school's homecoming football game.

During the ride to the house Dad wanted to hear about the aircraft we jumped from. Mom didn't want to hear about anything related to jumping. She instead worried about how skinny I was and asked why the Army couldn't feed us better. Both thought my uniform was smart and I cut an attractive figure. We sat up quite a while that night talking, and Dad and I swapped a number of Army stories. I learned Ed Mize, having turned eighteen, went into the Navy only a few weeks earlier. After talking and taking some time to wind down a little, I finally felt I could get some sleep.

Despite a late evening I was up and over at Minerva's early. Mr. Chastain greeted me, let me in and directed me to a chair. He seemed pleased to see me.

"Good to see you Sir," I told him. It was true. Although brief, I had enjoyed our earlier visits.

"Minerva has been sick I'm afraid, but I saw her a moment ago and I believe she's much better now."

"Yes. Mom explained to me at the station last night," I replied.

"Well, she'll be out in just a moment. These girls of mine tend to hide until they get themselves all dolled up. I imagine you're anxious to see her."

"Yes Sir, I am."

He said, "You know it reminds me of a time back when I was a kid. There was a fella who wanted to call on this young gal he was real sweet on. So one day he came visiting on his horse. It was a good-looking steed on its own but the guy also had a nifty saddle that really set it off. You could tell he was proud and he was hoping to impress this young lady he was so fond of. She came out on the porch; he was sitting on the horse. The horse was prancing around the yard, nervous maybe, because it suddenly kicked and bucked this fella off. He landed in the middle of their walkway headfirst. Knocked him out cold, didn't wake up for a day and a half and had to spend three days in the hospital." There was a moment of reflection in his eyes. "I've often wondered if he ever had the nerve to call on her again."

Just then Betty Jo entered to explain Minerva would be right out. She'd hardly finished speaking when Minerva came through the door, like a princess being announced. It was a beautiful sight. It was Christmas at last.

"Hi," she said softly.

"Hi." I hesitated a bit. Perhaps I was savoring the sight or perhaps the moment was slightly awkward due to the length of time spent apart, but it was brief. We moved together and hugged. I kissed her lightly.

Her dad spoke up, "Well, I'll move off and let you two visit for a spell. Betty Jo, go check those breakfast dishes will you? Make sure they get dried and put away."

They left and we kissed again. There was a hint of her past illness in her expression as she apologized for not making it to the station. "I stayed up till midnight hoping you would come by," she said.

"I wanted to, but Mom said you would be asleep."

She promised she was now fully recovered and was totally mine. She had taken two weeks leave of absence from her job so we could be together during all of my furlough, and we were together every day and all day.

* * *

On the 15th of July 1944, 895 men of the 2,056 Red Devils who
jumped on D-Day returned to base camp at Nottingham England. F
Company had been hard hit and lost eighty percent of its 129 men
through death, capture or heavy wounds; those of us returning,
including the walking wounded, were glad to be back on English soil.
As we pulled into the station, bands played and the town turned out
to give us a hero's welcome home. It was a nice surprise. Friends,
sweethearts and lovers jammed the station. Some were laughing and
all smiles, while others cried for troopers who wouldn't be showing
up.

The reunions made me a little envious or maybe a bit sad that I
once again didn't have Minerva there to greet me when stepping off
the train. Surely she would run to me, throw her arms around me, and
cover me with kisses. A lot of guys had English girlfriends and some
had married. They claimed they needed a distraction from army life
and the war. I didn't buy it at first but after walking through life in hell
the past month I began to understand. Those guys were sure getting a
homecoming now. Just the same, I also, felt good to get back.

Home base wasn't the same as when we left. New faces waited for
us, replacements who far outnumbered the old guys. Now, where an
old buddy had slept, a new bright-faced kid had taken over his cot.
Every one of them was a fresh graduate right out of the Frying Pan's
heat; the fire would be forthcoming.

* * *

When John, I, and thirty-three other California volunteers signed on
for the paratroopers, we were all loaded on a Pullman car for Fort
Benning, GA. From there the train followed a southern route thru El
Paso and Houston.

"You guys realize, of course, that it takes two days to travel across
Texas, my home state, largest in America."

One of the guys laughed, "Hell Burns, we got slow trains in
Georgia too, but we don't brag about it."

After five days of riding and sitting in switching yards we pulled
into the station at Columbus, Georgia. Army trucks with a sergeant in
charge were there to meet us. The sergeant, a member of the training
cadre, was the first real-live paratrooper we had seen. He stood there

in a firm manner, feet apart, unsmiling. He was a big guy and his face was suntanned to a golden brown; his jaw seemed to be chiseled from stone. His nose had once been broken and his eyes could look right though you.

With his legs tucked into dark brown boots shining like brass and a pair of silver wings pinned above his breast pocket, he carried himself with the air of a Roman god. We all felt like a bunch of slobs next to him, especially in our train weary uniforms. A voice you could have heard for two blocks gave the order to fall in. There was no doubt about who was in charge. The man left an impression and I could hardly wait to get started in his footsteps.

It was a short drive to Fort Benning from the town of Columbus. When we drove through the front gate, I could hardly believe the paradise waiting inside. Tall majestic pine trees grew everywhere, shading beautiful red brick barracks, manicured green grass and clean white sidewalks. There were clubs, a recreation hall, a chapel and a theater. All of the buildings appeared to be expertly maintained, like the grand estate of a large southern plantation. Everything looked absolutely picture perfect.

"Boy they sure know how to treat paratroopers," came someone's comment.

"Look at the towers!" John pointed at the jump towers rising just over the distant treetops.

"They look like the Eiffel Tower," a guy joked, as our transport glided along the pavement past the neat brick barracks.

I took in a deep breath. "Boy, John, this is going to be all right! I can take a lot of this; it's almost too good to be true."

It was too good to be true, for we drove right on past the perfectly trimmed green grass and the sidewalks and continued over a ridge to the backside of the camp, the area known as the "Frying Pan." What a let-down. If the camp had been a plantation then we were looking at the pigpens.

"Good God. Is this it?" a voice asked.

"Ugly, ain't it?"

"Is this anyway to treat paratroopers?" someone muttered.

This was nothing to write home about. Two rows of one-story barracks stood facing each other and looked like they were built out of used lumber from World War I. I could see a paintbrush had never touched the wood. The latrine stood at one end of the company street and the mess hall was located at the other. Two shabby wooden steps led up to the door of each barrack.

Inside didn't fare any better than the outside. The barracks had unpainted walls and floors and were furnished with double bunks made out of wood. The windows were wooden shutters with all the luxury of being propped up with a stick to let some fresh air inside, or closed down if it started to rain. It was all pretty primitive, yet this became my home for the next four months.

I later learned the first paratroopers of the United States were members of the Parachute Test Platoon. Shortly after their successful training Major William "Bill" Lee[xix] arranged for the Army Corp of Engineers to start construction of wooden barracks and a large consolidated mess hall suitable for a battalion of paratroopers. These barracks were intended to last only a few years so the procurement of building materials included a supply of well-seasoned, surplus lumber. They were left unpainted presumably because the first trainees, the 501st Parachute Infantry Battalion, were already in camp and needing them. It should be noted that these temporary buildings were used for nearly 24 years.

We still had the gorgeous pine trees, but sand took the place of grass and sidewalks, and it didn't take long to discover the sand got into everything when the wind was blowing. In the distance between the main camp and us were the three 250-foot jump towers standing like giant steel sentinels over the whole camp. East, beyond the pines and down a slight hill, there were glimpses through the trees of Lawson Field. A large number of C-47s were parked on the ramps in front of the hangers and we knew this was the field we would be flying out of.

While we were standing and waiting for some instruction I felt suddenly overwhelmed by all of the activity and enthusiasm in the camp. The place was buzzing like a hive full of bees. Several groups of troopers came marching down the road toward us counting cadence at the top of their voices. Other troopers came by running in formation. I heard one formation shout, almost sing, something to another formation as they passed by one another, but couldn't quite make out what it was. In the skies some C-47s flew overhead and men started spilling out the doors of each plane. They seemed so close I got the feeling I could almost see the expressions on their faces. Soon the southern blue Georgia sky was filled with beautiful white blossoms as they drifted down to earth.

The top sergeant bounded from one of the barracks used as company headquarters and began to call out our names. After he was satisfied everyone was present he gave us a brief rundown on some of the rules, both the written and unwritten.

"Men, welcome to Fort Benning. You've taken the first step to becoming paratroopers and part of the Army Airborne. Not every one of you will make it."

He then warned us how hard it was going to be. Anyone who couldn't take it had the chance to speak up and get reassigned. He didn't get any takers but he didn't lie about the toughness of the Frying Pan.

Perhaps a part of becoming paratroopers meant proving we could eat and live on anything, because the chow was terrible, far worse than anywhere else. Breakfast would always be the same: pancakes and fat bacon, apple butter if you got there before they ran out, and black coffee that would eat up the inside of your cup if you let it sit too long. We ate at picnic-type tables, forking food in with one hand and swatting flies with the other. To this day I still believe our cook was a German saboteur.

After chow that first morning, all of us new men had to fall out for a special test to see if we were physically able to be paratroopers. The test consisted of doing all kinds of strenuous exercises. Having done our share of calisthenics in California everyone I traveled with passed with flying colors. Someone started a joke, which spread around like a rumor.

"The final test will be the two-doctor exam."

"What's that," I said.

"The doctors will each look into one of your ears, if they see each other then you're fit material to be a paratrooper."

Besides all the morning runs we made, I soon found out push-ups were also going to be a way of life for us. Push-ups were handed out automatically for any infraction. Sometimes ten, sometimes twenty-five, sometimes fifty push-ups for things you did wrong, or that the cadre or superiors suspected you did. You didn't give them any argument as to whether or not you deserved punishment; that is, if you were smart. "Hit the ground and give me twenty," meant you did it and kept your mouth shut. If you gave them any lip, they would just add on another twenty.

* * *

I couldn't help but respect the new arrivals to Nottingham for their training. They had to be tough, but these guys all looked so young and wet behind the ears. I didn't understand how, at nineteen, I could have turned into an old experienced soldier so fast. Joe Ensminger was one of the new kids who moved into our tent. He was a preacher's son, a real decent fellow, and he would turn out to be a good friend.

Almost everyone returning from France was promoted by a rank and some by two ranks. Sergeant Wilbur Scanlon's position as First Sergeant was made permanent. It was he who came around everyone's tent with numerous promotions to hand out and he started with headquarters.

He told me, "Burns, I can either make you a sergeant or a corporal. Which would you prefer?"

There was no question what I wanted.

"Make me a sergeant," I answered.

"Good. I like the way you do things, you're not taking needless chances. By that I mean you think first, react second. Count on being promoted from PFC to T/4."

"Now Wilbur, I don't need your pep talk," I teased. "I just want the extra pay."

"Oh yeah, sure," he laughed. "Look, on a serious note, unless Ed returns, you'll need to count on remaining the Communications Sergeant."

"Have you heard anything?" I asked.

"Not a word and I'm afraid that no news may be bad news."

I had earned my first stripe at the Frying Pan. Now I had to sew on two more.

* * *

The day I released the homing pigeon during communications school we had field training all that day. Other than getting hit by that mock bomb everything else went well as we practiced all the items we had learned in camp. In early evening a truck came rolling into our area to take us back to camp. We traveled through fields and forest, down hills and around bends to reach the river. There was a ferry waiting on the riverbank. The ferry, used to carry troops between Alabama and Georgia, was a large raft reinforced with steel and cables. It could carry a company of men or two large trucks of troops. A small shed, large enough to stand in, was erected on one side of this big raft. From it a colored man stepped out and moved to the far end of the ferry to prepare our ride across.

Back in camp, with our three weeks of intensive cramming complete, we were pronounced "communication experts" and would now rejoin our outfits. The brief Comm School had put me a jump up on everyone else in my company, which was one of the best things about it. I now had some bragging rights because I was more experienced than they.

My outfit had moved out of the training area and into different barracks. They didn't appear any better than those we lived in during parachute training. After reporting in, the First Sergeant came by my barracks to see me.

"Burns, are you all educated with communication skills now?" he asked.

"Ask me anything, I know it all."

"Well good, but I'll trust you. Burns I came by to tell you that you've been promoted to PFC."

I thought, *first there was comm. school, a jump ahead of the others, and now I'm getting the rank of PFC. Yes sir, bragging rights and respect are mine.*

"Congratulations!" said the First Sergeant and he shook my hand. He made his way to the barracks front door but then turned back as he opened it.

"Oh yes," he added, "Burns, you are also on guard duty tonight."

"Gee, thanks a lot Sarg," I said. "And welcome home to you too!"

* * *

I already knew if the company wanted to keep me as Radio Sergeant for F Company, they had to give me three stripes. It just came with the job. It felt good to know that our new First Sergeant felt I was worthy, with or without the radio duty.

Lt. Colonel Lindquist became a full bird colonel and other officers made a higher rank as several reassignments were made within the 508th. Inside a couple of weeks, other major changes would effect the whole 82nd Airborne Division as it was transferred and became a part of the new First Allied Airborne Army, a dream creation of General Eisenhower. This Airborne army consisted of two Air Force Troop Carrier Commands, one American and one British, and also two Airborne Corps, likewise one American and one British. The new American XVIII Airborne Corp was comprised of the 82nd and 101st and a newly arrived but still forming 17th Airborne Division. The transfer was strictly a paper move and the troopers of the 508th never knew any difference. The Red Devils' sister regiment probably did, however, because the 507th was transferred to the new 17th Division, giving that Airborne command a battle-proven unit to strengthen its fighting ability. To command the first-ever American Airborne Corps, Eisenhower chose our 82nd Division commander, Major General Matthew Ridgeway. Then Ridgeway picked General James Gavin to replace himself for the 82nd's top spot. With his new command, Gavin soon had a second star that, at age 37, made him the youngest U.S. Major General since the promotion of George Armstrong Custer in the Civil War.

A Captain Harold Martin took over as F Company commander. Nobody seemed to know him or where he came from. We really liked and wanted Polette but he was only a 2nd lieutenant in Normandy, though after his performance he was made a 1st lieutenant and given leadership of the First Platoon. Lieutenant Goodale was also well liked and would have been a great choice, but he missed making captain. Vernon Thomas was given a battlefield commission and joined the 3rd Battalion's H Company. Vernon had been a strong squad leader and we would have loved keeping him in the Falcon Company. Meanwhile, Sgt. Don Burke came to F Company from the 3rd Battalion with a new battlefield commission and a gold 2nd Louie bar.

Five-day furloughs were issued to the Normandy veterans and I decided to skip out of town. I ran into F Company buddy Tony at the train station, so we teamed up and the two of us caught the train for Edinburgh, Scotland. We didn't know anything about the town. It was simply a good distance away from the war and sounded like a decent place to visit. I have Scottish ancestors and thought it might be fun to nose around and learn something of the old country.

When we arrived we found it was Scotch week and a big celebration with ceremonies was in full swing. They had bagpipe music, all types of dancing, drinking and eating. People had come to town by the thousands. We couldn't find a room anywhere, so we slept at the Red Cross Club sitting in a chair, or on a pool table or even on the floor.

Other than the sleeping conditions it wasn't too bad, because a lot of girls had come to town and there was a lot of fun to be had. Besides, we figured we would catch up on our sleep when we got back to camp. For two continuous days and three nights we went to the most glorious parties and to several dances in the park.

On the third day I awoke thinking I had taken all the noise and crowd and fun I could stand. So without telling Tony where I was going, I went back to the station and took the first train to a small town called West Calder. The ride was 30 minutes west of Edinburgh and I found the place beautifully quaint. The hills were green, the people friendly and the charming town was untouched by any war effort. I seemed to be the only GI in town and they treated me like a celebrity. I spent the whole day just looking around and visiting with the nice folks living there. They loved meeting a Texan and were sure I had a horse, and a pair of cowboy boots as well. But I found it hard to explain why there were no Indians or rustlers in my neighborhood.

I took a room for the night at the town's only inn and after an early dinner went up to my room, leaving a wakeup call for eight o'clock. As the peace and quiet settled over me I knew this was what I really needed, because I found myself exhausted both mentally and physically. I undressed and crawled into the biggest, softest bed I had ever been in. With its clean, white sheets and comfortable pillows this bed would serve a king, but I slept more like a child; warm, safe, without a care or worry.

The next morning at eight, there was a knock at the door. A maid poked her head in and I noticed she carried a wooden tray with a big, hot cup of tea.

"Pardon me, Sir," she said softly.

"Yes? Come in," I answered.

She walked in shyly and came over to my nightstand.

"Good morning, Sir, it's time to get up." Then she set the tea down. "Shall you have breakfast this morning?" she asked.

"Yes, I shall," I replied with a vision of fresh home baking running through my mind.

"It will be downstairs whenever you're ready, Sir. Do you need anything?"

"No thank you, just a little time."

"Then good day, Sir," she said and left the room.

I propped the pillows up behind by back, took a big, long sip of the hot tea and savored both its flavor and the lovely old town view out my window. Each was equally tasty. The bright morning sunshine had risen over the lush countryside and I couldn't help thinking this was real living. "Lord, thanks for bringing me here," I whispered to myself. "Maybe I should just go AWOL and spend the rest of the war in this place." After stretching my morning cup out as long as possible, I dressed and went downstairs to a breakfast of assorted rolls, buns, jams and more hot tea. It was true luxury—a leisurely spent morning.

I arrived back in Edinburgh around lunchtime and went first to the Red Cross club to look for Tony. Since I had left without a word, I feared he might have the MPs looking for me. I found him sitting in the lounge looking through a book. He glanced up as I walked in.

"Burns, where in the hell have you been all night?"

"It wasn't hell, Tony. I just got back from heaven, or maybe a place next to it."

"Gee whiz. You must have really made out!" His statement was more like a question, as if I should explain myself.

I nodded and said, "You wouldn't believe it." And I left it at that.

We spent another night courtesy of the Red Cross at Edinburgh, but early the next morning we had to catch the train back to Nottingham. There was a war raging full-bore in continental Europe, and no doubt the High Command had already planned another mission for the battle proven 508th.

* * *

On the first full day after everyone's return from furlough there was an incident in the latrine. I was sitting down at the toilet with another half dozen troopers after a full day of training. A few other guys were washing and discussing going into town. Two more paratroopers walked in, one carrying a grenade and the other holding the safety pin. I didn't know either of them.

The first fellow said, "Let me have the pin so I can put it back in."

"No, just hold the damn thing still and I'll put it in," replied the second.

From my point of view I didn't care who did what, but I'd really rather them do it outside. They huddled in the middle of the room and fumbled with the grenade until there was a sudden and unmistakable thump upon the floor.

One of them screamed, "Oh my god, I dropped it!"

They both hit the door running. Those of us using the can had watched the entire scenario unfold and as the two of them ran out we hit the door right behind them, pulling on our pants as we went. After a grenade is armed, there are four seconds before it explodes. I know we all made it outside with time to spare because most of us had our faces in the dirt when we heard a little "pop" as the primer went off. That was it. This pair of pranksters had unscrewed the grenade, poured out the powder, and put it back together again. It was a pretty damn funny stunt. But in the first moments after it happened, if we could have found them, the 508th would have suffered another two casualties.

* * *

July 29th was a rainy, dreary day, shortly after our furlough. That morning the Regiment had a memorial service for those lost in France. The battalion commanders read off their names and taps was played. Then the band started playing softly, and one trooper sang the song, "My Buddy." I had a bad time keeping my composure and I could feel the tears welling up in my eyes. I kept telling myself, *Paratroopers don't cry, paratroopers don't cry.*

The tears wouldn't listen. I glanced to my left and right to make sure no one was looking at me. All around me stood tough-looking guys with tears streaming down their cheeks. Even the new replacements were crying. At that point I could no longer hold anything back. As the last notes of the song played out, I stood unashamed and let the tears pour from my eyes and fall to the ground for those wonderful friends who did not make the trip back home.

✳ ✳ ✳

I tried to catch up on my letters. Minerva would always get one but it was time to send everyone else a note. Letter writing was a common problem to the veterans of combat. We couldn't write much more than the fact that we were still alive, giving some small comfort to family and loved ones. In past letters I had instructed them not to worry, but after witnessing countless deaths it was hard to continue writing that. I felt I would survive, yet there were heavy odds I would not. Far less than half the paratroopers returned from our first battles.

At certain times a soldier wanted to spill out his emotions in a letter home. However the army censors didn't allow much of that. Our letters sent home needed to project the positive when there was some, the truth as it might be allowed, and hope if we could find any. Yet to those who charged the hills, defended rain-soaked foxholes, and survived blasting artillery, hope and other positive truths were often hard to grasp, much less try to explain in words headed home.

I wrote to Minerva that I was in England because I believed we were meant to be, and that I felt the card with the 23rd Psalm had gotten me through. But inside of me lived an honest measure of doubt which I had acquired somewhere along the way. I kept this knowledge of doubt hidden, keeping it to myself and out of my flowing pen.

JUMP
Seven

"You're not killing anyone; you're shooting at a target."

Soon after my furlough I attended a party in Nottingham and met an English girl there named Jean Martin. She was very pretty, with her soft brown hair just touching her shoulders, hazel eyes, and a beautiful mouth with a full lower lip. Her figure was near perfect and quite capable of making me forget I had a girl back home. We talked quite a bit and seemed to hit it off rather well, so when the party started breaking up I offered to walk her home. She agreed. It was delightful to walk with her and to see her to the door of her home.

"Would you care to pop over for Sunday dinner?" she asked.

"Yes, I'd be delighted."

"You can meet my family and maybe we can take another walk."

"I would like that a lot."

After all the fighting and killing, a visit with a normal family and a little wholesome female contact might get my mind onto something besides war. On my walk back to camp I decided she might become exactly the diversion I needed. And of course the thought of a home-cooked meal wasn't hard to take either.

* * *

The job of training the new replacements to fight Red Devil–style got under way that same week, and the sound of pounding trooper boots on the run echoed over the English countryside once more. Foxholes were dug and filled along the fencerows, and the calisthenics went on as long as ever. It was during our miles-long runs that our new company commander, Captain Martin, earned his nickname. We called him "The Rabbit," but not to his face. He got this name because he

99

ran with a little hopping motion.

In addition to the physical training, special schools instructed the men in areas of technical expertise. I went back to communication school for two days of refresher courses.

On Sunday I arrived at Jean's home and knocked on her door at the appointed time of 10:30. I knew this would be early for lunch, but who was I to say what was proper in an English home? Jean answered.

"Uh-oh," I thought, "I may be in trouble." She was more beautiful than I had remembered. Not only beautiful, but she was clean and fresh with a healthy, just-scrubbed look about her. She held out her hand for me.

"Welcome to our home. Won't you please come in?"

I took her hand. "Thank you, it's very nice to be here."

She led me through the door into the living room, where she introduced me to her mother and father. I now saw where Jean's good looks came from. Her mother, with graying hair, was an exact older model of Jean. Her father seemed on the small side, but was a sturdy looking man with gray hair. He was a businessman in town, and Jean's mother tended to the house. Jean also introduced me to her little brother who was about six years old and had blond, curly hair. I thought he was as cute as any English button could be.

Their home was comfortable with nice furnishings; everything looked old, but well cared for. Mr. Martin took a blue plaid coat and an old hat from the closet by the front door.

He stated, "You, Jean and I are going to pop down to the pub for a pint of stout while Mother gets lunch ready."

"That sounds good, Sir," I said.

But it didn't really. I wasn't going to tell him that I had been unable to acquire a taste for beer. An Englishman just wouldn't have understood. Mr. Martin had a car but it was such a nice day we decided to walk. Besides, gas was rationed and hard to come by.

Typical of the local pubs, we entered an old, queer place that was absolutely full of character. It had high-back leather chairs, wooden tables smooth with wear, charming paneled walls and all the good smells that come with a great pub. The ever-present dartboard hung on one wall. I had grown to love these places.

We sat at a corner table to catch some of the morning sun. The barmaid brought us each a pint of beer. I took a sip. It was slightly cool with a mild bitterness; not too bad, but not the sort of thing I would normally drink in mid-morning. I had brought my pipe with me and Mr. Martin had one, so we each lit them. Pubs are conducive to conversation, and we sat and talked while watching the miniature clouds from burning tobacco drift across the room. We covered a broad range of subjects in our discussion: the Bible, local politics, and of course the war. Jean took my hand under the table and smiled at me; I smiled back. We were like two kids with a big secret. Mr. Martin, being a wise father, pretended not to notice.

It was nice sitting in that old pub and holding hands with Jean. The war seemed far off. I found myself wishing the day could go on for a week or a month or even longer.

After his second pint, Mr. Martin said lunch would be ready by the time we returned home. I paid the bill and we started the neighborhood walk back to the Martins' house.

As we entered their front door, the smells coming from the dining room reminded me of Christmas time. We sat down to Yorkshire pudding, green beans and boiled potatoes. There were fruit tarts and hot cups of tea. It had been a long time between home-cooked meals, and I had eaten army chow for so long I'd forgotten how real food tasted.

After the dinner, Mr. Martin and I sat in the living room talking — that is, he did the talking. I kept stealing glances of Jean as she and her mother cleared away the table and washed the dishes. I couldn't help thinking how beautiful she looked as she walked around the table with long, slim legs taking very business-like steps.

Almost as good as being home with Minerva.

It felt so good to be a part of a family. With amusement I watched as Jean's little brother pushed toy cars around on the living room floor. It seemed like only yesterday I had been a youngster. Where had all the years gone? I was grown and a soldier before I knew it. And had it really been less than a month ago when I was wet and muddy and pulling a trigger for the kill? What a contrast.

As I sat and meditated on this change in lifestyle, with one ear on Jean's father, Jean herself came in and suggested we go for a walk. I agreed. Even though I enjoyed her nice family, my original intention was to visit her. I thanked Jean's mother for the fine lunch and for letting me be a part of the family for the day.

"You are welcome here anytime. Please come visiting again," she said.

I shook hands with Mr. Martin. I told him, "It was a pleasure to meet and talk with you."

"The pleasure was mine, young lad. I look forward to our next meeting. Good day."

"Good day, Sir."

Jean and I left. We walked toward the edge of town and found a park with beautiful green grass and trees. On an old-fashioned bandstand, several horn players and some percussionists prepared to begin a Sunday afternoon concert. I took off my jacket and laid it on the grass for Jean and then sat down beside her. We held hands and listened to music. It was like a day in the park with Minerva back in Fort Worth.

There was no war going on here. But at that very moment, just a few miles across the English Channel, men were fighting for their life, maybe losing it, while I sat with a beautiful girl listening to music. In the time it took to hear the band play, there would be another American son wounded or killed.

At dark, Jean and I walked backed to her home. Upon reaching the front door she asked, "Would you like to come in?"

My mind said, "Yes, and stay until this war is over," but my voice declined. Instead I said, "I think your mother and father have had enough of me for one day. It's time I got back to camp. I'd like to see you again next Saturday, if you're free."

"I'll be free."

I decided to kiss her. Pulling her slender frame close, our lips touched lightly and briefly.

"I never know what might come up, but if I can get away from the camp, look for me about six."

"I shall see you at six then," she said.

I thanked her again for the day and then turned and walked into the darkness. I felt on top of the world. Eight months had passed since my last time with Minerva. I certainly hadn't avoided the opposite sex; I enjoyed my time with English girls. But until today I felt there just wasn't anything here to compare with what I had waiting at home.

"Yes, Jean Martin," I said to myself, "you're going to be quite a diversion."

*   *   *

Training intensified and some of our training and field problems lasted all day and all night. Open countryside in England was limited, however, and when working field problems, it was often difficult to take them seriously with townspeople standing around watching and getting in the way.

One night my squad was attacking an objective, and when our plans were established I took the lead in an exercise that involved a bold move forward. To reach a certain rock wall meant crawling on my belly for a hundred yards. A good flat crawl can be taxing, but I established a pace for myself and made it in fair time. I was pretty worn from it, but with the rest of the squad watching I gathered my strength enough to cautiously look over the wall for the enemy. I saw a figure, and as I pulled my weapon into position, a little boy of about eight looked back at me with big round eyes.

"What are you doing mister?"

Lowering my carbine I first caught a breath and then told him, "Look kid, just tell me you're English and I won't have to shoot you." He smiled back.

On the 29th of August a practice jump was scheduled but, to no one's disappointment, it was scrubbed at the last minute. A number of troopers held to the theory that you shouldn't actually do something as practice that you have to do perfectly every time.[xx] I could see where there was merit to the argument.

A few of the guys wanted to try out the new quick-release jump harness given us. These had a single knob you turned and pushed, and the whole chute and harness assembly dropped off together; far superior to the multiple buckles we had dealt with in the past. If we'd had them in Normandy some lives could have been saved—those poor guys who drowned and maybe others who were caught hanging from a tree.

With each day the new men were fitting in better and better, and it became harder to remember which guys hadn't seen combat duty. A few of the troopers wounded in action returned to fill up the last gaps,

and the 508th looked like a fighting outfit again. I was pleased to have
my buddy John Hurst rejoin us.

The days of training turned into weeks. We knew the longer the
new men had to train the better it would be for both them and for the
Regiment. The experienced men were in no hurry for another combat
jump. Although the horror of combat would live with us forever, time
helped to erase the pain of friends lost, the terror of it all fading into
a bad dream.

My new friend and buddy, Joe Ensminger, and two other fresh
replacements, Lou Slama and Lambert Siniari, came to see me one
night when I was hanging out at camp.

"Sergeant Burns, could we talk to you?" they asked.

"Sure, go right ahead."

They seemed unsure how to ask, but they wanted to talk about the
reality of making a combat jump and then having to fight.

"We're all scared of course, but what really scares us is letting
down our unit."

I explained as best I could, "Don't worry about the jump itself;
everybody jumps unless they get hurt. When the flak starts bouncing
the plane around, you're gonna want to jump. That part's easy.
Dropping into combat and knowing the enemy is somewhere below is
a feeling I can't put into words, and if I could you wouldn't understand it. It's something you have to live though, like making your very
first parachute jump."

Joe asked, "Well what about the killing? You know my father's a
minister. Taking someone's life is absolutely against everything my
parents ever taught me. I'm not sure I can do it."

"You will," I assured him. "Joe, it's very impersonal. You're not
killing anyone; you're shooting at a target. That's what you got to
think of it as; remember your training. Anyway, it's done mostly at
long range, so you don't really know what the guy looks like or anything. You can't even tell which ones are officers. Just do the job as
you were taught and try not to think about that side of it."

"We're still going to be scared."

"Everybody is scared. I'm scared," I disclosed. "Don't worry
about that. You're going to do all right."

* * *

On weekends I managed to see Jean, and her parents treated me like one of the family. I had no intention of falling in love. She was just someone to talk to and spend my spare time with. The hours we might share together were something I could look forward to, other than the next day's training or the next battle assignment. In some small way she was a replacement for John McGee, but Jean did not come dressed in olive drab or carry the stamp "U.S. Army."

I had grown oddly tired of the downtown action and needed a new English experience. Without John the pubs weren't quite the same. When I lost John, I lost a part of my normal army life. The other guys, Woody and Joe and John Hurst were great, but McGee was a link to home, a piece of Fort Worth I had brought with me to England. I relied on him after every week of training for talk of home and a distraction from the war.

Jean also helped fill that void, and in obvious ways time with her was a heck of a lot better than time with John. Saturday nights we went out, but on Sunday we still went to the pub and then back to the Martin's for lunch. Then she and I would walk over to the park for the band concert, where we laid on the soft green grass with our faces turned up to get as much sun as we could while listening to the music. We didn't have a care as long as we could be together, and soon we found that if we held each other real close all the fears of the outside world faded away.

Through Jean I learned just how scared the British people really were. The tide of war had changed, but only a couple of years earlier the Brits had lived on the verge of invasion and conquest. Destruction, which I had seen in France, could have come to Nottingham, and such a thought was hard to accept—Nottingham was my safe haven from war. The build-up of American soldiers had helped the English suppress those fears because we brought with us a fresh confidence that had been lost to the island.

As we lay sunning ourselves, I could dream that Jean was an English princess who had won my adoration, and maybe to her I served the part of a medieval knight with wings, her personal airborne

protector. Jean had matured and become a woman under the shadow
of a great threat. After they spent years worrying, the Queen's forces
and Her Allies finally had a hold on the great German dragon. If only
we could slay the beast. It was a dangerous assignment. Lying side by
side on the cool grass, holding on tight and listening to the music
helped us push the danger away, at least for the moment. Sometimes
we could block out the world so well we seemed to hear the music
long after the band had quit playing and gone home.

Jean never asked if someone waited for me back home. Maybe she
didn't want to hear the answer, and I never offered to tell her about
home, Fort Worth or Minerva. No words of endearment were ever
spoken between us and there wasn't a promise made that couldn't be
kept. I guess in our hearts we both knew it was a wartime fairy-tale
romance that would be over with the ending of the war or with the
starting of an aircraft's engine. I had good intentions to not fall in love,
but it became harder to be faithful to my girl back home. I didn't
know if I would return and it was difficult to believe in the future.
Minerva sent me letters religiously, stating there was a life for us in the
future. But Minerva also lived in another world, almost another lifetime ago. Jean was here and now, and the number of days I spent with
her would soon equal those spent with my fiancée.

*   *   *

In the last week of August, new jump orders came down from Division
Headquarters, 82nd Airborne. We didn't know the exact assignment,
but they would tell us at the right time. Camp became a beehive of
activity: equipment bundles packed, weapons broken down for operational inspection and cleaning, and ammunition distributed. Personal
equipment went into storage.

Each communication sergeant drew a radio from supply. I gave F
Company's radio a good checking and then packed it into one of the
bundles. By late afternoon we were on trucks and headed out of town
for the airfield. The Regiment divided by companies for the briefing,
and then everyone hit the sack early in anticipation of a dawn takeoff. Unlike the Normandy jump, we weren't given time to sit around
and worry about it. There were no sand tables staring back at us and
I liked it that way. Many guys had trouble getting to sleep; I'd say

Dwayne T. Burns,
Communications Sergeant of
F Company, the 508th
Parachute Infantry
Regiment, 82nd Airborne
Division, at age 20.
(U.S. Army photo)

A 30-foot jump
tower used for para-
trooper training.
The purpose of this
tower was to simu-
late the initial shock
of a chute opening
during freefall.
(U.S. Army photo)

Roy E. Lindquist and Thomas J.B. Shanley (both of whom would become colonels) during the 508th P.I.R.'s initial training.
Below, a practice jump. (508th History and U.S. Army photos)

When James Gavin took command of the 82nd Airborne Division, he became the youngest U.S. major general since the Cvil War. (U.S. Army photo)

Left, John McGee after completion of his paratrooper training. (Courtesy Marilyne McGee)
Below left, Lloyd Polette, a "soldier's soldier."(Courtesy George Miles)
Below, Lambert Siniari and Louis Slama, who came from the same hometown and took their training together. (Courtesy Louis Slama)

Above, a pair of C-47 troop transports in flight. (U.S. Army photo)

Below, Woody Phelps relaxing in France after hostilities had ended. (Dwayne Burns photo)

Above, Joe Ensminger and Dwayne Burns in a photo taken after the Holland Jump.

Joe would say prayers over the graves of fallen comrades until he, too, fell victim to enemy fire, in the Ardennes.
(Dwayne Burns photo)

Two views of the fighting in France. Above, U.S. tanks make their way through the hedgerow country. Below, troopers cautiously mop up a formerly enemy-occupied town. (U.S. Army photos)

A drawing by Dwane Burns of the 508th Parachute Infantry Regiment's flag, ribbons and other insignia.

Below, Colonel Charles H. Young's C-47, "Argonia." Young commanded the 439th Troop Carrier Group. His unit dropped the 82nd into Holland.

A drawing to symbolize F (Falcon) Company of the 508th Parachute Infantry Regiment.

Below, troopers waiting to board the "Argonia."

(Drawings on this and the preceding page by Dwayne Burns.)

This and preceding page: the initial stages of a paratrooper action. First, boarding the aircraft, flying into enemy territory, staying calm if possible, and finally the jump, as below, during Operation Market-Garden. (U.S. Army photos; above photo courtesy U.S. History)

Two depictions of the Normandy jump rendered by Dwayne Burns, after the 508th P.I.R. had finally been given a respite from combat.

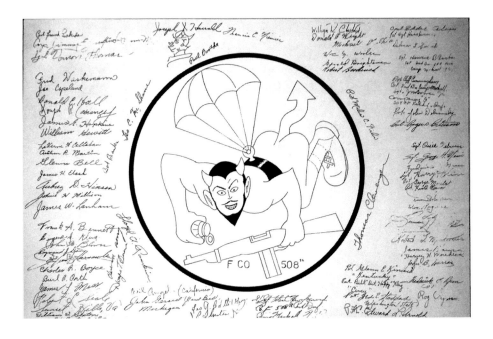

Above, the Red Devil insignia signed by members of F Company. Below, a watercolor by Dwayne Burns of the Holland jump.

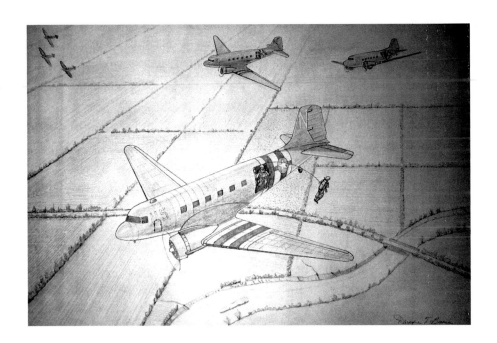

Paratroopers advance through a wooded area. (U.S. Army photo)
Below, four airborne lieutenants during a break in the Battle of the Bulge.
From left, Lts. Frick, Miles, Polette, and Trahin.
(Courtesy of George Miles)

Above, a paratrooper streaks down the street to throw off a sniper.
Below, another scene of street fighting in a devastated city near the
German border. (U.S. Army photos)

Above, captured Allied paratroopers are marched through the streets of Paris after D-Day. John McGee is in the foreground at right. This photo was taken from a German 35mm motion-picture frame.

All's well that ends well, as John made it back to the States and matrimony.

(Photos courtesy of Merilyne McGee)

√
Minerva Chastain. This photograph was sent to the author one week prior to the invasion of Europe on D-Day.

Below left, the author preparing for his last jump in France, 1945. Below right, as part of Eisenhower's post-war guard.

(Photos courtesy of Dwayne Burns)

Above, the co-authors of "Jump," Leland and Dwayne Burns, at a book signing for "All Americans All the Way."
(Photo courtesy Ellen Peters)

Left, Dwayne Burns at an interview for the 50th anniversary of D-Day.
(Photo courtesy the Fort Worth Star Telegram)

most were the replacements. Stories of home floated around as everyone shared a favorite memory.

* * *

My best day together with Minerva was at her high school picnic prior
to my reporting for duty. Not only did I spend it with her but also the
outing gave me a chance to say goodbye to some of my other friends.

I drove to her school late that morning, parked my car and went
looking for her. She had said her last class before the picnic would be
P.E. and she would be somewhere outside. I found her on the softball
field.

She was dressed in kelly green slacks and a solid white blouse, and
I remember thinking, "Boy does she look good." Minerva stood five-
foot-four, slim at the waist and didn't weight more than 105 pounds
soaking wet. She was playing left field and I sat on the rock wall surrounding the field at a spot near her, watching her and falling in love.

At the noon bell she was free and we walked to the parking lot to
meet Ed and Frances. The picnic was at Burger's Lake and most of the
kids turned out, ready to beat the heat and have a good time. It was-
n't like today's swimming pools. It was just a big round hole, about six
feet deep with a sandy bottom, surrounded by green grass.

At the end of the lake was a floating dock with a diving board on
one end. We bought food and cold drinks from the concession stand
and enjoyed them at picnic tables under plentiful shade trees. For just
a small price, all of this was available for the day. Some kids swam,
others danced or played ball.

I didn't know how to swim and was relieved when Minerva confessed she could swim no better than a lead sinker. Most of the day we
sat on the grass and talked. Or else we just walked around. Somehow
during that day I realized Minerva loved me, not by what she said, but
by the way she acted.

Toward evening we located Ed and Frances and the four of us
drove to Forest Park where we stayed talking until dark. Ed and I then
treated our girls to dinner and a movie. As I got into bed that night I
was so tired and sleepy I knew I'd be asleep soon. Instead I kept thinking back over the day, thinking of the memories I would hold onto in
the months ahead.

* * *

Early the next morning we learned our Drop Zone had changed. General Patton had overrun the selected DZ so an alternate drop near the town of Liege, Belgium was selected, but then this also became overrun with leg units. With a big sigh of relief and smiles all around, we loaded back into the trucks and returned to Wollaton Park.[xxi] All the paratroopers were in favor of giving Patton a medal or having him run for President.

Without any message, Jean stood waiting for me the next Saturday afternoon when I knocked on her door. I didn't have to explain why I had missed the previous weekend; it seemed the townspeople always knew what we were doing. Jean just said she was glad to see me back. It was a great weekend. We didn't know this would be our last together, but it couldn't have been more fun, and this way we said no sad goodbyes.

On the 14th of September we loaded onto trucks once again and headed to the airfield. And this time the Red Devils kept their return rendezvous in the Valley of the Shadow.

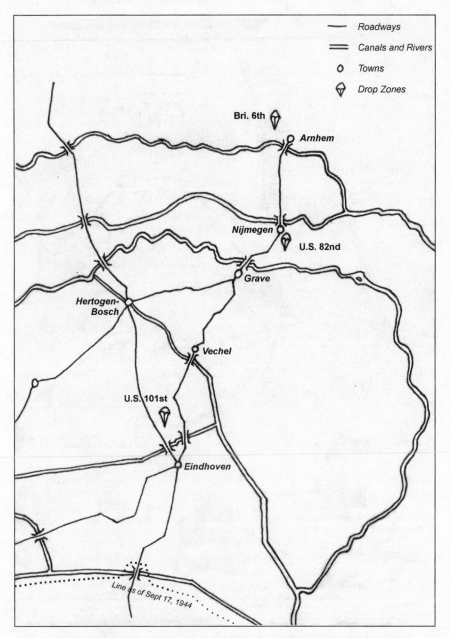

Operation Market-Garden called for the Allied airborne divisions to seize and hold bridges while British armor advanced from the south.

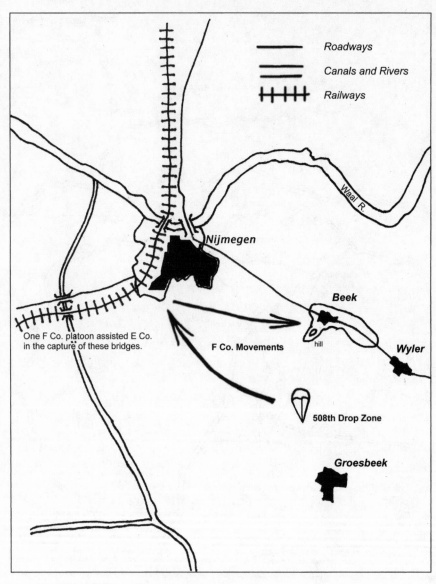

The 82nd Airborne's area of operations around Nijmegen, with its primary objectives the bridges over the Waal River.

JUMP
Eight

"My gosh, what are we going to do?"

They called it Operation Market-Garden, which made it sound like we were going to be picking apples or tiptoeing through Holland tulips. Of course none of us troopers ever knew who "they" were, lest it be Eisenhower, but we thought the campaign should have been called something more rugged. Nevertheless on Saturday, September 16th, 1944, the 508th was primed to go[xxii]

We were scheduled to jump the next day and everyone was feeling good and loose. An air of confidence seemed to overcome our apprehension. It was like a superior ball team getting ready for the playoffs. We knew we could lick 'em but we also knew that things sometimes go wrong. We had to play our best.

Some men indeed played ball on this day, while others laid on their cots, dead asleep to the world and oblivious to worry or noise. That night the regimental band performed. Some troopers danced while others clapped their hands in time to the music. The band made me dream of my own days on the electric guitar with Jimmy Warren's Kuhula Hawaiians down at the Blackstone Hotel. Mostly we played Hawaiian songs that were real popular during the war years. I reminisced about the night we played at Casa Manana on the revolving stage. Another time we went "on the air" during the Light Crust Doughboys radio show sponsored by Burrus Mills. No doubt I was good enough to join the regimental band, but who would of thought they'd let anyone bring a guitar to England.

Man, those days were gone, I decided. We'd be jumping into combat in a few hours and I wasn't here to pick out chords. Aiming a six-string electric National at the enemy wouldn't get me very far.

111

Sunday, September the 17th, dawned bright and clear. Our jump would be in daylight, and we thought this would be easier than the night jump into Normandy. After having a good breakfast of eggs and bacon we moved out to the planes. Just a short wait and we loaded up. Takeoff seemed very smooth and routine, and only a tad longer than practice.

After getting airborne I couldn't help thinking it felt a lot like a practice jump, only this time we had a fighter escort. A little before noon I watched the English coastline of North Foreland slip by 1,000 feet below. Our destination for this trip was Nijmegen, Holland, the objective of the 82nd Airborne. The 101st "Screaming Eagles" were jumping south of us into Eindhoven, and north of us the 1st British Airborne Division was to jump just outside of Arnhem. At Nijmegen each regiment of the 82nd had their own DZ and each attacked certain targets in the area. The 508th P.I.R. jumped into the area known as Groesbeek Heights.

As I sat looking out the open door, all the past memories of Normandy came rushing back. I wondered if this flight would be as bad or worse. If jumping in daylight was easier than at night, it would also be easier for Germans on the ground if they were there to pick us off. Briefings had warned us to expect heavy flak and there might be some opposition in the air. We lacked the cover of darkness but the day drop meant few, if any, missed drops. Our pilots could see the drop zones from miles out this time, and pinpoint jumps were expected all around.

Thoughts of home came to mind and I wondered what Minerva and my family would be doing when they learned the 508th had dropped into Holland. I took off my helmet and looked at Minerva's card still taped in the top. I read it through slowly, completely. Glaring reality returned to me as I saw the card for what it really was: heavy paper looking rather faded and dirty. It had been through a lot, but then so had I. Maybe I was sort of faded and dirty myself, not physically like the card, but mentally, emotionally, and spiritually changed by the war that surrounded me.

There were three ships in our formation flying in a V-pattern. I rode in the lead plane and would be the fourth man to jump. In line ahead of me sat our 2nd Battalion commander, Major Ortho Homes,

who had replaced the wounded Shanley, and next to him his radio
operator. Jumping third was my Company commander, Captain
Martin.

A glance down the aisle at the faces of the other men reminded me
that most of them were green and that this was their first combat
jump. I suspected the same of Captain Martin but hadn't asked.[xxiii] I
wasn't sure I wanted to know, since we'd had good leadership before
from Goodale and Polette and I wanted to see that kind of cool performance under pressure again. I knew that just because someone did-
n't have experience it didn't mean they were unable to get the job
done. Still, the memory of new replacements coming to talk with me
about fighting replayed in my mind. We ended that talk by my assur-
ing them that they "would be fine and, would do all right." Now as I
looked over the two sticks I didn't feel so sure. If only there had been
a little more time to train them. The old hands had had over four
months of advanced training before jumping into Normandy. Many of
these replacements had received little more than four weeks.

While the English coast was still visible, some of them were
already airsick from the ride and had thrown up on the floor. Combat
jumps were a much longer ride through the air than practice ones, and
when a man needed to heave on these trips there was no designated
place, only the floor in front of him. I knew how they felt from my seasickness while crossing the Atlantic. I wondered what made one man
sick at sea, another sick in the air, while some others have a problem
with neither. Maybe some are made to fly, some made to swim. Air
travel was never a problem for me.

Returning my eyes to the inside of my helmet, I prayed for safety.
Having come out of France without a scratch, I couldn't see how I'd
be so lucky twice in a row. Although I prayed for safety my real wish
was to be somewhere else. However, like any full-fledged member of
the 508th, I was damned proud to remain with my unit, make my
jump, and face whatever danger Holland presented rather than be left
behind. In fact, I'd jump right after my company commander!

The sun shone brightly as we crossed into Holland. So far we had
enjoyed an uneventful ride. The countryside below us had a wonderful lush beauty, and we could see some flooding near the coast. There
were also a lot of rivers inland, but on this trip there wouldn't be much

danger of our guys landing in water.

My eyes gave the Dutch horizon a studious look for windmills; I expected to see them everywhere, like in the books—but I didn't see even one.

The Germans started sending up a heavy layer of flak, but it didn't seem to come close. Flak appeared as small, dirty gray puffs that suddenly popped up all around the plane. It looked harmless enough, but it could be deadly. I hated the stuff because there was no way to fight back. I thanked God it didn't last long.

While continuing to watch out the door, I suddenly saw a plane drop out of formation—one of the troop transports could no longer keep up. I made out the three blades of the plane's twin props and was surprised that both engines had stopped. Inside our own plane every guy started pointing and shouting and then twisted and turned at the windows trying to watch the plane land. It fell miles behind our formation and would land a long way from our DZ. I could see no indication the troopers had jumped, and I wondered if they were riding the plane down. The pilot left the gear up, and I wondered if he remembered to drop his equipment bundles from the belly. I saw a little dust as he touched down and bounced back into the air. Then he came down for good and the ship slid along the ground on its belly. The craft looked fine, a smooth and straight landing from where we sat. It was a fantastic job from a great pilot. We flew on, leaving them to their troubles.

More guys threw up. If they were sick before, the flak didn't help. Now the inside of the plane began to smell pretty bad. Someone had to relieve his bladder coming over the water, quite a chore in full combat gear. First the man had to take off nearly all his equipment. Then, while standing up, hold on to the plane with one hand while the ship bounced around. He managed to get half of it on the floor, quite a bit on himself, and hardly a doctor's sample of it in the container. Now, after bouncing through flak and other turbulence, everything had spread itself around. When the ship nosed up, vomit and urine ran to the back. As the ship nosed down, it all ran the other way. I felt lucky to be sitting near the door.

The ready light came on and we all stood. Near the Drop Zone we started picking up flak again. This time the fighter planes accompanying us peeled off and went for the gun emplacements.[xxiv] All along the roads below Dutch people waved to us and danced around. The flak prevented us from feeling like waving back. We just wanted to make it over the DZ. We rode through the flak a few minutes more, but the plane took only one or two minor hits and we had no casualties. The skies then cleared of the gray explosions and the ride smoothed out a bit. The red light came on and we stood there more than ready to jump. Our standing time felt rather lengthy until the pilot at last hit the green light.

Battalion commander Homes yelled, "Let's go!" He jumped out the door, and the stick moved forward.[xxv]

After going out the door I saw the tail of the ship pass by overhead and I heard the crack of my canopy and reacted to the opening shock. All seemed smooth as I floated through bright sunlight with no sounds of gunfire, just the drone of the airplanes passing overhead. The time was 13:30.

I landed on the ground standing up, and with our new quick-open harness, I turned, pushed in the knob and the entire harness fell away.

"Outstanding!"

The terrain appeared nothing like Normandy—no hedgerows and no trees. All of F Company landed together in the middle of an enormous field. Eventually we learned that all the drops for the 508th went well, except for A Company's. As luck would have it, two planeloads dropped about two miles east of the DZ and landed in Germany. Lt. Rex Combs rounded up 22 of the jumpers, took command, and they fought their way back to battalion, killing an estimated 20 Germans and bringing back approximately 50 prisoners.

The C-47s made their turns and headed back for England, but other ships were still coming in for the drop. The line of planes stretched endlessly and the blue sky was covered with parachutes. The "Market" part of the operation used about 1,550 planes carrying close to 19,500 paratroopers and glider riders. There were nearly 500 gliders, the majority of them used by the British. By some accounts the trail of planes bringing in the 101st and 82nd Divisions, along with their fighter escorts, stretched 10 miles wide and 100 miles long.

Down below, troopers quickly tore open the bundles and retrieved their extra equipment. I found my radio and turned it on to see if it

survived the drop. It checked out all right. We met no resistance during our assembly, although we heard some very distant gunfire. We
joked and laughed as we moved out. Once again it felt like a practice
jump in England. I couldn't believe we were in German-held territory,
only a mile from the German border. We were fifty-plus miles from
our own front lines, and yet it was this quiet. Curiously quiet.
Something should have been happening, and I kept waiting for it.

Captain Martin formed up the company quickly and we headed
toward Nijmegen, our initial objective. Sgt. Giegold commandeered
two horses and a wagon from a farmer and brought up the rear, transporting our heavy equipment. After a few miles we stopped and several lookouts were posted while the 2nd Battalion officers had a quick
powwow. I looked around and briefly spoke with several of the new
guys to give them a little encouragement. I made a point to find Joe
Ensminger and the two inseparable buddies, Lou Slama and Lambert
Siniari. These two seemed a lot like John McGee and me in a way.
They seemed to do things together. I didn't know how long they'd
known each other.

Then the companies split off and Captain Martin led F Company
into a late afternoon march on its own. We stopped a few more times,
but only briefly to check our direction and survey the next immediate
mile. We heard distant gunfire off and on, but at no point did we cross
any Germans. The edge of darkness overtook us as we reached the
outskirts of town. We sent out scouts and moved within Nijmegen's
borders, meeting no enemy resistance. We didn't drop our guard, even
though the streets seemed still and silent on what became a dark,
moonless night. At one point our scouts stopped, so the company
came to a halt while waiting for word to move up.

Suddenly a German machine gun opened up right in front of us.
Our scouts had walked right past it in the dark. The captain and I
were at the head of the company and I saw the muzzle blast flashing
right before us with its aim a bit to the left. Tracer shots went right
down the middle of the street, the shots looking like a long finger of
light you could reach out and touch.

We scattered and hit the ground, trying to find some kind of cover
from which to return fire, but there was none. One trooper did a quick
draw with his rifle and started laying down a round of cover fire. A

grenade explosion suddenly erupted. Then all went deathly quiet. No one made a sound and I could only hear my heart pounding. Down the line someone split the silence with a familiar battleground yell.

"Medic!"

I knew someone had been hit, and the howler brought all of us back to our feet. We had gone too far, for too long, and we'd begun to think this mission would be easy. The Nijmegen jump by the 82nd Airborne Division would prove anything but easy. We lost one man who stood in the direct line of fire. The company was lucky, for if those Germans had aimed a little differently that night we could have lost half the company.

Martin did a quick survey of our surroundings and called a halt for the night. He ordered us to dig in and set up roadblocks. It seemed premature to stop here now that we had reached the enemy, but he was the Captain. I radioed our position to Battalion and we waited for other orders. Overall the 508th was meeting its objectives and setting up defenses on the eastern side of the 82nd's area.

On the western side of Nijmegen the 504th P.I.R.[xxvi] began setting up and grabbing some minor bridges. To the south was the 505th. North of us was the Waal River.

When you're 50 miles behind the German front, you learn to trust your own unit. You don't put a lot of faith into promises or other outfits. However, we knew the 505th and 504th were dependable. Both units had seen service in Italy and could be counted on to carry out their missions within the sector. The 82nd glider and artillery units would arrive on the next day to provide troop reinforcements and bring in some heavier weapons with their Waco gliders.

To the north of us, about fifteen miles across the Waal, the British 1st Airborne had landed a few miles outside their objective, Arnhem. Our sister division, the 101st Screaming Eagles, setting up in Eindhoven, was about thirty-five miles south. Each division had the same mission in their respective Dutch communities: to take all the waterway bridges intact and hold them until relieved by ground troops. The "Market" plan was to lay an airborne corridor all the way up through Holland. The "Garden" part of the operation consisted of armored columns simultaneously breaking across the Dutch border to cross the successive bridges, ultimately launching a powerful thrust into Germany across the Rhine bridge at Arnhem.

The ground forces chosen for this duty were British, a part of Montgomery's army along the Holland-Belgium border. There were—supposedly—2,500 tanks and other vehicles making the push north in a spear-shaped movement. These armored units were to link up with each airborne division on a fast timetable, all the way up to the Arnhem highway bridge, nearly 65 miles inside German lines. Knowing how things could get fouled up or go wrong within the system, we had no guarantee this would happen. That's why we only counted on our own unit. We could well be stranded in Nijmegen.

Within the 508th, Companies A and B pushed north into Nijmegen, their objective the bridge spanning the Waal River.[xxvii] This was the big bridge and the prize of the 82nd's mission. Fighting their way through a strange city on a dark night, Companies A and B both reached the center of the city, where German resistance suddenly stiffened. Our guys' attack turned into a monstrous ordeal. One platoon of Company A, led by Captain Adams, pushed ahead and reached the southern approach to the hefty Nijmegen Bridge.

F Company sent out numerous patrols on the first night. One group also reached the big bridge. Lou Slama was a part of this patrol. He told me later that the Germans were in control, but earlier a trooper from 1st Battalion named Bill Bauman had even walked out on the bridge.[xxviii] He looked for Germans and explosives and found neither.

One A Company patrol managed to knock out a building believed to house the enemy's demolition controls for the destruction of the gridiron structure, but then they got cut off from the rest of their company and had to hole up for awhile a couple of blocks away. Germans had moved in between them and the bridge.

At F Company's command post, everything remained quiet, but our patrols reported lots of German movement throughout the city. The next morning the Dutch people came out of their homes to find deep holes dug into their front yards, with the heads of U.S. paratroopers sticking up from them. They were friendly folks and quite glad to see us. We were offered both food and drinks.[xxix] Most of them wanted to talk and give us whatever information they could. A short, impromptu funeral service was held for our fellow paratrooper killed the previous night. Several of the guys dug a grave on a corner of a

vacant lot just across from our roadblock. Pvt. Joe Ensminger, with
the experience that comes from being a minister's son, read some
verses from his Bible and said a prayer.

"Father, he was devoted to his country, he was devoted to his unit,
and he was our buddy. We might not understand why he got it and we
didn't, but we're all better men having known him. And now God we
hand him over to You. Accept his spirit, comfort his family back
home, and give us the courage to fight in a manner worthy to redeem
him. This is our request in the name of Jesus Christ, Amen."

We, his buddies, covered our fallen brother and smoothed over the
dirt, placing his helmet and one dog tag on the grave as a marker.
Later the Dutch people in the area came and placed flowers from their
gardens on the grave.

By noon of the second day, our first full day, the Krauts had recovered from our surprise visit and were assaulting on several fronts.
Other than the large river bridge, the 82nd had taken all the smaller
canal bridges and other primary objectives, but General Gavin had the
division scrambling to hold them. The lead units of the 508th were in
the same fix. Polette had taken one platoon of F Company and most
of E Company and captured two bridges side by side: one roadway
and one railroad.

A, B and G Companies were all under counterattack from the
Germans. The other 508th companies were stationed in critical locations to discourage other attacks. I understand now that our commanders had to juggle the units around from point to point because
the Germans were trying to break into town from so many different
locations.

About this time the British tanks and troops, which had crossed
the Dutch border with a flying start while we troopers were making
our jumps, had been slowed down by one German attack after another. The first battle was with the enemy's deadly 88s hidden in the
woods on both sides of the road. The British XXXth Corps had to
keep to one major highway, which turned out to have hidden German
anti-tank emplacements along the way. The tanks were already a half-
day behind their schedule of reaching Eindhoven and joining up with
units of the 101st.

The defensive status of F Company at the south entrance to

Nijmegen was too good to last, and General Gavin had to pull every man he had to retain the ground already taken. On the afternoon of September 19th we moved out to help the 508th's 3rd Battalion set up a roadblock between the towns of Beek and Wyler. While the 3rd Battalion plus F Company went after any German resistance found on the way to the village of Beek, the Regiment's 1st Battalion attacked a place called Devil's Hill and also the town of Wyler. The remainder of our 2nd Battalion found duty fighting for the southeast glider landing fields that were now nearly overrun with German troops coming in through the woods.

That day our glider riders came in, and at some points we weren't there to greet them. The Germans were! Not only did we need the manpower those gliders carried, but many of those motorless planes also packed small artillery cannons, jeeps and the bulk of our supplies for the next three days. An estimated total of 15,000 men rode in on gliders, some of whom rode in on day one during the paratroopers' jump. So close were the Germans to overtaking the landing zone on the following day that riders landing at certain edges of the field had to come out shooting and fight their way to a friendlier side. Many supplies were left behind and had to be recovered later after the landing field had been secured.

Late in the afternoon, F Company joined in with units of the 3rd Battalion to attack Beek. The Germans threw some shells at us while we were at the base of the hill just south of the town. We swept into Beek with an easy start. Then the Captain sent a part of us to work our way to the top of that hill while G and H Companies finished up with the village. There was only light resistance and the Krauts left quickly. From this captured hill we had a view of the main road running east out of Beek town and the road that ran to the northwest going into the city of Nijmegen. Off in the distance, across the rooftops of Beek, we could spot the last major objective of the 82nd Division, the Nijmegen Bridge. It had yet to be liberated and during the early morning had received additional German reinforcements. The structure was a magnificent work of concrete and steel engineering, but physically not worth all the lives it would cost before it was taken.

Looking from our position to the northeast and across the road, we could see the flatland for a good country mile or better. As we stood atop the hill we were well concealed by the trees and bushes— it seemed we were in good shape. Part of the company remained in Beek, holding that objective with G Company and H Company. The larger part was posted on the hill. We started under the command of an old friend. Our lone officer in charge on this hill, one of the finest of the war, was Lieutenant Polette. As radio operator I made my place next to him while everyone gave the landscape a good survey. Before any time at all had passed we heard an ominous sound.

Up the road heading for Beek to counterattack the 3rd Battalion came what looked like an enormous slice of the German Army. My view was limited through the trees, but there were more enemy troops than I had ever seen at one time. They were walking along in three columns at route-step and they didn't even know we were right there above them.

A realistic guess would be that this was a battalion, maybe reinforced, or some other portion from a larger unit. What really set it off was the staff car with the top down and some high-ranking officer riding in the back, acting like he was number one.

Hollywood could not have created a better scene. They had come right up the road toward us as if they had never heard of the American Army.

With them right under our noses I found myself nearly afraid to breathe lest they hear me. Since we were limited in numbers I thought maybe if we stayed hidden they would just pass on by and go into town where the 3rd Battalion plus F Company could show them a real good time.

"My gosh, what are we going to do?" I said. "There are so many of them."

Polette was right beside me but I didn't really know who I was speaking to. I guess I was talking to myself, because Polette suddenly swung his Thompson machine gun off his shoulder. I looked over at him and he turned and looked back.

With a quick double shift of his eyebrows he said, "Let's go get 'em."

His voice sounded so casual and his expression so smug, one might think we were sitting in a pub and were going to try to pick up a couple of girls at the next table. I wanted to ask, "Get 'em with what?"

Without another moment's hesitation, and even though we were greatly outnumbered, he took off down the hill. I was still trying to ready my own weapon and join the run when Lieutenant Polette started firing his first shots. Now, it must be explained, all the troopers of F Company would have followed him to hell and back if the lieutenant said we could do it and would lead the way, so down the hill we went. This action isn't in the books and remains unknown in war history, except for the few troopers who were there and survived, but it had to be one of the greatest classic battle charges of the European campaign.

There were only thirty or forty of us on that part of the hill, but there were several hundred enemy soldiers at the bottom. Slamming down the hill, firing from the hip and screaming at the top of our lungs, we acted like crazed Indians on the warpath, and suddenly this hill was the Little Big Horn, with General George Custer waiting below.

Despite being few in number we had great willpower, and with each step, with each scream, our spirits became wilder. The Germans we unleashed ourselves upon must have felt our energy. They likely had sensed our determination and, not knowing our true head count, had surely visualized their own massacre. Our advantage was the tree cover and the Germans were in the open. The platoon was spread wide, and below it must have sounded like the gunfire came from the entire hill. The Jerrys broke and ran like whipped puppies. It almost looked like an organized move. That is to say, they all turned tail and ran as one. We started to cut down the hill at an angle and ran after them until we got to the road. There Polette called a halt.

He shouted his orders, "This is as far as we go! Pick your targets." He dropped down on one knee for better aim, and his Thompson jumped every time he cut loose.

I took a place at the roadway's edge and picked a target. Down on the flats the Germans were running for their lives. There was no cover. All they could do was try to get out of our range. There were so many of them I found it unusually hard to concentrate on one mark at a time.

Only one German seemed willing to stand and fight, and he was in the back of the staff car, madder than hell. His driver had turned off the road and was gunning ahead of the rushing retreat. The officer stood up, shouting and waving his arms, trying vainly to get his men to stop and reorganize. But the soldiers had the bit in their teeth and there was no stopping them. We urged them to continue on their way with a helpful repetition of small-weapons fire.

As the last Germans made his escape to a range of safety, we finally stopped firing and sat down to watch them finish their way across the flats. Between the two sides, one could see scattered pieces of equipment and dead or writhing Krauts for a thousand yards. The "devils in baggy pants"xxx—the German nickname for us paratroopers—had scared them off again.

After a brief pause from our mad sprint down the hill, we withdrew back to the top and set up an organized defensive position in a pear orchard. The view was good there. We knew it was only a matter of time, however, until the Germans would regroup and start back. Maybe this time they'd hit us with artillery fire. But we figured they wouldn't try coming across the open flats again.

JUMP
Nine

We ran for the lights and shot from the hip.

As the battle for Nijmegen unfolded in the first three days of Market-Garden, the 508th saw companies fighting at Beek, Wyler and Ber en Dal. Our 3rd Battalion's fight in Beek with F Company support was waged with plenty of Germans other than the ones we had chased from the hill. In fact, our platoon was lucky to sit somewhat quiet for most of a day in the orchard while the others had their hands full in town. However, our own job was very important because we were keeping anyone off their backside. The Germans soon realized that our command of the high ground was a big asset and they started sending in artillery. It didn't come our way very often but they seemed to cover the whole hill at one time or another and some guys took a good hammering. Likewise, they never brought forth any sizeable ground troops like the force that we had driven off with that crazy charge.

We could tell when the Germans were ready to hit the town because from our position we could see the enemy entering from the north end and I'd radio down a warning. After a couple of hours of weapons fire, we could also see the Jerrys leaving and then knew that the 3rd Battalion had held its own.[xxxi]

However, the Krauts didn't ever leave for long; they kept coming back and kept looking for new ways to overrun Beek. And each time they entered one could hear another round of intense fire. Every now and then, a German patrol that didn't know better would try to come around the east side of town. We'd watch until they were well within range and then our machine guns would open up and send them running back across the flats.

125

After a day, changes in personnel were made of both men and officers on the hill. I stayed in my position on the hill since there was no other radio operator. Captain Martin and Lieutenant Goodale showed up with a platoon and Lieutenant Polette led the others either into Beek or to establish a position elsewhere on the hill. Lieutenant Goodale joined my position as a platoon leader.

"You've got it good up here, Burns," the lieutenant told me.

"How's that Sir?" I responded.

"Beek is a mess. They won't give up."

"Well it's been mostly quiet here," I informed him. "But the Jerrys keep sending patrols and there's a short shelling every so often. Like you said, they won't give up."

Goodale replied, "We'd better keep our eyes open."

"You got it."

A scout came back to report he'd seen some soldiers digging in on the northwest side of Beek.

"They're way off in the distance but right at the edge," he said, "and I can't tell if it's Fritzes or some of our guys."

"Let's find the captain," Goodale said.

We discussed it and got on the radio to learn that newly commissioned officer Vernon Thomas was acting in his first command role. I smiled with some pride and the lieutenant grinned back. He understood; Vernon was one of us. He'd show H Company how to do it.

My own foxhole on the hill was located just behind our machine-gun nest. I think, or maybe just hoped, that Warren Zuelke, an excellent gunner, was in charge, but he may have been lower on the hill or down in Beek at this time.

The Germans sure wouldn't give up, and we had another occasion to provide entertainment when they attempted another review of the flats. Goodale, a few other troopers and I sat and watched a patrol circle the far side. There was a dike there offering them some cover and they could have gone undetected if they had crawled instead of stooping. The Lieutenant had six enemy soldiers spotted from way back through his field glasses. When the Germans reached the range he wanted, Goodale turned from his glasses.

"Someone man the .30 caliber."

I was closest, so without looking around for Warren or another gunner I climbed into the hole. I hadn't fired a machine gun since Basic Training.

"Set your sight for 300 yards. Fire when ready."

I knew what I was doing, but didn't know if the other guys knew that I knew. The weapon-sight was cranked up to 300; I lined up on the first man and pulled the trigger. Tracers launched from the muzzle flew instantly to their intended target. With a direct hit I pumped several rounds into the first man. His chest just exploded but his body was slow to drop; then it sort of melted to the ground. It was a gruesome death. I lifted my aim and before they knew what hit them, three more of the six-man patrol were laid on the ground. The other two ran for their lives in different directions. I stopped firing and let them disappear behind the dikes.

Lieutenant Goodale lowered his glasses and looked my way. "Damn, Dwayne, where did you learn to shoot like that?"

I tried to suppress a grin. "Us radio guys are taught how to send communications through the air. I figure they got the message."

Captain Martin came up to see what all the firing was about and Goodale filled him in. I felt proud when the lieutenant mentioned me, but then the captain started chewing us out.

"I'd better not hear that thing firing again. I don't want the Germans to find us up here, and they will if we keep shooting at them."

We were stumped. Goodale was outranked so he just answered with a weak "Yes, Sir," and Martin left. After watching him leave we turned and looked at each other; our jaws had dropped to our chests. In a battle that had 82nd Airborne forces stretched thin I thought this hill was an easy assignment, but when we did fight we got into trouble. In his defense, I think it was possible that the captain knew something we didn't, but if that was so we never learned of it. From this time on the captain and I didn't get along too well. On a different note, the sight of that first German dying is a memory that has haunted me often; the only long-term pleasure in the experience was to find favor with the lieutenant.

While the battle of Beek was only part of the 508th's duties, just a single fight when compared to the mission of the whole 82nd Division, the importance of the stand is well known and understood. If Beek had been lost, the Germans could have cut off our supply field and we'd be sandwiched next to their forces holding the south end of the big Nijmegen Bridge.

Losses were high in Beek and at points troopers had to temporarily withdraw from certain parts of the area. After the advantage of the battle flip-flopped three times, the town was finally secured for the Allies on the 21st of September. H Company, with help from parts of G Company and F Company, had done the job, but they were hardly functional as companies for the rest of the Holland campaign. F Company alone lost nine men in Beek.

The hilltop section of F Company did have one other rather foul problem during all this. It wasn't with the Germans, but with the half-green pears in the orchard and from some turnips in a field back south. We had been consuming these to supplement our rations. If the enemy had hit us on the hill at the right time, they could have really caught F Company with its pants down.

Meanwhile the 504th had drawn the assignment of trying to take the big bridge over the Waal River. After three days of fighting, the Panzer tanks still held the south end. General Gavin decided the solution was to assault both ends at the same time. The 504th's 2nd Battalion was picked to make a river crossing and take the north end. Facing a lot of small-arms fire as well as a barrage of light artillery, they made it to the north bank and had it secured in less than 30 minutes. Then they attacked the structure to secure the north end. The 505th made a renewed assault on the south end and both sides of the German resistance fell at about the same time.

The Germans' last defense was a handful of soldiers holed up in the bridge girders. On the 20th of September, several days behind schedule, the first British tank crossed the Nijmegen Bridge and prepared to move north toward Arnhem. The move north, however, never took place. At least not as soon as it should have. Instead, the remaining British Airborne soldiers were pulled out of Arnhem and the fight was abandoned. The 1st British Airborne, plus a Polish Airborne Brigade that had flown in to reinforce them, had been practically destroyed. These actions were learned through rumors and half-truths, and the common fighting man never knew the real story until long after leaving the front lines.

* * *

After those first early days the fighting became lighter for everyone within the division. The Germans had either given up on this patch of land and withdrew, or they were making plans to counterattack at areas not controlled by the 82nd. F Company had time to lick its wounds and to count its losses once again. There were more deaths than wounds in Beek town; I believe this was due to the close fighting where the battle lines were established by streets, not fields. Joe Ensminger once again conducted a brief service for our comrades in arms that fell during those battles.

He quoted from the Bible, "Hear these words from King David."

The LORD is my light and my salvation, whom should I fear?
The LORD is the stronghold of my life, of whom should I be
    afraid?
When the wicked, my enemies and my foes, come against me
    to devour my flesh, they stumble and fall.
Though an army may make camp all around me, I will have
    confidence and stand firm.

After Joe finished the Bible scripture he led a prayer.[xxxii] Then, having expressed our last goodbyes, we moved on. I was very pleased to have Joe with us in Holland.

In the evening we once again sat and discussed the recent fighting. Most of it was about Beek.

One soldier said in question form, "I heard Joe Hernandez got it before we ever reached the town." Hernandez had earned a Silver Star in Normandy.

"Yeah, he got hit with an 88, blew him up bad."

"Van Every got it in Beek, but he'll live."

"That's twice for Van Every. I saw him hit at Hill 95," Another trooper added.

"How about Lieutenant King, is he dead or wounded?"

And the answer was that this lieutenant, and "Sergeant Rex Spivey and a whole bunch of others were dead." Some died in Beek but a few, including Rex, were killed from the shelling on the hill. Those 88s had done more damage than I realized. These were the business discussions of a front-line soldier. Everyone knew and liked Sergeant Hernandez, and Sergeant Spivey had been a buddy of mine.

It was the 29th of September when we pulled out of Nijmegen and headed north, where we cleaned out some light German resistance. After the fighting died down, Lou Slama came to me for help.

"Sergeant Burns, could I have a moment?"

"Sure Lou, what's up?"

"I think my best buddy Lambert got hit back on top of the hill. He's not around here anywhere. Will you go back with me and help me find him?"

"Of course, let's go," I said.

A lump of fear started to grow in my throat as we walked back. I was reflecting on the visit that Lou and his buddies, Lambert Siniari and Joe Ensminger, had made to me for advice. Each of them was a real good guy and I had since taken an interest in their well being. But I didn't get a chance to think about it too long. About 200 yards back we found Lambert lying under a tree. He always looked quite young, and here it struck me he was just some Huck Finn-type sleeping in the shade for a spell. His youthful face could have fooled anyone into guessing him as no older than sixteen years of age. We sat down beside him. Other than a little puddle of blood in the hollow of his neck there didn't seem to be a mark on him.

"Oh boy, oh boy, this is going to kill his mother," Lou grieved. "We grew up together, joined up together. His mother used to treat me just like I was one of her own sons."

As Lou recounted stories of he and Lambert growing up, I gently unstrapped the dead soldier's chinstrap and pulled away his helmet. Lou took his buddy's weapon and smacked it into the ground, the barrel down, the stock sticking up.

"Damn it, damn it, damn it! Why is it like this?" He cussed in a harsh whisper.

"Seems like the best kids are the first to get it," I said, but I really didn't know if that was true or not. It just seemed like the right thing to say.

We balanced Private Siniari's helmet on top of the rifle butt, so he would be found and picked up and his body properly buried. We walked back to the unit in silence. I felt I should find something else to say, but while I couldn't, I knew Ensminger would.

* * *

Most of the 508th's 2nd Battalion relieved part of the 504th P.I.R. which had dug in west of Voxhil. Some of the guys called it Fox Hill. As the communications sergeant I had the immediate duty of checking out the field telephones. Running field phones from company command to every platoon had started to become routine in Holland. Then we ran a line to either battalion or regiment. I don't recall having to correct or add anything at Voxhil when we moved in. For the rest of September, F Company spent its nights patrolling the front lines. This could have been a quiet area except that the Germans had it marked as a target for artillery shells and screaming meemies.

So there wasn't much ground action, but on October the 1st, early in the morning, a heavy barrage began. We had the rude awakening of an incoming whistle, a deafening crash, and then flying shrapnel, dirt, tree limbs, and anything else that managed to be in the path of the plummeting steel shells. We slept in foxholes, which offered some protection, but all the debris started raining down on us.

I tried to make myself as small as possible in the bottom of my foxhole. You just don't get used to artillery. Like flak, it is very impersonal and you can't fight back. At least with flak you expect to fly out of it and your pilot has some control over the plane's destiny. With artillery there is never any telling how long it will last, and there isn't a darn thing you can do about it.

Shells started coming in four and five at a time, and the pace continued all day. We couldn't move out of our holes. With the landing of each shell I dug in a little deeper. After awhile I began to feel so isolated and lonesome that I called over to Joe in the next foxhole.

"Hey Ensminger!" I screamed. "Are you alright?"

"Yes," he called back between the blasts. "But I wish they would stop this—I need to take a leak."

"Try using your helmet," I suggested. Then I turned to the other side and yelled again, "Hey Woody! What are you doing?"

Another round hit nearby, with tree limbs and dirt whistling just over our heads. I heard Woody cry out.

"I'm digging!"

I paused a moment at his words and then hollered, "Try using your helmet."

Any humor within the banter was left unacknowledged by all because the terror was too great to accept it. My own thoughts were mostly prayers, and I felt I had reached my mental limit.

God, please don't let them send any more. I just can't take another series.

But another series came in and somehow my nerves held up. Why any of us were still alive was beyond me, because the Germans had dropped enough artillery to kill every American paratrooper in Europe.

Then I wondered if maybe they had killed everybody. So shattered was my thinking that I began to imagine our small pocket of F Company soldiers was all that remained. In another few rounds we too would be joining our fallen comrades.

Then the shelling suddenly stopped. I could hardly accept it; perhaps the constant pounding had only made me deaf. I sneaked one eye open and saw the air starting to clear. I heard others turning in their own foxholes and checking the area.

We started creeping out, everyone moving timidly at first. It might be a false alarm and at any time we'd have to hit the holes again. At first, when I looked out, all I could see were helmets and eyeballs. Then with a little time we ventured farther out. Finally someone broke the ice and men started popping up. Joe was out with the early ones and he started an immediate dance to the bushes. We started working out the cramps in our legs and backs.

Someone commented, "Boy, that sure was some heavy shooting."

"It lasted a God-awful long time," another added.

One trooper explained, "Well, of course it lasted a long time, the Jerrys are such rotten shots they have to keep trying it again and again."

"He's right, why if those were our boys shooting we'd have all gone at the first incoming series."

The men had found themselves again, and it didn't take long for the talking and joking to take over. The unit was in good shape personnel-wise but I believe one man was killed. Ralph Burrus and Lou

Slama and at least one other were injured. With a quick inspection, we found every tree in the area had been hit and most had no limbs left at all. And all our telephone lines were cut up. I'd have a big task ahead of me if we stayed here.

Then I learned the lines had been cut right as the shelling began. There had been no communication with Battalion to inform them of the artillery while it was happening. We would now have to send a runner or wait for them to send one to us. We decided to wait on them. Just before dark, Major Holmes and his runner showed up at F Company headquarters. All members of company headquarters were there.

"Captain Martin, how you holding up here?" the major asked.

"We're in good shape considering the pounding the Germans dropped on us today. We've sent our wounded back and our spirits are holding up," he replied.

"That's great," Major Holmes said. "I'm thinking we may have to pull you out to aid E Company; or we might need to pull back to keep from getting your company cut off."

"What's going on?" asked Captain Martin.

"A German battalion hit E Company and overran their position today. They took a bit of a hurt and had to withdraw 500 yards. So keep your men prepared and ready. Lindquist may call for a counter-attack." The major started pulling a map from a leather pouch at his waist. "Let me show you the current lines of our position on . . ."

The major's speech stopped and everyone's eyes widened. A mortar round swished in with a scream. The thing almost landed on top of us and it was exploding before we were halfway to the ground. Dirt and bushes flew in our faces. My left arm and leg felt numb. "I'm hit!" I was thinking.

Amazingly I crawled back to my knees. I started feeling around, looking for blood, but couldn't find any. I paused to think about just what my body was experiencing and was startled to realize I was already standing. Slowly, the acceptance that my body was still in one piece and contained no gaping holes came back to me.

Likewise, Captain Martin and Major Holmes were both OK and back on their feet. But their runners each took a hit in the back and had to be evacuated. Others in headquarters were okay as well, except for John Hurst. He left with the others but his injuries were minor and I knew we'd have him again soon. This was John's second Purple Heart.

* * *

As the evening crawled into night we all grew a bit edgy. Everyone sensed something was about to happen. Every other man had orders to sleep, but few of them could. After the shelling of the day we all needed rest but the tension was too thick.

Just minutes past midnight the orders came over the horn, "F Company, counterattack and restore the line." We hated to leave our nice, safe foxholes, but who could sleep? Attacking in the daylight is bad enough, but at night—be it fact or just perception—an attack can really get nasty.

After creeping forward into the blackness it didn't take us long to find the Germans. They opened fire on us and we began firing back as if on cue. The trooper next to me went down. In the dark I didn't even know who it was.

"Medic!" I called out.

I stepped to his side and dropped to one knee. Before looking at him I first finished my clip by aiming toward a spot from where I thought the enemy shots had come. Then I looked down at the trooper to see if I could help, but no one would be able to do anything for him. At least two rounds had struck him in the left side of his face. He had died instantly. He was one of the replacements but I can't recall who it was or if it was someone I knew.

I know there was blood on my hands when I jumped up running, slipping a new clip into my M-1 as I went. In the dark I spotted a muzzle blast through the foliage. There were other quick flashes up and down a tree line. Oddly, it reminded me of fireflies on a Texas summer night.

Adrenaline rose another degree; we ran for the lights and shot from the hip. There was no way to know which of us found a target.

Our legs carried us into smoke hanging close to the ground. The smoke clung to the smell of gunpowder and death. This mixture of odor, or the taste of fear, caught in the back of my throat and up into my sinuses, making it hard to get a breath.

When I came close enough to hear the Germans moving, I slowed down my pace by a third and looked for a hard target. Firing from both sides became sporadic and finally died down as the remaining Germans withdrew. I found the dead remains of a machine-gun crew in front of me. After the quiet set in, we stopped to once again bandage our wounds and count our missing.

They said it was a brilliant attack. Once again I didn't know who "they" were, but figured the attack was brilliant because "they" were all still alive. Among us, twelve troopers had been killed and another sixteen wounded. I would have bet those troopers' view on the attack's great fame would be different. However, when votes are taken the dead don't get to participate. The count against F Company was low, though Ensminger still had his work cut out for him and somehow he always found the right words. The high status of the battalion's charge was probably due to the winnings that resulted from it. German dead numbered about fifty, with twenty-eight others taken prisoner. We captured one tank plus some light armored cars. This battle proved to be the last of the fierce fighting for the 508th in Holland.

On the sixth of October, the Red Devils marched back into Nijmegen, where three amphibious Army DUKWs were waiting for us. I couldn't help but wonder where these "ducks" were when the 504th's 2nd Battalion was trying to get across the Waal River and attack the bridge from the north.

After we got aboard, these amphibious craft carried us north beneath the big bridge and then along the river's edge. Delivery of the 508th was to an island so large it absorbed the whole regiment and we were now attached to the British 50th Division. The island was bordered by the Waal on the south and the Neder Rijn on the north and F Company drew its assignment in another apple orchard. We felt lucky here. Not only were the apples ripe and delicious but also we were far enough from the front lines that the chow truck could bring us up hot food. This made a big boost in our morale.

With no incoming artillery and living in the quiet of a peaceful orchard, our jittery nerves began to heal. After only a few days we were relieved and trucked back to Nijmegen for a real rest. Billeting was in a schoolhouse, with real bunk beds, showers and movies. Everyone received a new pair of socks and no one minded that they were four sizes too large. We even got mail and the *Stars And Stripes* again. It's just amazing what little things in life can do for a trooper's shattered nerves.

However, the powers in charge knew combat soldiers couldn't be exposed too long to this soft life. So, after a few days it was back across the Waal and to the front lines. We again took up defensive positions. The action had moved farther on and mostly we sat and looked across no-man's land in the daytime and sent out patrols at night.

Some of our patrols went deep into enemy territory, staying as long as 24 hours and then coming back the next night. There was always some spasmodic artillery fire going on. The Germans wanted us to know they were still there. Life on the line here was quiet, but it was really a miserable existence. It rained almost every day and each day the water became a little deeper in our foxholes.

Woody and I always shared one together. This one we dug beside a large drainage ditch. We covered the entire top with logs and dirt and placed its exit into the ditch. As the water grew deeper in the hole we put down ammunition crates to sit on or lie down on so that our bodies kept dry.

One day while inside the dugout we were cooking our dinner over a small camp stove. Woody was at the far end and I sat with my back to the exit.

"Hey, look at this big crack in the wall," Woody said. "It wasn't there yesterday."

"Must be all the rain has soaked down," I commented as I studied the dark crack. It was of some interest to me, but I had a greater interest in our dinner.

"Gee whiz! It's getting bigger all the time," Woody observed. "I think we better get the hell out of here before it caves in on us!"

I backed out at his command but then stopped at the ditch and reached in for the dinner and the stove. The dugout's wall did not look good.

He yelled, "For God's sake, Burns, hurry up! I don't want to be buried alive in here!"

As I pulled the stove out, Woody started to crawl for the exit. He didn't make it. The whole side of the dugout fell in and chunky mud the texture of thick chili buried him up to his armpits.

"Oh dear Jesus, help me!"

He was yelling like he was snakebit. Returning inside as far as I could, I started digging him out.

"You're okay," I told him. "It's not going to cave in any more."

I called for John and Joe and some others to come over and help. In a couple of minutes we were able to free Woody's legs and pull him out. Then we all sat down in the ditch and started laughing.

"You know that used to be a darn good foxhole," I joked.

"Stop laughing at me," he said, laughing just as hard. "I'm the one who got buried."

On closer inspection we found our hole still serviceable, but it was agreed we would live in the ditch, and the dugout would be used only when artillery fire came in. There was no way we were going back in there to sleep.

Life in the ditch really wasn't any worse than in the foxhole, except we had no cover. Both were equally dirty. And so it was here in the ditch that I celebrated my twentieth birthday. For a paratrooper I was getting to be an old man.

I said to the guys, "You better start showing some respect for my age. I ain't a snotty nose teenager like most of you dirt smudges. And remember, I've got three stripes on this arm also."

Some of them answered back, "Aw, shut up."

"Yeah Dwayne, go find somebody who cares."

A package came from home that week. It was a pen and pencil set with the U.S. Army eagle on it. Everyone admired it.

Sergeant Scanlon said, "Burns, if you get killed, can I have it?"

Guys were always claiming or giving away stuff when the worse happened.

"Sure, Wilbur" I replied. "It's yours. Just as long as you're not the one pulling the trigger."

* * *

After another few nights of our sleeping in the ditch, the 508th went back into reserve for a second rest. F Company headquarters was given an old farmhouse to stay in. Being in headquarters had some small perks.

While giving the house a good inspection, we found a package of what we thought was either cake mix or pancake mix. We couldn't read the packaging and had to go by the pictures printed on the side. After way too much discussion and debate we decided to make a single pancake as a test. First, however, we needed some syrup and one fellow brought our attention to a five-gallon can under the sink. At first we didn't know what it was. Someone tasted a drop's worth, and sure enough, we had about two inches of syrup-like substance in the bottom of that big can.

"On with the pancakes," I said.

We dumped the whole sack of mix into a pan and then very carefully added water. We didn't want to get it too thin. Two guys had been heating a big frying pan on the wood-burning stove, and some of the batter was poured in. All of us stood side by side in a full circle around that frying pan to see what was going to come out. After plenty of time to brown, it was turned over.

"It looks like a pancake."

And it did. By some miracle it looked like we had something. It was golden, it was beautiful. The many shades of brown were perfectly mingled together. I could feel my mouth watering.

Thoughts of home flashed before me. My dad always cooked the family's breakfast on Saturday mornings and we always had pancakes. It was one of my favorite breakfasts. I knew pancakes, and this had to be one. But I was cautious. Once before, many of us troopers had worked together to make a really special pot of baked beans. Not one bean was eaten from that experience. This pancake looked good, too good; something was bound to go awry.

The pancake came out and we let a little syrup flow across the top. Everyone took a bite. It was wonderful! We all smiled but I had to tease the guys.

"I don't know guys, after we cook them we might want to just send them down the Dwayne."

They just rolled their eyes and ignored me. So then we really started cooking. Another frying pan was pressed into service so the cakes would come twice as fast. We ate all we could hold and still had pancakes on the table. It was a great time and everyone had more fun than they'd experienced in a long time.

* * *

After too short a break, F Company found itself back at the same ditches on the front line with the rest of the Red Devils. By now all our foxholes were just big mud puddles, so most of us were taking cover in the ditch.

On one day when the skies were clear and the temperature as warm as could be expected for an October day, we were all laying out in the sun trying to dry. It was calm and it was quiet. From behind us we heard the sound of incoming aircraft. Allied fighters, we figured, and sure enough, two P-51s passed overhead and crossed the German front lines. Their line of flight seemed so lazily executed it projected all the excitement of an old farm dog moving from one shady sleeping spot to another.

"Boy, that's the life," I commented. "Go out for a little flying, shoot up a few Germans, then go home and have a nice dinner with your girlfriend. Then, at the day's end, you have a soft warm bed to sleep in at night."

Joe asked, "How do you know he's got a soft warm bed?"

"Joe, where did you sleep last night?" I asked back.

Any place would have been better than where we were just then, except of course the battlefield. Joe laughed softly. We watched the flying pair move steady at about 1,000 feet, growing smaller to the eye.

"Yeah boys, I tell you, that's a helluva way to fight a war." Then I made an open wager. "I bet he don't even know we're sitting down here in this mud wearing the same clothes we jumped in over a month ago."

Suddenly we saw that flak had started exploding around the two flyboys. I guess we hadn't even known the guns were out there. The two Mustangs maintained a straight course and went on for about two miles until the flak ended. Then the pair made a 180-degree turn and came right back through the flak again. It was as if the pilots were saying, "You dumb Germans can't hit anything."

But as the planes neared the lines the shooter had found the correct range. One of the planes was hit and fell off on its right wing. At 50 feet it looked like it might level out, but then the right wing fell again. I figured the pilot must have been hit since the plane showed no signs of damage. We just stood there, staring, as the aircraft dove straight into the ground.

A terrific explosion shook the earth on the plane's impact. Fire shot into the sky and then black smoke billowed so thick and dark it blocked out the wreckage and most of the flames.

Nobody said a word. The remaining P-51 crossed over into Allied airspace and did a zigzag along the front. Her engine sang a different pitch with each turn. It was like a bird crying for its mate. But the mate was not there, having been shot down by an evil hunter from the Black Forest. We were stunned and I don't know why. This was a war after all, and people died every day. Maybe we just couldn't believe it had happened. Air combat was not a daily experience to us. I felt I was the one who needed to speak up, and finally broke the silence.

"Boy, its sure good to be down here on the ground where it's safe."

* * *

On the 11th of November we were relieved and moved back to Nijmegen. We had been on the front line for 34 days and had hardly moved a foot forward since landing. At least now Nijmegen was considered safely in Allied control. Rumor had it that we were done, our fighting was over, and that the unit was going home to Nottingham. Based on the time it took to train replacements and plan another airborne attack, nobody could argue against it. The war, as many expected, would be over by Christmas. True to expectations, we began a hike to the town of Oss. There, we were told, trucks waited which would remove us from Holland and take us to the rear, to France.

We were all smiles. Not even the fact that it was a 22-mile hike to Oss bothered us. At Oss the trucks were waiting. It seems they could have met us on the road a few miles sooner, but we didn't much care about that either. Everyone was so charged up about returning to England it would have taken an awful lot to upset us. We slept for most of the 36-hour truck ride. Dreams of a reunion in England filled my mind.

On November the 14th we unloaded our cramped bones from the trucks and were told our location, Camp Sissonne. It was near Reims, France. We were told this would be our new home.

JUMP
Ten

*"We've been ordered to move up
and stop them."*

The 508th PIR paid a price for the liberation of Holland with 147
killed and 549 wounded or missing. I thought it sad that certain members of the Normandy jump had lived through that travail only to be
killed in Holland. I wondered if any of the old guys would be around
to turn out the lights when the party was over. But if you listened to
some troopers, the war was all but won and the 508th—indeed the
whole 82nd Division—wasn't expected to see duty again. That pleased
us a lot.

Not one trooper was happy about staying at Camp Sissonne.
Everyone wanted to go back to Nottingham. Reims was too close to
the war and evidence of it lay scattered everywhere. We blamed our
assignment on Eddie, the company clerk.

"Eddie, what is this place?" I questioned. "You were supposed to
look after the camp. We should be in England."

"Hell, Burns, don't blame me, you've got more stripes than I do!"

He had me there. When I moved from PFC to Sergeant I had
passed up several of the guys who had been with the regiment from
the start, but when Wilbur came around passing out promotions again
most of the old guys caught up. Just like before, there were a few new
replacements waiting for us when we came back. Once again many of
them looked way too young.

There was a good side to the new camp; we were living in brick
barracks now instead of tents. That of course also meant indoor
plumbing and we sure did like that—luxury, man!

Overall, Sissonne was more of a military camp than Nottingham.
It had a big house where movies were shown and an NCO club. Of

course the new men joining the regiment thought France was just fine. Being green troops, they were a bit more gung-ho for fighting and this was close to the war action. They didn't yet have an actual combat jump behind them to provide the correct insight.

Additional new men continued reporting for duty in small numbers. Some new officers also moved into our company, but we regrettably lost Lt. Polette. Lloyd Polette, who had earned the Distinguished Service Cross in Holland, was transferred to E Company as its new commanding officer. Good for him since I knew he'd make captain soon, but bad for us in F Company. I learned a few of the newbies had made it to Nottingham before our camp had broken and moved over the channel to France. Replacements were always needed to take over for those killed or staying in the hospital. The youth of the new guys kept bothering me and I wondered if it was possible I was just seeing them through battle-weary eyes. Two combat jumps and I was old at the age of twenty. Billy Ward was one of the new men assigned to company headquarters. We became good friends and he soon picked up the nickname Billy the Kid.

Captain Martin didn't take long to get the company back to basics with close order drill, beautification of the area and night problems in the surrounding hills. After a short number of days, 48-hour passes to Paris were handed out to the Holland vets on a rotating basis. As the first group came back, the stories began to circulate and I could hardly wait for my shot at the big city.[xxxiii] Otherwise, events settled into day-to-day army life rather quickly. I personally grew to believe the Red Devils would be stationed here until the war was over. The army had stage shows sent into camp. One of them starred Mickey Rooney, and the others featured very good French touring companies. All the shows were quite entertaining, which helped make routine army life better.

On many occasions we were allowed to go into the city of Reims. Christmas was coming and things were looking up. I planned to get into Reims and do some Christmas shopping on my next pass. After a month I started thinking like the new men—this wasn't too bad of a place to sit out the rest of the war.

It was almost certain that the 82nd Division was done fighting. New divisions were still coming over from England and even more units were still forming. Our old sister regiment, the 507th, was reassigned to the 17th Airborne Division after Normandy, and that unit was just now obtaining full strength in England. History confirms that ✓General Gavin was arguing for the All Americans to pull back. Gavin had to be a very brave man because I had seen him at the front more than once reviewing battle problems, and he was known to crawl from one company to another while under fire. But there were men in our sister regiments, the 504th and 505th, who had seen action in Italy and had earned four jump stars. The General believed there was only so much a country could expect from its soldiers. The only thing we enlisted guys knew was that rumors kept floating around that we were done. Our war was over.

I began reflecting on what a wild ride it had been. Only a year ago I was in communications school with fresh wings on the breast of my shirt. Countless memories with John and many others who were close friends at the time came to mind. Most of them were now scattered and several were dead.

* * *

The morning John McGee and I started our military duty we'd boarded a bus for Mineral Wells, Texas, a town 50 miles west of Fort Worth. It would have been easier if they had sent us a thousand miles away. We were so close to home, but in truth we were living in a whole different world.

We spent two weeks in Mineral Wells. Long enough to be outfitted in new uniforms, go through more processing, and get tested in a number of ways; the state of our mental and physical beings was important. When it came to emotions I don't think the army cared, but some inductees were still hurting at being pulled away from home. Everyone went through the hundred and one things it takes to turn a civilian into a GI. We were busy all day, every day. Nights were free but we were restricted to base. We used most of our time writing letters home or showing off our girlfriend's pictures to the other guys.

I had mixed feelings during this time in Mineral Wells. I was young and looking forward to being free from my family and setting out on my own for the first time. Being in the service was new and exciting and it brought the promise of high adventure.

However, I was taking on some responsibilities. It meant growing up, becoming a man and making my own decisions. No more running to Dad or Mom and asking them what they thought. Of course the army felt compelled to make a lot of decisions for me.

On June 1st they had us fall out with all of our equipment. We marched down to the train station, where we climbed on board and headed west. Only our locomotive engineer and the good Lord knew where we were going, but neither of them was talking just then.

Our first stop was Clovis, New Mexico. It was a beautiful Sunday morning. We would be here a few hours and anyone who wanted to go to church was allowed to fall out beside the train. We all walked into town and attended church as a unit.

Most of us went, but for several it was only for the walk and to work the kinks out of their legs. I thought it was a welcome break from the train and the townspeople were friendly. They treated us like we were something special.

By the middle of the afternoon we were rolling west again. Throughout New Mexico and Arizona we slowed or stopped at every little desert town, most so small and poor looking I said a silent prayer, "Please Lord, don't let them unload us here."

As we entered California the train passed through beautiful citrus orchards and several much more modern towns.

"We're going to be all right, John," I said. "Things are looking up."

"I hear you talking, Buddy," John replied. "We've made it to the Golden State. The West Coast is going to be home for a while. It can't be too bad."

We finally reached our destination at the small town of Paso Robles. Camp Roberts was our new station and we would be there for the next seventeen weeks, going through basic training. Our camp sat twenty miles from the Pacific Ocean, approximately halfway between San Francisco and Los Angeles, with lots of little but interesting towns in the area.

Camp Roberts was one of the largest infantry and artillery training camps in the world, covering 47,000 acres. The camp had all the comforts of home such as service clubs, theaters, bowling alleys, recreation halls, chapels and a hospital. Rows upon rows of two-story barracks lined the hot, dusty streets. High, grass-covered hills surrounded the camp. In the middle stood a parade ground so long and wide an airplane could land on it from any direction. The parade ground was also hot, and during the day you could see the heat waves shimmer above it.

I was in the 1st platoon of our training company and John was in the third. Some of the boys didn't know their left foot from their right and it took weeks for them to learn to march and to do the manual of arms. I'd had four years of R.O.T.C., so it was very boring to spend weeks waiting for the rest of my platoon to catch up.

We spent weeks on the firing range learning how to fire the machine guns and mortars and our own M-1 weapon. Other instructors taught us basic infantry tactics, bayonet attacking and dirty fighting. Treks through both the infiltration course and the obstacle course became almost daily occurrences.

Running the infiltration course wasn't difficult. Rather I should say crawling through the infiltration course, because it was comprised of seemingly endless ditches and tunnels. Anyone caught running where they shouldn't received the opportunity to start over from the beginning.

The course was a test of your nerves. At one point we had to crawl across an open field where machine-gun fire kept singing just over our heads. It would have been near impossible to get shot, because we also had to crawl under multiple strands of barbed wire at the same time. Anyone getting shot would first have to find a way through all that wire. Still, it seemed too real.

It's hard to explain just how or when the boys who started began turning into men. In addition to the heavy weapons we trained with we also pitched a thousand pup tents and dug a couple hundred foxholes. Each task played a part in pushing us toward maturity. Every one of us had taken apart the M-1, machine guns and mortars and then put them back together so many times we could have done it blindfolded. We spent so much time on the parade ground under the burning California sun, our lips cracked and bled and our skin turned brown.

Besides the physical exercise every day, we had regular kitchen police duty to pull. At night, if they couldn't find us some other work we would scrub the barrack floors, wash our clothes and get ready to meet the next day.

We were men now, who could both drive a large truck and walk our post in a military manner. We were men with training in multiple skills, hard in muscle and tougher in spirit. Each man stood tall and proud, and collectively we became even more. We were a battalion—a force to be reckoned with.

Mail call was the big event each afternoon. I received letters most of the time, one from Mom and one from Minerva. Once in a while Mom sent a box of brownies. I opened the package, took out two and passed it down the line. I didn't look for the box to make it back, but neither did other guys who passed down their own stuff. Share and share alike!

It wasn't all work and no play. We also enjoyed some fun times, spending many happy hours in the battalion recreation hall singing around an old piano. All that music made me wish I had my guitar around but I didn't think the army would allow such a thing.

Starting about the first or second Saturday of July[xxxiv] our training battalion began receiving weekend passes. If you didn't have duty on Saturday or Sunday you could have a pass. John and I went to Santa Cruz on our first pass. We went out to the boardwalk where there was an amusement park and a swimming beach. A group of us walked up and down the beach carrying a camera. When we saw a pretty girl, a couple of the guys got her to stand between them to have their picture taken. We never did have any film loaded, but one by one the group got smaller as the boys met girls.

John met a nice girl at Santa Cruz who invited us to come up to Santa Clara on our next weekend pass and have Saturday night dinner with her parents. We were able to return the following Saturday. We had a good home-cooked meal and a wonderful time. They opened their home to us and treated us like family. The invitation was extended to come back any time we could. It sure was nice to have a "home" to go to and we learned to love the family very much.

When John and I began training for the paratroopers that kind of family connection was missing. I guess the Airborne thought they should be your family, but they sure would kick you out fast if you failed to live up to their expectations. After we had that first five-mile run in our new jump boots I thought the dropouts might be over. Far from it.

With the understanding that we would have to wait a month before we were allowed to start the A Stage, I couldn't blame a couple of the guys when they threw in the towel. Facing more running each morning, our sore blisters were telling several of us to do the same. But we somehow blocked out the pain and kept at it. The delay was very disappointing because we'd been counting the days until our leave. The cadre cared less and if we didn't like it then we could just leave. The worst part was breaking in our boots.

"Didn't anyone tell those guys that jump boots were made for jumping?" came a complaint.

"Are you kidding? These guys are just making it up as they go. There ain't that many troopers out there so they don't know anything yet."

Another guy chipped in, "There's a brigade already out there, North Africa or somewhere. I read it in the *Stars and Stripes*."

"Hell, that don't mean a thing, those guys haven't been in much longer than us and we'll be shipped overseas with them before Christmas," the first shot back.

"I wouldn't say that," another added. "We gotta start the damn school, and we ain't even had our first jump."

I said, "Yeah they lied, told us we would have only four weeks here, but now it has changed to four weeks for school and another four until we can even start the school. I don't trust them very much."

"Speaking of jumping, why does everyone yell Geronimo coming out of the plane?" one of the guys asked.

"Because it takes too long to say Chief Sitting Bull, stupid."

One guy swung off his top bunk and yelled out, "No, you're the stupid one. Don't listen to him. It was a bet. One of the very first jumpers said he wasn't scared. His buddies said he was a liar and he'd probably be so scared he'd forget his own name. Then when they jumped the next day the guy forgot his name and yelled Geronimo instead. He lost ten bucks."

"That sounds like crap to me, sounds more like sitting bull. Where'd you hear that?" someone asked.

"It's the truth," said the man off the bunk. "True story, a sergeant told me and he was here when it happened."

The true story of the Geronimo yell is this. On the night before their first mass jump (third actual jump), Private Aubrey Eberhardt of the original Parachute Test Platoon went to the movies with several training buddies. A western was playing that night telling a story about the renegade Apache chief Geronimo. After the show a foursome including Eberhardt went across the street to a beer garden where a large quantity of brew was consumed in a short time.

While walking back to their tent encampment the group compared the risk of several men rushing to the jump door in a single mass exit versus the timed-out jumps they had made before. Eberhardt made a comment that the mass jump should be no different than the first two; in other words, no big deal. The remark brought on instant hassling from his friends and one of them claimed Private Aubrey would likely be so scared he wouldn't even remember his own name.

The remark and laughter so angered the test platoon member that he promised not only could he remember his name but also the name of the Indian chief seen in the movie. During the morning of the jumps on the following day word got around about Eberhardt's oath and when the platoon began spilling out of the plane there came a loud "Geronimo" followed by wild war whooping. During the fourth jump on the next day the entire test unit picked up the shout and it continued from there to the following jumps. Thus the tradition of paratroopers yelling "Geronimo" while going out the door began.

There were many reasons for jump school washouts. Several students just plain lacked the physical ability, and if you couldn't keep up you were shown the door. Trainees who fell to injury, mostly broken bones, were removed from the unit. I knew the paratroopers didn't want anyone who had broken anything but I wondered if second chances went out to other kinds of injuries. Seems like a true accident might be viewed differently, but I never knew and I sure didn't want to find out the hard way. The biggest reason for dropouts, as I'd learn later, was from a fear of heights.

Although not formally in jump school, we did have members of the paratrooper training cadre who led us on double-time marches every day down to a field beside the jump towers. And every day I looked at those towers and the men training on them and burned for the day I could go up there myself and give it a try.

Here in this field we did our calisthenics, which included all those we had learned in basic training plus some new ones they made up. The one they seemed to enjoy the most was where you held your arms straight out and inscribed small circles with your fingertips. At first it seemed easy but they would keep us at it until it felt as if our arms would drop off and every muscle in our arms would start to tremble. Part of the displeasure came from the lack of countable repetition; nobody knew how much longer it would last. The instructors must have been doing it for years because they never seemed to get tired. I think they got their kicks from the grievous expressions on our faces. For me, rope climbing was the hardest exercise, always a challenge to reach the rope top and slap the supporting crossbar. However, our upper body strength increased tremendously during this time and I became better at the rope before school finished.

October the 21st came,[xxxv] my birthday when I turned nineteen. Minerva sent me a beautiful silver bracelet with small gold para-trooper wings and my name engraved across the faceplate. On the reverse side was another inscription, "With love MC." The guys tried to tell me I couldn't wear it because I hadn't made a jump yet. That may have been true. I didn't ask, but I did wear it on our town trips. I didn't show it off like I wanted to, but I knew it was there and it had come signed with her love. That was all that mattered to me. It was the greatest gift I had ever received; nothing short of God Himself could keep me from earning my wings now. No longer was I doing this for me; jump school was for us—Minerva and I. And only a few days later, the last week of October, we finally started the A Stage of our training.

I had already figured it out when the announcement for A Stage came, but it was John who quickly vocalized it. "Hey, in four weeks we'll get leave and then we can be home at Thanksgiving. A Stage is starting at a great time."

We had more calisthenics, double-timing and rope climbing, but at this point we didn't care any longer, we were in tip-top shape and those of us from California Basic already had the muscle. We figured out that the exercises here were just working our bulk in a slightly dif-ferent way; we could now do anything demanded of us. We were anxious to start jumping, however, and then we wanted our leave to go home. Going home sure had a good sound to it. Six months had passed, one full month ahead and then we could see our families and loved ones again.

Another part of A Stage was the issue of our jump suits and those famous baggy pants. Some guys thought they looked funny but all the real parachute classes wore them, so we didn't hesitate to put them on. They weren't really baggy at all but appeared that way because the pockets were on the legs.[xxxvi]

Maybe it was standing tradition or maybe it was just something that got started, but whenever our lower class, or any other "A" would pass alongside a class in D Stage marching in formation, the D Stage class would sing out in unison, "You'll be sorry!" This always brought on smiles. One day it would be our turn and one day soon we would be the class doing the jumping.

In retrospect I found A Stage was a weed-out stage to make sure every student was physically fit enough to be paratrooper material. Since we had just gone through four weeks of the same, there were no dropouts here.

Our class entered the B Stage on November 1st. This consisted mostly of learning how to tumble, exiting from an airplane, controlling the chute, landing, parachute packing and, of course, more calisthenics. After our morning run and chow, we could take a trail through the woods, across a little dry creek, up the bank on the other side, out of the woods to reform and double-time to Lawson Field.

Then we went on to the packing shed. We were allowed to sing on the way. Of course our favorite song was "Blood On The Risers."

Parachute packing was a good part of the training. The packing shed we used was a converted aircraft hanger so the ceiling inside was very high. Row upon row of polished wood tabletops filled the bulk of the space. At the end were some supply rooms, offices and a large towering structure that was a special room used by D Class.

In this room parachutes could be hung to their full length and shaken to rid them of dirt, grass, and sometimes even bits of tree limb. On the side of the packing shed was the Sweat Shed but at that time I didn't know anything about it.

The packing shed was cool inside and we would sit on the tables while the instructors showed us how to untangle the chute, how to fold the panels and lay out the suspension lines, and then how to stow the suspension lines to the backboard with rubber bands. But you weren't allow to call them rubber bands unless you liked doing push-ups; instead they were called retaining bands.

Functions of all the parachute parts were taught: the canopy, the risers, connectors, panels and go rods. All of these were new words in our vocabulary. We were shown how to pack, lace up the chute, and tie the break cord. Each of us was assigned a packing partner who would work on the opposite side of the table. The partner would assist in packing your chute and then you would help him. In this way each man packed or assisted in packing two chutes after each jump. Joe, a short New York City Yankee fellow, became my packing partner.

There was no horseplay in the packing shed. This was serious business: dead serious. Everyone paid very close attention and made sure he knew what he was doing. This was the time to ask questions, not when you were in the air. The chute you packed was your own and was the chute you would jump with. It was a matter of life or death. If the chute had a malfunction and didn't open, it was nobody's fault but your own.

We would be using a twenty-eight-foot chute called a T-5 assembly. A static line inside the airplane opened it automatically. It also included a reserve chute that you could open manually if there was an emergency. Tools such as shot bags, folding irons and packing paddles were used in packing.

On our first day in the packing shed we lined up and were issued two chutes each. My main chute was beautiful, an almost new nylon chute. My packing partner Joe drew an old silk one.

He said, "Burns, I don't like the looks of this one. Look at all this."

He showed me where it was turning gray with age and he also pointed at some tiny holes in it where something had been chewing away.

"I'm going to take it back," he said and carried it back to exchange it.

"I'd like another chute," he told them.

But the personnel in charge of the equipment supply asked him,

"Why? Are you afraid to jump this chute?"

"Well look at it, look at these holes," he explained.

"Are you afraid to jump this chute?" they asked again.

My partner wasn't about to say yes. He just kept trying to show them the holes and the discoloration and they, hardly looking at the chute, just continued to repeat the same question.

"Are you afraid to jump this chute?"

He finally gave in, "Hell no, I ain't afraid to jump the damn chute!"

"Good," they answered in return. "Go over there and get it packed."

After lunch we practiced tumbling either to the left or to the right, whatever the instructor called for. The tumbling would help us land when we started our jumps. From this we graduated to a wooden mock-up door where we learned how to jump out of airplanes. You had to stand in the door with your left foot forward and then kick out with the right foot while turning in the air to face the tail of the ship. At the same time you had to assume the correct position of having your feet together with knees slightly bent. Your hands were on the reserve chute and your head was down while counting "one thousand, two thousand, three thousand," and you landed in a sawdust pit.

After each turn we had to run to the end of the line and do it all over again. I was amazed at how uncoordinated some of the guys were. Some looked more like a ruptured duck learning to fly. As the days wore on, however, we became better at all the points of jumping, and were beginning to perform together more like a smooth operating machine.

We also had started our harness training, which we received while suspended above the ground. As we hung in the air, strapped into harnesses called "ball busters," we were taught how and which risers to pull to slip to the left, right, forward or backward. The instructors taught us how to turn around and face the other direction and how to assume a landing position.

Our knowledge of both jumping and landing would be tested on November 2nd. This would be the day of our first jump from the thirty-four-foot towers. That doesn't sound very high, but this was the point in the training where the greatest number of trainees had been known to quit. Our instructors jumping from the tower door made the descent look graceful. However, some of the troopers had trouble letting go of the door and making the jump.

The tower was just a little two-door room on top of thirty-four-foot poles. The first door was reached by climbing a ladder to the top of the platform. The other, which was the shape and size of the door in an airplane, was on the opposite wall. A steel cable ran from the mock-up door and angled down to a short pole in the ground. Risers were attached to the cable and to the jumper's harness. This tower would show us what standing in the aircraft's door was like and it provided a short free fall like the one experienced when making a parachute jump.

While climbing the ladder I reflected back to when I was about twelve years old. My childhood buddy Ed Mize and I with a few other boys built a trolley in the woods. We had worked most of the day getting a cable secured to the top of the tree. We installed a piece of one-inch pipe to use as a handhold. Because I was the oldest, as well as the instigator and designer of the project, I was chosen as test pilot for the first ride. I must have stood up in that tree for twenty minutes or more, working up the courage, before I flung my fragile body into outer space. As I finished my climb up the training tower I told myself that they weren't going to give me twenty minutes to make up my mind here. *Just don't look directly down at the ground. Stand in that door and look straight out at the horizon and don't think about anything but going out. When the instructor slaps you on the butt, don't hesitate, just go.*[xxxvii]

The instructor told me to stand in the door, I stepped to the edge. I had done a good job of talking myself into going, and at the given command I was jumping out the door while turning myself towards the tail of the ship with my hands on the reserve chute, head down and feet together, knees slightly bent.

To this day I don't remember any sort of fall, just going out the door and seeing all of the faces below looking up at me. But when I came to the length of those risers there was a sudden and abrupt jolt and I went sliding down the cable with a silly grin on my face. I released the risers, then ran them back to the tower where the jump trainer would hook up the next student in line.

Then I sat down with the other troopers and watched John make
his jump, which he did in good form. Everyone was giving each other
slaps on the back, congratulating them for making it over the first hur-
dle and boasting about how great we all really were. Every once in a
while somebody looked rather poor and there was no end to the hassle
we would give them.

During the time we started our jumps from the thirty-four-foot
tower we also received an introduction to the Plumbers' Dream.[xxxviii]
Some thought it was more of a nightmare. It looked like steel ladders
welded together at right angles. It was about twenty-two feet in
height. You were to climb up through it, over the top, back and forth
and up and down through this thing in a prearranged course. It was
built to tone up every muscle. On some parts you used only your arms
to swing from one rung to another. On other parts you used both arms
and legs. At the very top, you used only your legs and it took only a
single mistake for you to be labeled "one of the girls."

At night and on weekends we had diversions to get our minds off
training. The movie theater at the main part of camp was a good one
and recreation halls offered a lot. Those who wanted to talk to a girl
for a change could visit the WAC's day room where there was usually
a female available for conversation. John, always a champion at meeting girls, had met a WAC by the name of Gwen, so we had someone
to ask for by name. Most weekends we went to Columbus or across
the river to Phenix City, Alabama.

Phenix City was a warren of business establishments designed to
meet the carnal pleasures of life. It was one of the most corrupt cities
in the nation during the war. It was there that most troopers went for
a night out on the town: fighting with the MPs or with the armored
boys, or just drinking and carousing. But we had discovered the town
also had one of the best skating rinks to be found anywhere and John
loved to skate. I was strictly a novice at it, but John and I usually did
things together, so most Saturday nights would find us at the rink.
Besides, you only saw a few servicemen, but there were always lots of
girls.

The start of C Stage began on November the 7th.[xxxix] It was cold,
rainy and too muddy to jump from the massive two hundred and fifty-
foot towers. So it was back to the packing shed for more practice at

packing chutes, and of course more calisthenics that afternoon, rain or no rain.

November 8th dawned clear and bright. After our morning five-mile run, our pancakes and our coffee, we marched over to the towers. We really were looking forward to getting off the ground. Anticipation was running high and we were up for it, but the wind was blowing so strong the jumps were delayed for one more day. C Stage was getting off to a slow start and we knew we had to go through C Stage before we started jumping for real. I was already looking forward to my two weeks at home after I received my wings. It had been a long time. I wanted to see home, but mostly I wanted to see Minerva.

November 9th we still couldn't jump but we were introduced to the wind machine. This was an airplane engine and prop mounted on wheels with a wire cage around it. This was to teach us how to control our chutes after hitting the ground on a windy day. We took turns putting on a parachute and lying on the ground belly up or belly down, whatever the instructor wanted.

The machine was started and the parachute billowed out, dragging each man across the field until the instructor ordered "Recovery." Then you were to rotate 180 degrees, come up on your feet and collapse the chute by pulling in on the upper or lower risers. Some of the men just couldn't get the hang of it. They were dragged across the field so many times they got holes in their fatigues. Heaven help them if they ever had to jump in high wind conditions.

November 10th gave us good weather. It was sunny out with no wind; a beautiful golden Georgia day. As we made our morning run I knew this was the day we would start jumping. After morning chow, we all marched out to the field. Half of us went to one tower and half to another. An instructor stopped us at the base of the tower.

"All right you men, listen up," the trainer announced. "These are the two hundred-fifty-foot jump towers. You've been staring at them every day since you arrived."

"Heck yeah!" came an excited voice from behind me.

The instructor stopped speaking while his eyes searched out the source of the comment. "Shut up soldier!" he barked. "Did I ask you to speak? Now get down and give me a twenty-count."

A head in the back suddenly went down and I could almost see the guy through the legs and bodies of the others. After three or four pushups I heard the instructor bellow again.

"Count them. I want to hear you . . . no that's not six, start over and count them out loud. The rest of you, eyes forward unless you want to join him."

I turned towards the tower pronto.

"One," came the voice from behind.

"Now then, listen up," our instructor continued. "Today we will use the two hundred-fifty-foot towers to continue our simulation of an aircraft jump. In an actual jump you'd never jump at a two hundred-fifty-foot altitude, that's too low. But our tower allows us to start with the parachute canopies already open. The thirty-four foot towers showed you what to expect after jumping from the door. From it you have felt a jerk like the opening shock of a chute deployment. Now you'll experience the drift that occurs when you descend to the ground. We will harness each of you in turn to a chute that will be hooked into the large rings at the cable's end. You will then be hoisted to the top and stopped just short of the release point. The sergeant will ask you, "Are you ready?" and you will answer with "Yo" or "No." When you're released you must climb the risers. Give them a really hard pull so that you will slip away from the tower, and we don't want anyone crashing into the tower, so pull the correct risers."

He paused and looked us over before walking a couple of steps towards the tower side. There was a brief pause as the outspoken trainee knocked off his last couple of repetitions. Then, the instructor announced, "Seeing as there are no questions then, I want a single line starting here," and he pointed straight out with both hands.

We rushed to form a line.

"Is everyone going to jump?" he hollered.

"Yeah!" we answered.

"Any girls out there?" he asked and paused. Then he said, half smiling, "Let's knock this thing off."

One at a time we put on chutes, the canopies were hooked into the large ring connected to the tower, and we were lifted to the top. The sergeant would ask, "Are you ready?" but no matter what the answer was you got a release. A no sounded like yo; there were no dropouts in C Stage.

When my turn came, I stood there as they fastened in the chute, and then the ring was pulled up a little. I looked straight down between my boots. I could see all the troopers looking up. They looked awfully small down there and were getting smaller all the time. I stopped near the top. The view up there was fantastic. I could see all over camp and all the way to town.

"Are you ready?" I heard the sergeant yell.

"Yo!" I snapped back and felt the cable pull me up another few inches. There was a click-click, and I dropped. I was free!

"Climb those risers!" came a scream and I reached as high as I could and pulled them down to my chest. I slipped away from the tower and then let go. Boy, this was great! This was the most fun I had experienced in training and I knew it was only the start of things to come. By taking up the correct landing position I landed very light. I did my tumble anyway, got out of my chute and ran to get back in line.

We each made two jumps that day to make up for time lost to the bad weather. All went well until one trooper grabbed the wrong risers and slipped backwards into the tower. He just hung there, 150-feet in the air, and all jumps were discontinued while two of the sergeants climbed the tower to help him get down. He was lucky not to be hurt and was only bruised where he had hit one of the crossbeams. His ego may have been bruised a little but the rest of us did a lot of bragging.

The rest of the week went fast, and before we knew it we were through C Stage. Just one weekend now separated us from our first actual jump. That weekend John and I went to town on Saturday morning and had a good breakfast. Afterward we walked around town, which gave us a chance to talk to some of the local Columbus girls. Since football season was in full swing we asked and learned where we could go to watch one of the high school games. We rooted for the home team. All of the weekend activities made us feel more at home. Life really felt good during these times and we were trying to enjoy it to the fullest. But of course all this was occurring while most of the world was engaged in a raging war. We knew before too long that these good times would end and we would find ourselves full combatants in that war.

* * *

In France, on December 17th, 1944, Woody and I decided it was a good night to take in a movie and then stop off at a nightclub on the way back. We returned to the barracks very late, after midnight, and I was looking forward to a long sleep in my reasonably soft bed.

As we came up the company street we could see all the lights burning. Everybody was up. We walked into our room and there was equipment stacked on the floor and on the bunks. Even my bunk was piled with a stack of equipment, and that didn't much please me. Barrack bags were turned upside down and the contents were being separated into Bags A and B. Ralph Burrus and Lou Slama were back from the hospital and I saw them and John Hurst standing there in the middle of all the turmoil with a look of uncertainty.

I said, "Hurst what in the blazes is going on?"

He looked up and answered, "Where in all hell have you guys been?"

"Around," quipped Woody in a rather melodramatic voice, but from John's expression we needed to avoid humor.

John explained, "We just got the word. Yesterday the Germans started breaking through the Ardennes, in Belgium,[xl] and now we've been ordered to move up and stop them."

JUMP
Eleven

Christmas just couldn't get any
worse than this.

The German counterattack had actually started on December 16,
1944, with three armies directed at the U.S. VIII Corps. The hardest
hit were the green 106th Division and the battle weary 28th Division
that had been thinned out to an easy breakpoint.

"Hitler must have found out the 508th had pulled back for a rest,"
commented Woody. "The Germans would do anything to ruin our
Christmas!"

"This is sure as hell going to spoil our holiday," John added. The
Regiment had been looking for special ways to enjoy the Christmas
season this year and inquires had been sent to each company, though
no definite plans were made that I knew of.

"Damn," I exclaimed. "Is this fair?"

"Probably not," said John.

"No stinking way," said Woody.

"I knew we were too close to the war here," I complained. "A
month's rest and now they're sending us right back to the front. I
haven't even made it to Paris yet!"

"It does seem they could send somebody else," John added.[xli]

We, of course, didn't realize then that the generals were sending
everybody they could find. Woody and I started right in with the
work, at one point we each had to get out of our Class A suits and into
combat gear. We worked all night getting ready to move. Weapons had
to be cleaned. After his jump boots, a trooper's weapon gets the most
attention. My M-1 was a tool of the trade and had to be oiled and
cleaned with loving care. Many of the guys had pet names for their
weapons. Our work through the night seemed to move quickly, but

not one of us old-timers was looking forward to this trip. Our fresh replacements, who started out excited, soon realized this and they grew just as concerned. Packing up now seemed a lot like our pre-jump moves before Normandy and Holland, only this time we knew the schedule. The trucks were due to roll in at dawn. There would be no jump.

* * *

Packed and on time the next morning, but weary with fatigue from a lack of sleep, we reluctantly loaded and climbed aboard the column of arriving trucks. Space was limited. Trucks for only a brigade were on hand and a whole division had to be moved, so we learned we would have to stand up throughout the whole trip, an uncomfortable arrangement since these trucks were uncovered.

Despite the unforgiving travel arrangements and our zombie-like mental state, the jokes and banter began and we felt a bit of relief at finally being on the way. Still, most of us remained in a small state of shock at having our world turned around so unexpectedly.

Someone complained, "This is no way for an airborne regiment to go into combat."

"Damned disgrace if you ask me."

Billy the Kid said, "I've earned my wings. I haven't earned any wheels."

"Hey that's right! We're not qualified for this mission."

"Forget it," muttered Woody. "Haven't you heard about earning wings with a single combat jump? This is called OJT, on the job training."

"Gee Sarg, does that mean I'll get silver wheels to wear with my wings?" Billy laughed.

"Yeah, Kid, they're like jump stars," Woody teased. "One for every time you roll into action. Joe has one for Holland, Burns and I each have two stars, now we're all going to earn a wheel."

We rode those trucks all day and into the night, standing like a bunch of cows being transported to the slaughterhouse. Fort Worth has a slaughterhouse, I remembered. *If they take us there I'll jump out at Minerva's.*

The cattle trucks of this chilly December continued to roll, our destination unknown. Unlike cattle however, and lucky for us, the drivers stopped occasionally to let us out for a break.

The country people were great, first the French and then later the Belgians. Whenever we stopped wine bottles came out of nowhere and circulated around. I decided wine must have been to the French what beer was to the English, ever present and always warm. I didn't drink a whole lot of it, but it was better than English beer and a little bit of antifreeze couldn't hurt.

In places where we couldn't stop, the townsfolk lined the street to wave and cheer. They also threw bread and apples. That was how I might have earned a Purple Heart: as we went through one village, I turned to face a small crowd just in time to get hit in the eye with an apple.

"Yeow!"

"Burns are you all right?" Joe was sympathetic.

"Yeah, I guess. Whose side are they on?"

"Someone out there must have a good right arm judging from the way it came in."

"I'm not bleeding or anything unusual am I?"

Joe grinned. "No, but that's too bad. You could've earned a Purple Heart."

"No thanks. I'd have to tell the medics I was hit by a flying missile. And if they asked what type, I'd have to answer it was a 'Red Delicious'."

The road trip continued into the night. I believe we went past Bastogne[xlii] and kept going northeast. Bastogne was a critical junction in the area, with a convergence of seven major roads. Werbomont to the northwest was a steep bluff with a natural defensive position overlooking the shallow Ambleve River. Traveling six or seven hours behind us on the same road was the 101st Division. Everything was in a state of confusion and no one could say where the Germans were. Hitler's troops advanced rapidly. Shortly after we traveled the north road out of Bastogne the Germans flooded into the region. The 101st Airborne reached the town just minutes ahead of the enemy, detrucked and set-up their positions. Within a few hours the German LXVIII Panzer Corps surround the town and the 101st Division began their famous stand for Bastogne.

A little before dawn on the 19th, the road-grit and dirty, bone weary and mentally depleted 82nd unloaded near Werbomont, Belgium. We were to establish a defensive position, but didn't know if it should face the north, east, or south.

Mostly we tried to stay awake. Several couldn't.

Later, orders came for us to move east near the town of Chevron. On the 20th we got orders to move again. By then the 101st at Bastogne was surrounded and the brass began to understand through reports where the Krauts were and were not.

Our move on the 20th was a morning march that started gray and cold, with dense fog and a strong hint of snow in the air. Each of us had grabbed a little sleep, but we weren't prepared for the long march that took the rest of the day and continued all night. As another dawn began to break, we found ourselves digging into positions along Thier-du-Mont Ridge, near the town of Goronne. Far below was the Salm River.

We were in the middle of the north side of the Bulge. The 508th with the rest of the 82nd had pushed a long finger into the middle of that north side and the 508th was at the tip of the finger. We still hadn't seen anything of the German Army.

Next day, December 21st, winter weather unleashed the first great snowstorm at about midnight. We shivered and watched as the hills around us turned white. The intense cold became our worst enemy. We still lacked winter clothing, so we wore what we had: long johns under O.D. pants and shirts from our Class A uniform, under combat suits, two pair of socks and anything else that would help retain body heat.

The 7th Armored and the 106th Infantry Divisions had been over-run in the first days of battle and we were to supply them with an escape route back to our newly established lines. We actually sat several miles out ahead of our own lines, as a bridge of firepower making it possible to evacuate anyone who could reach the river. The miserable cold had us spending most of the day just trying to stay warm. We wanted to build a fire and there were a few at the back of our lines but up front we thought better of it.

Patrols were constantly on the move; they were looking for the first sign of the Germans. Stories spread among the troops about atrocities committed by German soldiers at Malmedy. More than 100 captured Americans had been machine-gunned down.[xliii]

We swore then and there they wouldn't take anyone in F Company alive. If we had to die, we'd give the Krauts a helluva fight. It seemed the higher-ups really believed the enemy would come our way, considering how they kept us in that snow.

Another day went by, the rough weather continued. By midday of the 23rd, we'd still seen no action but many, many vehicles and assorted material from the 7th Armored and the 106th Infantry Divisions had passed through the 508th's position. The personnel marched along in one or two never-ending columns. Every once and awhile you could notice a platoon's worth of forlorn men who were looking wretched and defeated. They went safely to the rear to reorganize and serve as possible reserve units.

With the retreating divisions behind our position, a demolition team blew all the bridges in front of us. No sooner had the blasting thunder died out when we heard the unmistakable grinding sound of some tanks. I wondered if some unit had been delayed and was now cut off, but in fact the tanks were German. The bridges had been destroyed just as the first Jerry soldiers arrived. That was too close.[xliv] We figured on an attack anyway and it was just a matter of time before they hit us. Late in the afternoon orders came down for the regiment to withdraw that night under the cover of darkness to straighten out the line. We'd leave a cover force of one platoon per company and start back around midnight. Falling back was not a pleasant or agreeable move because the 508th had never given up ground or retreated. Our position was on high ground and well dug in, and we wanted the line to move up to us. But the brass said otherwise.[xlv]

We spent the rest of the day looking down those snow-covered slopes for Germans and waiting for the word to pull back. I mused that if the regiment could have some cozy cabins with big fireplaces and large picture windows, then the landscape would have been considered beautiful; the kind of winter scene that advertises a ski lodge. There was a deep blanket of snow over the earth and the trees were so heavily laden their limbs touched the ground.

Well after dark, under bitter cold conditions, we silently climbed from our foxholes and started on the road back. Our covering force remained behind with orders to hold until 03:15. I suspect the Krauts must have heard us and figured we were up to something, because as the withdrawal moved out, a few rounds of artillery dropped in. Had they fired a littler earlier we would have been caught without cover and in range of the shell burst. It could have cost many lives.

We tried to stay quiet while moving down the road but a full regiment of men creates quite a rumble. Such a dark night made it hard to see and, although the snow helped muffle the sound of tromping boots, there was a steady amount of grunting and mumbled swearing as here and there someone slipped and fell. Back at the ridge we heard shots fired; our covering force was taking the hit while the rest of us moved back.

We were all too tired to say much and it took every effort just to get up and move on. This was our first retreat since entering combat in Normandy. Nobody liked it and the travel seemed a lot longer going back than it had going forward. As we trudged through the snow, I wondered how many days it would be before we had to fight our way back for these few miles we were now giving up. How many men would die to retake that same high ground?

We felt our way along the road in the dark, hoping it was in the right direction. Suddenly the two men walking point hit the ditch and all the rest of us followed. It went deadly quiet. There weren't supposed to be any Germans between us and our own lines, but hell, things were always getting fouled up! We had walked into an unexpected roadblock.

As I squatted in the snow I could hear the gun safeties being snapped to the off position all around me. So everyone was thinking we might be fighting our way back if we wanted to see the rest of our division again. Our hearts were pounding, our breathing had stopped, and everyone waited for a signal. Each man was a quarter second from action, everyone had a finger on the trigger, and each pair of eyes remained focused on the road ahead. Who would fire the first shot? Give any of us a hard target and it was dead.

Then a voice, loud and clear, broke the chilling silence with a sentence I have never understood.

"Is this your dog?"

Chuckles of relief went down the line. We didn't know what was going on, but thank God, at least the words were English. The road-block was ours, and we were back to our own lines.

By late afternoon on Christmas Eve the covering force was back in the Regiment with little loss of life. A farmhouse in our area was used as F Company's command post with the 3rd Platoon taking up positions on the left, the 1st on the right, and the 2nd back in reserve ready to jump to the aid of one or the other. Captain Martin wanted phones set up and he needed a radio operator stationed with the 3rd Platoon so he sent me down to fill in at that position. We had a new communication guy who could stay with the captain.

Joining two others at a platoon C.P., I spent Christmas day helping to dig a three-man foxhole as part of a new defensive position. This would not be a day for either rest or joy, but at least it was quiet.

I thought back to last Christmas; it too had been quiet. In Columbus I had felt so alone.

*   *   *

The Christmas holidays of 1943 were almost on me and while in communications training I had been too busy to shop for Minerva or family. So the following Saturday John and I got together and headed into town. We left early that morning so we could have breakfast at our favorite café. It was a very small place, they knew us well and we always had the same thing; waffles and bacon. Those waffles were the thickest ones I had ever seen and I really liked the thin crispy crust the chef cooked them to. As soon as the waiter brought them out, we told him to put two more on the griddle. After breakfast we got on with our Christmas shopping. I had never seen Columbus so crowded. The city looked good. People were everywhere and smiling, and it sure put me in the holiday spirit.

As the day went on we ran into other troopers and somehow started a game where we placed about six or more troopers in a line with each man about fifteen feet apart. Then we would catch an officer coming down the sidewalk with his arms full of packages and make him try to return our salute one right after another. The officers knew what we were up to, but all they could do was grin and bear it, returning our salute if at all possible. If both arms were full they would just nod their heads and smile back.

For the Christmas weekend we were all given a three-day pass.

"Do you think we could make it to Fort Worth?" I asked John. He gave me a look of disbelief.

"And make it back? No way!" his voice was stern. "It'll take two days to get there. What are you gonna do then, have Minerva walk you from the inbound train to the outbound train?"

"What do you think they'll do to someone who doesn't make it back?" I was no longer asking, but just wondering aloud.

"Well you can kiss that new stripe goodbye. Then they'll probably lock you up until the end of time, or at least until the war is over. You do remember there's a war on don't ya? John gave me a long look, and then he added. "But if you're going to try it then count me in."

"Ah, it's crazy," I said. "We would never make it."

"Maybe if we got lucky they wouldn't miss us at first." John's mind was kicking into high gear, always a dangerous sign.

"It's 750 miles one way. With all the luck in the world there still isn't enough time. What we need is a car."

And if we had owned a car, we would have tried it. Even if it meant getting back a little late it would have been worth it. This was Christmas; even commanders have some red blood.

So on Christmas day I found myself all alone. Everyone else had gone off to the main part of camp looking for something to do. John tried to get me to join in, but I had done it all before. Instead I caught the bus and went into town thinking I might find someplace open to have lunch. There wasn't a soul in sight. I don't believe anybody was working except the bus driver. I left him at the main bus station on the edge of the downtown area and started walking.

After traveling the full length of town I still hadn't seen anyone. Two days before these same streets had been overflowing with happy smiling people rushing around to do their last minute shopping. Street decorations, which had only recently put me into such a good spirit, now seemed a little sad and forsaken, there was nobody to enjoy them and their desolation was a suitable reflection of my own holiday mood. Thinking of home I could picture Mom putting Christmas dinner on the table.

That would be happening right about now. I could see her setting out a perfectly baked chicken with southern dressing, green beans, potatoes, salad, pies, cake and all other kinds of good things. And there's Minerva sitting beside me, her image so strong I was tempted to reach out and touch her. Home. Then again, maybe we would be having dinner with her family, so I dwelled on that thought for a while. Minerva's family was large. Her two brothers were the oldest and had young families of their own. One was a minister; I figured he would say grace. Her mother had died while she was young but there were four daughters in the family. Her sisters were Johnny Lee, Georgia and Betty Jo. I found each of them a beauty, but to me Minerva was the pick of the family. Her dad was a great guy and I never tired of his storytelling. Her family or mine—either one would be great for Christmas dinner. What a torment to know what pleasure I could be having!

I crossed over to the other side of the street and started my long walk back to the station. I passed the place where John and I often had breakfast; I sure could use one of those big waffles now. My walk continued, I kept wishing. I was wishing I were home, wishing I was with Minerva and wishing this day would end. One thing was for sure Christmas just couldn't get any worse than this.

I was wrong, for Christmas 1944 was very much worse. It was a lot colder and there was no place to go to get any warmer. The enemy was coming my way and bloodshed could be expected. Death was forecasted on a day when most of the world was rejoicing.

It didn't seem possible it had only been a year, so much had happened. The 508th P.I.R. had covered a lot of territory in '44. On this holy day, despite the number of army buddies around me, I once again felt strangely alone. Every man seemed to feel the same, and conversation was light. I know I helped build a foxhole that day, but my actions were switched to automatic repeat, and my mind was busy elsewhere.

It seems that we dug out a trough four feet wide by six feet long and about five feet deep. This was a common size. I do remember two of us returning to the farmhouse and confiscating a mattress from one of the beds. We carried it back and laid it in the bottom of our foxhole. The entire hole was then covered with logs and dirt leaving only a small entrance and a few firing slits. Then we laid out our GI blankets.

I set up the radio in one corner where I could easily hear it, and I also ran a wire to Company headquarters for hooking up field telephones. I made my wire run out the back of the foxhole and took it directly to the rear, and then I turned and ran it parallel to the firing line and up the small hill to headquarters. The other communications man, new to the company, took it from there and ran a line to battalion.

I'd been told the Germans loved it when they could cut our wire because they would then wait for someone to come out and fix it so as to take them prisoner. I wanted my line to run backwards where the Germans wouldn't see it, and if they reached it they'd have to go through me first. At the end of the day I was surprised at everything we had done. Nightfall arrived and the place looked like it had been home for several days.

On the night of the 25th the Germans overran an outpost and got the jump on several companies. It was a large force and the fighting lasted for more than two hours before the enemy drive could be repelled.[xlvi] The 25th was also the evening Bed-check Charlie started coming by. Just before dawn a German plane would fly slowly along the front line at about 500 feet and then turn to head for home. Everyone decided we would wait for him and take a pot shot at his plane. Not that we expected to hit him, but it did break the monotony of a cold, gray day. After all, if you can see the enemy, why not shoot!

The next morning dawned cold and cloudy again. We had the liberty of enough time to assay our new position. More importantly we were better rested than we'd been in a couple of days. Mines were laid, extra ammunition was issued, and artillery and mortars were zeroed in on specific targets. Geographically we were positioned on the north side of a road near the small town of Erria. In front of our position the ground sloped up gently for about 100 yards and then trees cut off our view. To the rear it was flat with trees approximately 50 yards away. Company headquarters was to one side up a rise.

Directly across the road from our 3rd Platoon C.P., far out in the field, was a stock water tank, frozen solid. When most of the work was done, and since boys will be boys even in time of war, half the platoon started playing a game on the ice. The guys took a running start on solid ground to see who could slide the farthest from the bank. This was done with lookouts of course. Some lookouts were for the Germans and another was to watch for any officer who might not appreciate our sporting nature.

Even though it was late, we did get a Christmas dinner this day. A truck came up with turkey, dressing and most of the usual trimmings. Better yet, it also brought mail. I got a lot of letters to read while enjoying my holiday meal. I also got a package from an aunt. We all tried to guess what was in it, and of course everyone just knew it was something good to eat and that it would make a great dessert to our turkey. I tantalized everyone by reading my letters through our meal and then opened it last. Boy, were we surprised when I opened it up and found a bottle of aftershave lotion! All was not lost, however. The lotion was packed with dry roasted peanuts that really hit the spot.

3rd Platoon, to which I was now attached, dug another foxhole as an outpost about sixty yards in front of our road position. It was in line with, but just short of, the frozen stock tank. On the night of the 27th I held outpost duty with three others from various parts of the line. Captain Martin had ordered me to move out there with the others and we took up position while it was still daylight. I hooked up another field telephone. A telephone was smaller and easier to carry than a radio with all of its built-in tubes and heavy battery. As darkness fell over us we began a close watch toward enemy lines. Word had spread that yet another company outpost had been wiped out and we weren't going to let ourselves be overrun.

Just before midnight we heard some faint sounds filtering through the trees in front of us, and I called in the activity. Before long we saw spooky shadows moving on the right. The stock tank would keep anything or anyone from coming directly at the outpost, but we were beginning to get a nervous twitch. The guys wanted to get out of there while things were quiet and they started giving me the look because I had the rank. Fully concurring, I hit the field phone again to report we were coming in. The communication lines broke with a quick jerk on the phone and with it in my left hand and my weapon in the right I rolled out behind the others. We took up as quick a pace as silence

allowed and recrossed the road, each of us into the safety of his own
foxhole. At 1:15 in the morning the Krauts hit F and G Companies
head-on with their main force.

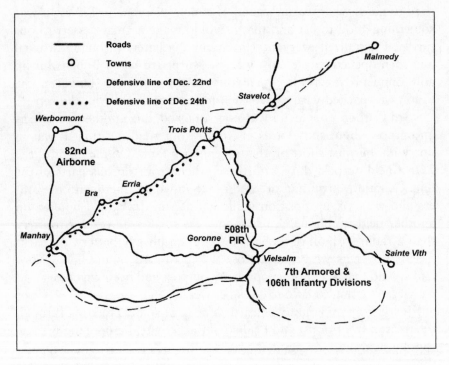

The 82nd Airborne's initial area of operations during the Battle of the Bulge, on the northern shoulder between St. Vith and Werbormont.

JUMP
Twelve

"Fox Three, do you copy?"

Ralph Burrus, who had been wounded at Hill 131 and then earned a second Purple Heart in Holland, had our machine-gun crew plot out a haystack in the field close to the forest's edge. When the first shots started he requested they send a string of tracers into it. The hay flared up to provide a huge bonfire light. In the field, all we could see were Germans. There were hundreds of them down on their bellies crawling towards us.

"Good Lord almighty!" I exclaimed. "How did they get there so fast? Another minute and they'd have been in our foxholes, crawling down our shirts." It was a shock to everyone, but the emotion was cut short as our small arms opened fire. F Company radioed back for artillery and mortar fire. Fighting was now at a fevered pitch and there were rifle flashes seen up and down the line.

We heard the fast-firing Kraut machine guns open up, and then the deeper-toned American ones answered back. The F Company C.P. took the worst of what the Germans were throwing. On the right, where there had been a lot of movement in the woods, all hell erupted. To the far left it remained nearly calm. Through all of this flying lead we had artillery and mortar shells landing all over the field before us. I didn't see how anyone could come through it alive but the Germans still tried and some succeeded.

Thanks to the burning haystack we could see them crossing the field. We radioed again and had the artillery and mortars drop their shells closer to the front lines. Germans, dead and dying, were scattered across the field, but still others came on.

One had to admire their determination, for there was no cover for them to get behind. They just kept coming right into our fire until they were able to reach the ditch on the other side of the road. It looked like they would overrun our company C.P. by the sheer strength of their numbers.

From my position all I could see were silhouettes against the burning haystack but I knew anything moving out there had to be a German. Between the three of us in the foxhole we kept up a steady fire. If it moved, we fired on it. The line around us was holding but I knew the Germans had to give up soon or we were going to need help. Surrendering wasn't an option. Those Malmedy stories had us committed to fight until death, be it theirs or ours.

Everyone was firing. There wasn't even a half-second of silence. Some of the men who were dug in at the road's edge lobbed grenades into the opposite ditch.

I heard another radio call made as a final correction for our artillery and mortar fire. This time command ordered it to be brought in right on top of our position. Almost instantly the whole area started exploding in flames as our artillery shells danced up and down the road.

I had sat through a lot of artillery fire over the past year but I hadn't seen anything like this. The night sky was blasted away and an artificial daylight prevailed. It was fantastic, and a part of me wanted to watch. However I also wanted to keep my head, so wisdom forced me closer to the bottom of my hole.

We began timing our shots. One man would look up and fire, the next would crouch in the hole ready to fire, and the final man would reload. All of this was staggered between the ground-level detonations of our heavy shelling. Look up at the wrong time and you might not look up again.

When the artillery slowed up, we found substantially fewer targets to aim at and the firing died down to a normal raging battle. Our foxhole firing rotation fell apart as the three of us sat back to catch a quick breath of air, and for a moment I found I had forgotten how to breathe. My lungs seemed to fill slowly and erratically. There was squawking on the radio. Suddenly I became aware someone was calling for the 3rd Platoon. I picked up the microphone.

"This is Fox Three, over." I could hardly manage the words. My voice was more of a whisper.

"Fox Three?" called the radio again.

"This is Fox Three, go ahead." I felt stronger on the second try.

"Listen up, Fox Three, this is Headquarters." The voice sounded frank, controlled. "We have a break in the phone lines running to you. A man was sent out to repair it several minutes ago but he's failed to come back and the phone is still out. Do you understand? Over."

Small arms fire was picking back up so I had to shout my response, "I understand, the wire's been cut, over."

"Fox Three, we want someone to start from the 3rd Platoon and work their way back toward Company headquarters, to see if they can find the break. Over."

Now its funny how when there's a dangerous job to do they never use any names, just someone had to do it. This time the someone they were talking about was me; I was the only communications man with the 3rd Platoon and it was therefore my job. Besides that, I had a perfectly good operating radio next to me. I thought someone was trying to get me killed.

The voice came back, "Fox Three, do you copy?"

One of my fighting partners was peering back out the foxhole, preparing to start firing again. I caught the eyes of the other. Even in the dark he read my face and knew something was up.

"I copy," I hollered into the radio. "Fox Three out."

Telling me that they had already sent a man and that he hadn't returned wasn't much encouragement. However he might be lying out there wounded and waiting for help. I looked over the edge of the hole. Mortar fire was still dropping on the road and small arms from both sides was anything but light. Through the dark I mentally visualized the wire run, tracing it back to Company headquarters several hundred yards away. In truth, I couldn't see anything moving out there. I pulled my gloves from my pocket and slipped them on. The other guys had started rotating their fire again. I took one by the shoulder.

"I have to go out and check the phone line. See you later."

He nodded but I think I told him "see you later" more for my own benefit than for his. I hoped saying it would make it happen. I slipped out of the hole and took another look around.

It is my job. That's why I'm wearing three stripes.

Lying flat and facing the rear, my hands reached up and touched the sides of my helmet containing my good luck card. I told myself "I believe, I believe, and I will not fear." ✔

When the ka-whump, ka-whump of the artillery shells slammed into the ground again, I expected there was going to be a break in the firing. Reaching back for the phone wire coming up out of the fox-hole, I took a deep breath and took off on a dead run.

I let the line slide through one hand and held my weapon in the other.

After hitting my stride I doubled over to keep as low as I could in an effort to make the smallest target possible. It was good I had been cautious enough to run the wire to the rear several extra yards. Somewhere out here in the field was a break. If I were lucky it would be really close.

As I ran, the ice and snow started building up in my hand. At the point where the wire made a ninety degree turn and headed uphill I stopped and shook the ice from my glove. I started again but every thirty or forty yards I'd have to stop once more. One hundred yards up the hill the wire went slipping out my hand. It was the break. And there, lying in the snow was the communication man headquarters had sent. He had found the break as well, but hadn't even started the splicing job required to make the phone operational again. He was dead, and as cold as the ground on which he laid. I couldn't tell in the dark if this was our new soldier or not, but I didn't have time to think about it.

I stripped off my gloves to make the splice and dropped to one knee. It was difficult to tie the line together and watch for Germans at the same time, I was only forty or fifty yards back, and a sitting duck for anyone who saw me. Artillery landed in the road and at each explosion I'd duck and lose the wire.

God, if you get me through this, then I'll go home after the war, marry Minerva, and never ask you for anything again.

After the two ends were twisted together they had to be wrapped with tape to prevent shorting out and I began that job. A shot sounded like it was fired in my direction, but a glance around showed nothing. The artificial daylight no longer existed and I could only see a few shadows unless a mortar was pounding the ground. I was scared but continued wrapping. Then, even though it felt like a long time, the job was done, probably tied and taped in record time. Another shot fired, hitting the dirt just to my rear. Some Kraut did indeed have his eye on me. Good thing I was ready to leave.

On the run back I followed the newly repaired phone line downhill, then I cut the corner and didn't even slow down when I reached the skinny foxhole entrance—I just went in head first and plowed into one of the guys there. Those 3rd Platoon members and I didn't know each other very well, but it sure was good to see them and to join in the firing rotation again. That hole felt like a safe haven. After another twenty or thirty minutes the fighting slackened greatly and I felt I would survive yet another battle.

We learned that Germans had overrun G Company's 3rd Platoon and from there they were about to overrun 3rd Battalion headquarters. Most of the battalion had to fall back. F Company machine gunner Warren Zuelke of the 1st Platoon was set up next to G Company where the Germans broke through. Upon hearing the burping of enemy guns to his right and right rear, he and his crew pulled their gun out of the foxhole and set it up where it could fire both forward and to their right. After making this adjustment Warren said the Germans came so close some of them died in the foxhole he had just vacated. His ammo bearer was killed.

Lt. Colonel Louis G. Mendez, 3rd Battalion commander, called for all the troopers who were in reserve. This was E Company, now commanded by Lieutenant Lloyd Polette, a platoon out of I Company, and F Company's 2nd Platoon. It is known that Polette and his Exec., George Miles, were both feeling cocky and teased the colonel about having to bail him out when they reported. Mendez, however, grouped everyone together and led the counterattack himself while there was still darkness. Many Germans, thinking they had won a night's sleep, were captured in their bedrolls.

At my position we watched for Germans the remainder of that night. Nobody went to sleep and we were still keyed up when the night slowly turned to dawn. Destruction lay everywhere and smoke hung like fog over our position. With the morning light we learned just how much hell we had kicked out of the Germans. They had withdrawn, taking their wounded with them but leaving a lot of dead. It would be a long time before they would try that again.

3rd Platoon did a head count. We had several walking wounded but only one man killed in the fight. I believe this man was Pfc Bob Clegg. A patrol sent to the other side reported more than 100 enemy bodies dead in front of F Company's positions. G Company reported 66 dead in front of their area. Some Germans had gotten within 20 feet of the Company command post before meeting their death. The farmhouse being used for Company headquarters looked like it had been hit by the best storm Hitler could conjure up. It was heavily riddled—really shot up. Weapons and equipment were everywhere. A dead cow, collapsed in the backyard, was missing its head.[xlvii]

Our hats were off in great thanks to the 82nd's 319th Glider Field Artillery, a battalion of 155mm howitzers, which had been attached to the 508th, and also to our own Red Devil mortar squads. Those units really saved our skins. Without their excellent support the German's would have overran us for certain. However, the field guns sure made a mess. We had to spend the rest of the day rebuilding and strengthening our position. At one point we took a quick break, and Joe Ensminger found words to share from his Bible for the man we lost out of the 3rd Platoon.

* * *

Over the next three or four days we kept busy playing cat and mouse with the Germans, first one regiment then another, but the attacks lacked the effort and urgency we had witnessed on the 27th. Our Red Devil Regiment fought well with little injury, but one of those killed was long time Tech5 Sergeant Harold Hiner.[xlviii]

The push to pinch off the Bulge was started on January 3rd, 1945. F Company stayed in reserve until the 7th, and then we went back and retook our old position on Thier-du-Mont Ridge, the same one we had withdrawn from two weeks before. G Company led the Regiment and attacked across open ground after a barrage had been laid down. Camouflaged German 88mm artillery held their fire until the troopers were in the open and well within range. Then the Germans proceeded to blast G Company apart and it withdrew.

Tanks were called in, but they were soon destroyed. Artillery and mortars opened up on the enemy positions, but the German fire continued when G Company made another attempt. It looked bad, although the troopers knew that if they stopped they would be massacred where they stood. They pushed on through the 88s and small arms, with very heavy casualties, and drove the Germans back. The 88s were captured along with a few of the German wounded. General Gavin said the attack was one of the finest jobs the 508th had ever undertaken. However nearly two-thirds of G Company had been lost by the time they got into position. Some of those were men only wounded in the attack but who died from the freezing cold before they were found and evacuated.

Just after this battle we came upon a couple of troopers who had been run over by tanks, probably our own that had tried to help. At first sight it was just a slimy pool of blood and mud and rags. If it hadn't been for the two pair of jump boots sticking partially out of the gore you'd have had a hard time telling just what it all was.

I looked away and choked down an impulse to vomit. I wanted to throw away my weapon and tell them I was quitting—no more. I couldn't take it any more. I fought with my churning stomach while tears came to my eyes, and there was an overwhelming desire to drop to my knees and cry. I wobbled and then suddenly felt like the others were watching me.

You must not show your feelings, I thought. You're one of the old men. You're a true veteran with two combat jumps under your belt. There are many here that are fighting through their first mission; how do you think they're going to handle it? This is your third; you are the example for many. Be tough. Get mean, get real mean. This may be war, man, but you are indestructible, so shake it off!

I captured a gulp of cold air and forced my mind elsewhere; to home, Minerva, and everything sweet and lovely and good. Anything except what lay back there in the road, and somehow, one step at a time, I managed to walk away. Holding onto the hopes and memories of a life long ago, I increased my distance from the gruesome mess of former human life that was around me now. My weapon was still in my hand, the other troopers were still beside me, and each of us would fight yet another battle.

At night, after everyone had dug in and settled down, we could do some talking about it and we would learn that each man had the same problem and felt the same way, but it was going to be a long silent road until then. Physically we could walk away. Mentally the road would never be quite long enough to leave it behind. I still walk on that mental road from time to time.

* * *

Three days later, on the 10th of January, the 75th Division relieved us and we moved into a rest area near Chevron, Belgium. It sure was good to be able to sleep indoors beside a warm fire. On average the outdoor temperature still hovered around zero. Company headquarters had been assigned the downstairs portion of a farmhouse. It had a big wood-fueled cook stove in one room and we kept a good hot fire going day and night. Hot chow was trucked in twice a day and the cooks left behind bread, cheese and canned fruit for lunch. We made toasted cheese sandwiches on the stovetop. For dessert we went to the basement, where the farm owners stored five-gallon cans of sweet cream. This cream was so thick you needed a spoon to eat it. We'd get half a canteen cup full and add our canned fruit to it. This, boys, was living in high society.

Since order had been restored to Chevron, we were asked to keep cleanshaven, and so every morning we had to go out and break the ice at the well before we could get water. At night we sat around the stove with our chairs propped back and our feet up. At first we talked about the recent battles and it was here that we learned that Lieutenant Vernon Thomas, former sergeant in F Company, had been killed on Christmas Day, and the old guys were saddened. After reliving the past fighting, the evening hours became our story time. Everyone swapped yarns about funny things back home and half of what was told was a whopping lie. Somebody wanted to know what each man had been doing before entering the Army. I confess to feeling a bit boastful at my own story.

* * *

The day after John and I had our induction into the Army I reported early to work at Consolidated Aircraft. I had been employed there as a draftsman for the last six months and was assigned to work on a new aircraft bomber. I told the guys there they would have to build it without me. I told my boss it was quits because I was now in the Army.

"They gave me seven days before reporting," I explained, "and I'm sure not going to use it working." He understood and wished me well. I cleaned out my desk, signed the necessary paperwork, and told the gang to hold down the home front.

Now I was free to have some fun and there was a full week ahead to enjoy. Minerva was in her last week of high school so I had the days to kill before I could pick her up in the late afternoons. Time with her became a week of memories that I would carry with me through all my training and beyond—it was all we would have to share for sometime to come. Since school was letting out soon there were several planned parties. We saw movies together and had dinner out, but most of all we talked and really got to know each other and I really liked what I learned about her. Besides our long talks about family or school friends, Minerva and I also shared our hopes, dreams and ambitions. Talking with each other came natural and those were precious minutes. Sometimes no words were necessary; just sitting alone and holding each other was enough. One could argue that we packed each day with a lot of living because we knew that all too soon I had to report to camp. This new romance had to grow fast because it didn't have long to grow.

* * *

Some of the troopers didn't know I was engaged so I was pleased to share how special my girl was and pull out her picture again. I got a chance to retell Thanksgiving Day of a year ago.

Everyone else shared their good times and then we started laying out plans of what we would do after getting back home. One of my favorite fantasies was about the car I would buy when I returned to Fort Worth. It would be a 1941 or '42 Packard convertible: powder blue with white top, white sidewall tires and a boatload of chrome. I could close my eyes and see it sitting in the driveway all washed and shiny. I could feel the road beneath me as I accelerated out of a lakeside curve, one hand on the steering wheel, the other holding Minerva close. I would take another aircraft design job and the two of us would raise a family of two boys and two girls, and I wanted them born in that order.

For eleven days, men of the 508th Regiment enjoyed this luxury of living our future dreams. On most of the days it snowed and soon the area was packed under a waist-high powder. The 508th finally received a few sets of white winter suits, but I don't recall anyone in F Company getting them. They wouldn't have been used much until the 21st of January. On that day we reluctantly gave up the warmth and safety of our farmhouse to return to the front lines in the area of Deidenberg.

On January 28th the entire 82nd Division attacked due east toward the village of Holzheim, Belgium. Snow came down hard and high winds made the going slow. It took up all day to cover a very short distance. These were very memorable days of war—not for the fighting, but for the intense cold and the extreme fatigue caused from walking through waist-deep snow. Knowing that if a trooper were wounded he would probably freeze before he could be evacuated didn't help our morale.

A renewed Allied attack began at noon of the next day. The 508th's 2nd Battalion's objective was Medendorf, and the 1st Battalion led the way into the village of Holzhein. After a hard battle, each town was secured and defensive positions set up. In Holzhein, First Sergeant Leonard Funk of C Company and his men captured 80 Germans and left them under the guard of four troopers while the main body pushed forward and finished mopping up the village.

In Medendorf, a patrol from our 2nd Battalion was sent to contact the troops of the 1st Battalion and link up communications. Three lone German paratroopers led by a daring German officer captured this patrol. Evidently this small enemy force believed Holzhein was still in their hands, for they marched their prisoners into the town.

They soon realized their mistake but continued on anyway, in hope of disarming their American counterparts in C Company. The Krauts were in the rear of their captives and all were marching in single file. As the lot of them reached the four Allied soldiers standing guard, the Jerrys got the jump. They managed to do this partly due to the fact there was great similarity between the enemy's snowsuits and those worn by our 1st Battalion. While the C Company guards were still being disarmed, Sergeant Funk returned to the scene with several other troopers. Things didn't seem quite right to Funk's men, though again, the troopers were puzzled by the close resemblance of the snow-suits. They hesitated in their reaction just long enough to give the German officer time to close in on Sgt. Funk.

He shoved his machine pistol into Sgt. Funk's stomach and demanded he surrender. Funk pretended to follow his orders at first and reached up as if surrendering his Tommy Gun, but a quick reverse of direction and a blaze of fire at the officer turned the cards around. The German crumpled in a heap and the other enemy paratroopers surrendered. C Company was in control again. If Funk's action had failed the German prisoners would have retaken control of the town and then they'd have been set for a successful ambush of the 2nd Battalion. The battle for the town of Holzhein would have to be fought again. For his heroic actions Leonard Funk received the Congressional Medal of Honor.

At the same time the patrol from 2nd Battalion was ordered to meet up with the 1st battalion in Holzhein, F Company received independent orders. The small village of Eimerscheid lay just a quarter mile from Medendorf and we were sent to take it. The attack was through heavy woods and the deep snow again made for slow going. The German resistance was strong. Billy "the Kid" Ward positioned himself near me and we urged each other on. As we came within a hundred yards of the first building, a trooper on my right took a shot and fell face down without a sound. I knew he was hit hard and yelled out for the medic, but I kept going myself because this was no place to stop.

We wanted the village, thinking we might spend the night there, but the Germans wouldn't give it up. Our ammunition ran low, so we dug in and held what we had gained, waiting for rations and supplies to move up. Before I dug in, Billy and I went back through the woods to see about the trooper who had gone down beside us. He had taken a head shot and was bound to be dead, but Billy knew him from jump training and wanted to make sure. If he were only wounded we couldn't let him freeze to death.

When we returned to the spot, we saw a medic had moved him under a tree and was still with him. The man was sitting up with his back against the trunk. His head had bandages in both the front and back. He was smoking a cigarette and smiled as we approached. Billy kneeled down and spoke to him.

I asked the medic, "How bad is it?"

"Looks like he'll make it," the medic replied. "But he should be dead; the bullet hit him below his right eye, passed through his head and came out below his left ear. He's doing okay. I don't know why, but he's doing okay."

"Nothing in his head to hurt," Billy laughed.

No doubt this paratrooper had passed the "two doctors looking in your ears" exam.

The next day, the 2nd and 3rd Battalions attacked east, toward Lanzerath. With heavy loads and deep snow, it was all we could do to move forward. Jerry sat behind his defenses knowing the terrain in front of him was inaccessible and no one could get through in such hard weather conditions.

He was almost right.

However, this mistaken belief was probably the largest contributing factor to our success. Since they weren't looking, we showed up unannounced, and the town fell to the 3rd Battalion after only slight resistance. Meanwhile the 2nd Battalion moved forward, meeting only a light defensive fight.

*　*　*

During these days I was splitting my time between duties with the 3rd Platoon and Company headquarters. There didn't seem any code that would determine when, where or what. So when Captain Martin sent me on a one man mission it made sense. He wanted me at another company but I have forgotten the details. What I haven't forgotten was how scary the trip was. I followed the captain's directions but realized I was behind enemy lines. I didn't want to turn back so I kept going, but with a careful eye out. Things remained quiet and the road turned back to the battalion's own area. At a roadblock the guards gave me a funny look so after I finished my business I asked about the route I had traveled.

"Why on earth did you come that way? That road is unsecured," I was told.

I also learned it was a much longer trail and that I could return to my own company in a third of the time by taking a different road, which I did. Why the captain sent me in the other direction I didn't bother asking. I just decided not to trust him.

All our days weren't bad. Even on the front lines there were good days and funny things happened. Even with our brothers in arms getting shot up, we often found things to laugh at or that brought us pleasure.

One day we set up Company headquarters in a farmhouse with the platoons dug into a defensive position across the road. John Beadling, who had fought in Holland, and I had been up the road on outpost duty all afternoon. It was a cold and miserable day. Snow piled up about three feet deep and grew deeper by the minute. It seemed we were out there for days until we were at last relieved. Heading back to the farmhouse my thoughts raced toward the nice warm stove it had in the kitchen.

Unknown to us, some enterprising soul in F Company had butchered one of the farmer's cows and he ground the entire cow into hamburger. When we opened the door a wonderful smell instantly hit us. Going into the kitchen we found several troopers busy frying hamburgers for the entire Company.

Joe Ensminger, the preachers' kid, was right in there, being the ever-helpful type he was. Since our guys didn't know how to pray, much less say grace, I imagined Joe blessing each burger as it came off the grill.

The atmosphere seemed so different from battle, my mind couldn't help traveling back to Fort Worth and my favorite hamburger stand where Ed Mize and I hung out with all the other kids. This was usually around midnight after the late movie at the Worth Theater downtown. The Worth was built originally for the opera around the turn of the century, and it was a massive place with velvet seats, shining brass and chrome rails, and the biggest chandeliers in the state. Students got in for thirty-five cents.

Now it all came back to me.

I couldn't believe the fantastic aroma in the kitchen. I thought I had died and gone to hamburger heaven. Burgers had never come this fresh before, and they were stacked all over the place—you could have all you wanted. Beadling and I went to start right in. Another trooper teased us.

"Aw, you two probably won't like them."

I told him. "Yeah, I'm going to send about a half dozen of these patties right down the Dwayne."

John laughed and popped me on the arm. "You always say that."

Needless to say, F Company went to bed that night with a pleasantly stuffed feeling.

Woody and I felt so good we decided to chance sleeping upstairs. There was a full-size bed up there which looked absolutely beautiful, but everyone else avoided it because of Jerrys' habit of throwing in artillery at dawn. Upper levels weren't too safe for sleeping.

This farmhouse had part of its roof missing so we knew the German gunners had already found the range. However, Woody and I talked it over and agreed between us that there wouldn't be any artillery shots in the morning. What a luxury to sleep on an honest-to-goodness real bed. The other guys were all piled up on the floor downstairs.

At about five in the morning, a soft scream came whistling in from a distance. Like a set of twins we sprang to the floor, grabbing our packs and weapons. The first shell exploded somewhere outside as Woody and I hit the stairs. We took those stairs two and three at a time. Just after flattening ourselves to the floor, a second round exploded and once again it was outside somewhere. After that, silence fell again. Jerry had missed the whole house and then given up after only two rounds.

"Maybe it was just an unfriendly wake-up call, nothing personal," said Woody.

"They're reminding us there's still a war going on, no comforts allowed," I said.

Outside of a few snowsuits, good Arctic equipment like boots and gloves were not available. I don't know why we all didn't freeze to death. Frostbite took its toll and at every other stop we heard of someone sent to the rear to recover. Ralph Burrus was one of those and we never saw him again. As a Texan I didn't really know what frostbite was, but I'd heard a bad case of it would cause you to lose a foot or hand, or even your nose.

* * *

On the 26th, F Company marched to a small town for a two-day rest. Company headquarters and each platoon were billeted in a separate building. A choice was given me, to stay with the 3rd Platoon as a communications man or return to Company headquarters. Since the Bulge began, I had fought mostly with the Platoon, but whenever we went into reserve I returned to Company headquarters.

There were good friends in Headquarters. Woody and I had been through a lot; John Hurst was always there, too; Joe Ensminger had become a close friend; but the Captain and I didn't really see eye to eye. I kept thinking he had sent me on that wild goose chase just to get me killed. I felt he had it in for me. The 3rd Platoon felt comfortable, and something inside said they needed my rank and experience because they were really short of old timers. I elected to stay and for the first time took my billeting with them.

An order came down to collect all grenades so they could then be stored in a safe place. This had never been done before and it puzzled us. The war alone was one those things that was hard to make any sense of, but with the Army, sometimes making sense of orders was flat impossible. There had never been any problems with grenades before, so a rumor started that our action was over and we would soon return to Sissonne, France. The collected grenades were stored at Headquarters, a three-story building made largely of brick.

The next day came with no mention of returning to the Sissonne camp and we knew it wasn't going to happen right away. Still, the end of the war once again seemed close at hand, and everyone felt good to have survived.

Late in the afternoon of our first full day in the village, everyone settled down and we were glad to have a chance to take it easy. I was down in the basement shooting the breeze with most of the others in the platoon and was getting to know them better when there came a titanic explosion, one that rattled all the windows and shook the ground. In a single movement we all made for the door to see what had happened. We didn't think it was the Germans because we were too far back.

The view from the door was quite unbelievable. Company headquarters was gone, all three brick floors; in its place stood a pile of rubble not more than six feet high.

Everyone started running because we knew somewhere under all that pile of brick and mortar were buried the men of Company headquarters. Captain Martin, John Beadling and Billy Ward were just outside the building and two of them were starting to stand up from the shock of the blast as we arrived.

Like mad dogs we tore into the debris with the only tools available: our bare hands. Throwing bricks and moving great chunks of wall, we dug down through the destruction and found the first man. First Sergeant Scanlon was alive but was bloody and beat up. John and Woody were right near him. Each of them was hurt, John more so than the other two, but they would each heal. (This was John's third Purple Heart.) Billy claimed three more were missing so we kept at it.

Our hands began to bleed from cuts and scrapes but there wasn't any slowing down. Then we found Joe Ensminger. From the looks of him he must have died instantly. He was burned black and his left leg was gone from the knee down.

I had always meant to ask Joe why he volunteered for the paratroopers. He didn't look the part and sure didn't act the part. Joe seemed more like the studious type with his GI-issued glasses and small stature. But that didn't keep him from carrying his part of the load, and he fought as bravely as anyone.

Someone said, "He must have sat on the grenade box."

Those who had a hold on him carried Joe out to the grass and snow. The rest of us resumed digging. There were two more troopers to find, but I, for one, kept glancing at Joe's body. Since Holland it was Joe who always read scripture and voiced a prayer over those we sent off for burial. Now that he was dead, who could we get to say a proper prayer for him?

Another buddy gone, and of the green troopers who had visited me after Normandy, two of the three were now gone and Lou Slama was in the hospital. I wasn't doing too well looking out for them. Lou Slama had taken a hit from an 88 shell a few weeks earlier.

Our hands by now were really beat up and ripped. Our efforts were slower now, not a lot, but we had lost some drive. We had gotten stung. The farther we dug, nobody really wanted to find what might be hidden in the pile.

"Who are you looking for?" Sergeant Scanlon asked.

But he was so dazed we ignored him, and the captain had him loaded on a jeep that was brought over. Then after we had turned over almost every brick, Captain Martin yelled to stop, that the two missing men were coming down the road.

Big Jim Bartlett and a buddy had been out trying to score some booze to host a Company party that night. They'd missed the whole thing. This was one time that being a drinker paid off, while the Christian man lost his life. I didn't expect the Army to make sense but sometimes God didn't seem to either. Not one man was able to voice a word of prayer for Joe, at least not out in the open. I guess we didn't measure up to his standard. I felt a bit of guilt but there was some relief in believing he didn't need our prayers anyway. Heaven already had a special place for him. The fact that I had chosen to join the 3rd Platoon also made me wonder, for this very simple decision may have saved my life.

all - Gernades destroyed at Hdqt

explosion building

why 3 story building?

cause of explosion?

fear of frassing?

Relationship Sgt + Captain?

German shell hit the Hdqt

JUMP
Thirteen

"Are you trying to take me out with an 88?"

Somewhere thereafter the places through which we fought became German. We had crossed the border but didn't really know where. The fight became just a long series of towns with names all the same. Most were small villages and they were so damaged from the war they offered little or no shelter. Maybe the next one would offer a complete house, or the next town after that.

The towns, the snow and the time we spent moving through them became one long nightmare. It was a struggle to keep yourself moving. Day after day you went through the same motions, fought the same enemy with the same carbine, wearing the same clothing.

I came to expect it would never end. It was possible I had died weeks ago and something had kept me out of heaven. This was hell. We fought and we killed, but there was more ahead, always more ahead.

On the 30th of January we reached what we hoped was our final objective—it wasn't—located just inside the German boundary. On moving into the area we walked past some dead troopers that had been laid out beside the road for the grave detail. One of the bodies was that of Lieutenant Goodale. It shocked us and we had to tell the new guys just how much he had meant to the company. No one knew what had happened.

I was working with the 3rd Platoon now and we sat up a C.P. in a German dugout. The Germans had put a lot of work into the dugouts in this area, and they were real works of art by war standards. Made out of large tree trunk logs, they were more like small earthen houses. Each had built-in bunks and a ton of dirt over the top. It looked like someone planned on staying for the winter. The dugouts provided enough room for what remained of the 3rd Platoon with space left over.

While moving in I found my radio was dead; it was the battery most likely. So when the platoon was about settled, I slung the radio over my shoulder and headed down the road to headquarters. The sun shone and the bright day made for a fair walk so long as I stayed wrapped up well enough.

As I walked along, I gazed at the snow-covered hills in the distance, it was territory still held by the enemy. Everything sparkled with white and for the first time in a long while I saw the beauty of it. All was quite, nothing moved. At headquarters the communications operator told me they were having the same problem—the hand-held mike was freezing up.

"Set it over by the stove and wait a while," he said. "They thaw out quick, but water stays trapped inside. The heat will dry it out."

It made good sense and the stove felt good after my walk so I took a seat.

"How'd you learn that?" I asked.

"Oh I don't know, Canyon maybe, or someone from regiment. Hey, that reminds me; I heard a good story from those guys."

"What's that?"

"It was at Lanzerath, I guess. We had taken over a farmhouse as an outpost. The old man who owned it was sent away. Well the ol' coot didn't really leave and he kept getting in the way. Captain Nation would have him thrown out again but he'd come back to sit in his rocking chair. Then he'd want to know what was going on and get in the way again."

"So how'd they get rid of him?"

"They didn't. Jerry did. An 88 shell came whistling in and exploded right in the main room. When they got up and looked around nobody was even hurt except the old man. He was dead."

The two of us continued shooting the bull back and forth for about an hour and a half. Then we checked the mike and decided it should be good for several more weeks. I loaded up and headed back to the platoon's dugout.

The weather had held during my visit and I was enjoying my walk back. It was still early enough that the day remained bright. During the most serene part of my trip I unexpectedly heard an artillery round. So trained was my mind that I slid into the ditch without thinking and the shell dropped in about 50 yards to my left. I got up and easily found the spot in the snow where it had hit. From the sound I knew it had been an 88 but couldn't imagine why it had been fired. There wasn't a darn thing around me to shoot at.

I started back up the road thinking it could be "just one of those things" when I heard another one coming in. So I made for the ditch again. This one came pretty close, missing me by ten yards. Sitting up in the ditch, I looked over the road and toward the hills behind German lines. Now I knew what was going on.

"You crazy S.O.B.!" I screamed across the lines. "Are you trying to take me out with an 88?"

I couldn't really make them out or know if they could hear me, but they were there. Those Krauts must have been bored to tears or else thought I was real important. I moved back to the road and made a quick decision. If they were going to fire again, it would come soon. Looking back to the German hills I thought about testing them with a game.

I cut across the field on a dead run then made a slight diagonal turn. I figured this would throw off their aim. Sure enough another round came and dropped in on the road about where I would have been had I stuck to walking the road. It was so far away I just kept running. At the edge of the woods I stopped and turned toward the artillery fire once more.

"See," I laughed, "you're not so smart after all."

I entered the woods and used them for cover while I could. The 3rd Platoon C.P. was close by and when I reached the dugout I was still thinking how clever I had been to outwit the German gunner. Before crawling into the dugout I took off my radio, and just then a fourth round whistled in. It landed before I realized it and I was only halfway to the ground when the explosion came. The force of it rolled me over into the snow.

I felt numb all over and I couldn't hear too well. I just lay there trying to ascertain if everything was still connected. Determining there weren't any holes in my body that God hadn't created, I thought to myself, "Burns, you're starting to get cocky. That German was smarter than you gave him credit for, and it almost cost your life." I realized Jerry likely had the dugout plotted on his map and had figured out where I was going.

* * *

On the 4th of February, the 99th Division took over for the 82nd and F Company marched to the town of Rencheux for some rest. Rencheux was a small village well back from the front. Warmer weather started to melt the snow. We liked the change but the roads and fields turned into small inland seas of mud. Then at night everything tended to refreeze.

After only three days rest the 508th P.I.R. made a night move on February the 7th, heading east of Aachen near Schmidt, Germany. Here we would make a spearhead drive for the west bank of the Roer River. We had to travel through the Huertgen Forest, but the name forest no longer applied. This area had been leveled to several hills of splintered tree stalks, caused by constant shelling from both sides. It was also a valley full of wrecked-out, burned-out vehicles and a lot of twisted, decaying bodies, American and German—left from December when the Bulge began. Falling snow at Christmas had covered them completely. After six weeks the thaw started and the dead reappeared. There was no escaping the stench, which hung in the air like poison gas.

The Roer River remained the last obstacle before American armor could make a run across the plains for Cologne. Leading the way, 1st Battalion jumped off at two o'clock on the 10th of February. They ran into an anti-personnel minefield and were peppered with mortars and machine guns while charging Hill 400. After sustaining heavy casualties they pulled back and the 319th Field Artillery went to work raking the minefield with intensive fire.

The engineers laid out a path and then A Company had a go at it. The casualties were heavy, but they finally managed to get through. The Germans used wooden Schu mines here and our mine detectors just couldn't find them. Several of our Red Devils took it from the Schu mines that day.

At 09:30 our 2nd Battalion pushed past the 1st, and by nightfall

all fighting west of the Roer River was over. The Germans had flooded the river, so we held our positions. Either the weather turned cold again or else it seemed chillier by the water.

After a couple of days I developed sore feet. On the 15th my feet were hurting so badly I took time to take a close look at them. They were white, blistered, peeling and cold, the normal stuff. Thinking First Aid might have some cream to put on them I put my boots back on and told Captain Martin I'd be right back.

At this time the 508th was just sending out lots of patrols, so there was plenty of time to visit the medics and get back prior to the action starting up again.

But the medics didn't see it that way. An ambulance arrived and before I knew it the Aid station had me in the ambulance with two litter cases and five walking wounded. It seems frostbite had done what the German Army couldn't. It put me in the hospital.

We rode most of the night and it was very late when we stopped at a small field unit. Two of us with frostbite got out and the rest went on to a major hospital in France somewhere. The other soldier and I were led into a doctor's office and the doctor took our papers.

He was pleasant and talked to us for a few minutes, asking us what part of the States we were from and what kind of action we had seen. Opening a desk drawer, he pulled out a bag of marshmallows and gave us two apiece.

After days of eating K-Rations I felt amazed at seeing these marshmallows. I hadn't seen or thought of a marshmallow in over two years. They were so white, so pure looking, like they had fallen from heaven. Little bite-size pieces of heaven. I bit off half of one and it was unbelievable how good a simple thing could taste. It was the sweetest thing I had eaten in a long time and already I felt much better.

The doctor called an orderly and then told us he would see us first thing in the morning. We were each assigned a bed and, as per the doctor's instructions, ordered not to get out of bed at any time for anything.

This really was heaven! I could sleep as much as I wanted. All my meals—hot meals—were carried in for me. If I wanted anything, all I had to do was ask an orderly and he would get it for me. I just had to lie there with my feet elevated and enjoy it. So I spent the days sleeping, reading, eating and then sleeping some more.

For two weeks this treatment continued until the doctor allowed me to take my meals in the mess hall. By then I was relieved. I hadn't gone quite stir-crazy yet, but paratroopers were accustomed to a more active life-style.

Although separated from the Regiment, I learned I wasn't missing any of the action. From the 15th of February, when I walked back to the First Aid Station, until the 18th of February, the 508th took up strictly defensive positions and saw no more fighting. On the 18th the 78th Infantry Division crossed the river in an assault and the Red Devils loaded up for the long-awaited trip to Sissonne. They arrived back at the home station on the 20th. 134 men had been killed in action during the Bulge. More than 600 others were wounded or injured, several badly enough to be discharged. Many more friends of mine did not return, and this time the list included Lieutenant Polette and Lieutenant Goodale. Both had served with F Company at one time or another and I was proud to have fought under them and beside them.

In time I learned the story that was going around. Polette had become E Company's commander. On January 22nd he had his men digging in at a defensive position. After overseeing the establishment of his command post inside a building Polette returned to his men. He was walking up the slit trench giving the dig an inspection when Germans dropped in a couple of mortar shells. He wasn't hurt bad and most expected him to recover but Polette turned fatalistic. He told his men to "take care of George." George Miles was both his Exec. and his best friend since the establishment of the regiment. Lieutenant Polette died the next day.

On the 29th of January Lieutenant Goodale and his platoon were marching into a town that had been cleared out ahead of them. A German patrol, however, was just returning and didn't realize the town was in Allied hands. The two forces walked into each other and a fight started. Eight German soldiers were killed. The last two turned to run. Someone called to "get those two." Goodale answered that he had them and had no sooner left the road to give chase when one of the two Jerrys turned and killed him with a single shot. I was told that it happened so fast that the two Germans got away at first, though the whole platoon minus Goodale and one other shot trooper gave chase.

Our regimental adjutant, Captain Bill Nation, was also killed, during the shelling of a newly established regimental headquarters by German tanks. When the tanks moved in, Nation called for artillery fire against them. That was the last they heard from him. I didn't know Captain Nation myself, but I knew he was another of us good ol' Texas boys from the Fort Worth-Dallas area, and by all reports a really outstanding officer. All these men were heroes.

As soon as I started taking meals in the field hospital's mess hall, I knew there would only be a short wait before I could return to my outfit. Three days later I was sent to a replacement depot to wait for transportation to Sissonne. There I was assigned a bunk, "just for the night"; but the night became several nights and then a week. I got tired of this. There were no duties—fine with me—but there was nothing else to do, no entertainment, no parties, nothing. I had written and rewritten home while I was in the hospital.

I knew my fellow Red Devils were in France now and getting those passes to Paris. I needed to get back so I could keep up. Paratroopers weren't made for sitting around waiting, and I had taken all I could stand. I would have gladly given up a toe or two from frostbite just to remain with the unit.

After ten days the arrangements were finally set and I traveled by truck with several green soldiers right off the boat. They were full of talk and excitement and had a thousand questions about the war. I answered their questions politely although I didn't really want to talk in detail. They seemed a little awed by my presence but I didn't much enjoy it or their company. I had lost too many friends to start making new ones.

On arriving at Sissonne in early March[xlix] I learned we had lost our old billets and were now back to living in the same Tent City we had in England. It appeared the major hospital, that I had heard mentioned a month earlier in my ambulance ride, had taken our barracks. Many of our own troopers were recovering there. If I had been wounded I could have traveled straight to base camp from the first aid station. Instead, as one might expect in the Army, I took the long way around.

Living in tents didn't bother us; we had spent plenty of time with less. My own feeling of being off the front and out of the replacement depot was so good they could have put me back on the front. Of course, France was a whole lot better because there was no lack of things to do there. Shows were coming in for those who wanted to see them. A few of the older hands got passes to England, Brussels or Paris. What I enjoyed best in those days was just pulling a little light duty and talking to the old men of F Company. At one big gathering we took a head count of men who had started with the company's original formation in Ireland. Only twelve of us buddies remained and of the twelve, I was the only one without a Purple Heart.

John Hurst asked me, "Burns, you and I are always near each other during the fighting. How come I've got three Purple Hearts and you ain't got a one?"

"Well heck, John, when I hear those shells coming in I jump out of the way. You need to stop standing behind me."

John chuckled. He told me that when the company headquarters building blew up and killed Joe Ensminger, it was from German shelling.

"I thought we were too far to the rear for any shelling," I said.

Hurst replied, "I thought so too but I saw it come in. I just happened to be looking out the window when the first one landed. It was so far off I didn't even think about it. I hadn't even heard it come in. The second one landed about halfway between the first and the headquarters building. I heard it barely and wondered if they were shooting at us. I figured one more and I'd know for certain. Wish I'd said something sooner but I don't think it would have changed a thing. We'd all just squatted where we were and the shell would still explode on top of our grenade box. If we hadn't collected those grenades Joe might have survived the shell blast. Too bad."

"Yeah," I agreed. "We get a lot of that."

JUMP
Fourteen

Nothing was too good for
Eisenhower's Red Devils.

Soon after I returned, the higher command decided we should make a
✓ practice jump, having gone six months without one. I was now among
those who didn't understand why they called it practice. You had to
do if perfectly every time. Something always went wrong and someone
always got hurt because of it. However this was what we did to earn
our extra jump pay, and it did have a very fun element. I just didn't
think there was anything about it that could be called practice. It was
either a jump or it wasn't.   ↓

The day started out really pleasant and it looked to be anl enjoyable time. On the ground the atmosphere was a lot like a picnic.
Anyone with a camera had it out, taking pictures, while we waited to
load up and take off. It sure was a lot different than that first jump at
school.

* * *

November 15, 1943, is a day I will always remember. I had only been
flying once in my life, when I was about eight years of age and it
thrilled the daylights out of me. Dad worked for Bowen Airlines,
which used Meachem Field in Fort Worth as its home base. I think the
plane Dad and I went up in was the single engine Lockheed Vega.
From that day on I knew I was in love with the airplane and someday
I would learn to fly.

On this November morning the sun had just risen above the horizon and the trees were casting long shadows on the path to the hangers. All the hours of running and training were going to pay off. The
day was cool and still, it was going to be a great day for jumping.

Inside the packing shed we drew our chutes from their storage bins and took them outside. As we strapped them on the instructors counted us off into "sticks" of ten men each. Then they marched us into the Sweat Shed.

I discovered it was a long room built on the side of the packing shed and it had crude wooden benches running the full length of the room. We entered and sat down as a "stick," waiting for our turn to be called to lead up. This first jump would be from twelve hundred feet. As we sat there I thought about all of the time and training we had gone through. I recalled the morning five-mile runs, bloody blisters on my feet, the never ending calisthenics, the mockup doors, the tumbling and all the parachutes we had packed again just to get to D Stage. I felt a great sense of pride, however, while looking around, I could see a lot us had butterflies and were feeling a bit weak in the knees. Our long running curiosity had turned into uneasiness.

I watched as the men on the far side, two sticks, were instructed to stand and file through a single door leading to the aircraft ramp outside. Everyone watched them go. Any outsider seeing us for the first time might have thought we were awaiting execution and those leaving were the first to face a firing squad. Not too many jokes to say the least. As the last man of each stick disappeared to the plane we began to move up. It was like a wave running down the length of a long rope when you give one end of it a snap; we all stood up in turn and moved twenty places closer to the door.

I sat down and wiped my brow then I looked at the others. Regardless of the cool morning, sweat had begun to bead up and trickle down a few faces. Now I knew why they called it the Sweat Shed.

From outside an aircraft engine powered to life, then another. You could hear them rev up and easily visualize the C-47 begin to roll down the ramp. The roaring engines faded away as the plane made its turn and began its taxi to the end of the runway. The men inside were lucky; first to jump, first to land. The rest of us would have to sweat a little first and allow the shed to live up to its name.

Another sergeant entered. Two more sticks stood and filed out in a single line. The rest of us watched them go. Then we all resumed our motion of moving twenty places closer to the door. And again the roar of a C-47 coming to life was heard from outside.

I looked back to see where John was sitting. He winked and I gave him a grin in reply. It looked like he was about four sticks, two plane-loads, behind me; we would likely be in the air at the same time. My buddy and I were going to do a little flying.

Then came turn for my stick. We went out the door and into a large hanger. The shade and openness of the hanger was like facing a cool breeze under a large tree. It restored our confidence. A C-47 was waiting for us, it was smaller than I had expected. My stick was the last to get in.

We climbed aboard and began taking places on the right-hand side. This meant we would be the last stick to jump. Bucket seats lined each side of the exposed bulkhead rings and stringers running the air-craft's length. I took a full look around as I eased to my seat. It was an all-metal aircraft. It felt good to sit there, and through my nose I took a big breath. There was a pleasant smell about it. I may have only flown once in an aircraft but I had seen plenty of others back at Meachem Field and it seemed all airplanes have the same smell, it's a good smell, and this was a good airplane. It was also destined to find a special spot in the hearts of all paratroopers.

Everyone inside the plane began talking about the plane and the coming jump.

"Man o' man, we're gonna do it now," someone said.

"Well I'm ready, let's go!"

One fellow close to the door leaned forward in his seat. "Hey guys I just want to say I think you're all OK and good luck to everyone of you."

Then we all started to wish one another well but were suddenly cut short when the number one engine started to whine. It caught hold, shot out blue-black smoke and shook itself to idle. It was loud! All talking stopped and we just looked across the isle at each other with weak grins on our faces. Number two engine was brought to life and we started to rumble down the taxi strip to take our place in line with the other aircraft waiting to take off.

At the end of the runway the pilot checked the engine magnetos by stomping on the brakes and pushing the throttles forward. The noise inside was awesome. The aluminum fuselage began shaking and I wondered if the plane was going to come apart. Then the engines were throttled back and the shaking died down. The pilot released the brakes and we rolled forward.

Rolling down the runway, the noise was as loud as before and the shaking returned. It sounded like a great battle between aircraft and planet; our plane fighting to take off while the ground was fighting to hold on. The roar of the engines, the rattle of the airframe and the sound of the tires against the runway made a deafening combination. Then the plane lifted off, the whining wheels went silent and the airframe became calm. Except for the mighty roaring engines, everything seemed quiet.

It wasn't quiet at all really but there was a certain peace and the noise was a beautiful sound. A thrill of excitement spread through me as we became airborne. I turned in my seat, looked out my window and watched mother earth drop away. There was a tingle at my fingertips and toes and I suddenly felt akin to the airplane. The big craft was in its element, and I became one with it. ✔

After that first jump it seemed everyone believed they had command of the world. We were it, Uncle Sam's best, and the Germans had best watch out.

Weather for the following jumps stayed good. The whole week was beautiful. Our pancake breakfasts were successful business meetings; the morning runs a religious service. Now when we marched by a company in A-stage the instructor gave us a cue and we sang out in unison. "You'll be sorry!" And we tried to suppress a smile.

Jumps two, three and four went smoothly as the first except we didn't sweat it quite as much. Of course there were a few mishaps each time and we were not entirely free of injuries. There was always that one account of torn ligaments or a broken bone but I gathered this was to be expected when several hundred men were jumping every day. One trooper was seriously hurt. He somehow tumbled head over heels going out the door and a chute suspension line came up between his legs. When he got his opening shock the suspension line cut through his groin and into his stomach.[1]

My only scare occurred in jump four. While still 500 feet in the air my packing partner nearly landed on my chute. There I was, enjoying the descent, when up above me someone started yelling.

"Get out of the way, get out of the way!" he screamed.

I looked up and caught a glimpse of my packing partner Joe, his knees pulled up under his chin, slipping onto the top of my chute. I reacted with a handful of riser and slid to my left, Joe slipped himself a little backwards just missing a dead hit on my chute. We landed side by side. With hardly a glance at each other we rolled our chutes and walked to the truck. It was part of jumping and we found we could handle it.

I had to smile about riding in the truck after each jump. One of the stories passed around during training was about a trooper jumping for the first time. He was told if his main chute were to fail he always had his reserve and when he completed his jump there would be a truck on the field to pick him up. He made the jump and by-heck the main chute failed. He pulled his reserved chute and it failed as well. The ill-fated trooper then said to himself, "I'll bet that dang truck isn't there to meet me either."

* * *

This French "practice" jump I figured might well be the last for many of us. Sergeant Red Thomas, a veteran of Normandy, was jump leader in the plane I rode and I was jumping second behind him.

When the red light came on and everyone stood up, I placed my hand on the door opening. Red filled the door and had one hand on its opening as well. His other hand rested on the switch that would allow him to drop our equipment from the plane's belly. Waiting for the green light we hit a bit of rough air. With the plane bouncing around Red stuck his head out the door and looked back. I started to grab his shoulder, and then he looked at me.

"There goes our equipment bundles, hope we can find them," he said.

Red had inadvertently tripped the switch in the turbulence. We flew for another two minutes before the green light came on.

"Let's go!" yelled Red. I pivoted to my right to go out the door behind him.

I watched Red ahead of me. Every time I jump, the person's jump in front of me looks like slow motion. The static line goes taut and then pulls the cover off the chute. The canopy snakes out into the air stream with the static lines following. When the harness keeps the static lines from sliding through the air any further, the chute slowly blossoms out to a full open position and the trooper starts a gentle ride to the ground.

My own chute jerked me with a pop and I snapped back into real time. As was my habit I looked up and checked the canopy. It was full, all the panels were where they needed to be, and I hadn't any rips or broken lines.

"I love you," I said. "You great big beautiful sheet, I love you." I looked down to check the drop zone. What I saw caused me to suddenly cry out, "Oh my God!"

There was the wreck of a C-47 sprawled out in the middle of our landing field. Its burned out shell, still smoking, and the fresh plowed dirt surrounding the ship told me the crash had occurred earlier in the day. Riding the trucks back to camp it was all anybody could talk about.

Later we were told the accident happened that morning while dropping the 1st Battalion. Command thought it best not to let us know much about it. However, we later learned even more details. The movie actress Marlene Dietrich, a fan of American airborne, just happened to be visiting the regiment during this time. The training jump was already scheduled but the officers started calling it a parade jump for Miss Dietrich and she believed them. When the plane crashed she was very hysterical and afterwards quite distraught.[li] The ship had thrown a propeller just as the first stick started making their jump. The planes always slow down to a bare minimum before a jump and, when the propeller flew off, this plane was unable to generate enough power to maintain flying speed.

The jumpers inside had gotten out fine but as the ship lost air speed it began to crash-dive through the descending men who had jumped before it. There were some guys who got picked up on the wings of the diving plane and carried to their deaths.

* * *

On March 24, 1945, hundreds of C-47s and the new double-door C-46s, filled with paratroopers, flew once more into the enemy skies. Their destinations were drop zones across the Rhine River.[lii] However this time, the first since entering the European Theater, men of the

✓

82nd Airborne were not involved. The 17th Airborne was making its maiden combat jump. But not all the troopers were green. Some were pressed into limited action during the Bulge and the 507th Regiment had been a sister unit during Normandy. The All Americans got lucky and sat this one out.

On the fourth of April the 508th Red Devils, recently detached from the 82nd, immediately packed up and went by train to an airfield outside of Chartres, France. Here we were placed on a 48-hour alert. First Airborne wanted us ready in case we were needed to liberate prisoners of war who might be held as hostages. I thought of John. It was time he was liberated, if he was still alive, so I didn't mind this duty at all. We had already proven we could move a lot quicker than 48 hours. If we jumped the action was expected to be light, and for John I would readily jump once more, but it turned out the regiment wasn't needed. After the alert, our assignment in Chartres turned out to be one of the best assignments yet. Every morning we received a briefing on how the war was going and we could see on a map where the Americans and British would soon meet up with the Russian Red Army. That meant the war would soon end. Most afternoons we were free to play cards or write home and often we got a baseball game going. A beer party always followed a game. There were passes to Chartres every night, and it was a nice town.

The 508th P.I.R. also served MP duty. This was an interesting change. If there was a dance in town the MPs would go and make sure there wasn't any trouble, and they'd see to it the GIs were cleared out in time to make curfew. Then the MPs would stay around for another hour or so and talk to the girls. They even had to escort a few home to determine they made it there safely.

The best thing about this time was a three-day pass to Paris. I had looked forward to going for so long it was hard to believe it when I finally got there. They took a whole truckload of us in and I thought it was well worth the wait. For three glorious days we went all over the city, looking at the sights and forgetting the war.

One time a few of us entered a rather fashionable club and were shown a table. When the waiter came by, one of the troopers with us said, "We want a bottle of Champagne and some girls." It seemed a rather brash order for such a swanky, chic place, but sure enough several young ladies were shown to our table and visiting with the French girls was a thrill.

The end of the war came as no surprise. Victory Day in Europe found us sitting around the airfield once again in case we needed to jump for the POWs. We were glad to be there on this day in particular because it was the safest place to be. In town there was a raucous party going on as both the French and the GIs celebrated VE Day and I understand the medics were kept busy.

* * *

Shortly after VE Day we packed up and moved back to our tent city at Sissonne. Even before getting resettled, most of us were interested in only one thing: how soon we were going home. However, it turned out that the 508th was slated for Army of Occupation service.

In early June we moved to Frankfurt-am-Main, Germany. The 508th was stationed as guards for General Eisenhower's headquarters and personal home, as well as the homes of all the general officers assigned to European Headquarters.

We were billeted in Heddernheim, a suburb of Frankfurt, in four-story apartment buildings. There were four men to an apartment, each completely furnished and with hot and cold running water. I was now back with Company headquarters so John Hurst, Woody Phelps, new replacement Tom Clevenger and myself had one apartment. This seemed like a great deal of luxury, but suddenly nothing was too good for Eisenhower's' Red Devils. We were destined to become a spit and polish unit.

Getting cleaned up for Honor Guard duty felt really good for a change. Each trooper was issued a set of white gloves and scarf, a white utility belt and even white bootlaces. The big worry was not if we were being shot at, but how good was the crease in our pants and how we could get a better shine on our boots. The 508th proved it could be more than a top-notch fighting regiment; we were good garrison soldiers as well.

As for sharpness of uniform, we had no equal. We had a great deal of pride, having gone through the worst of the European invasion and some of its greatest battles. After the test of fire we had come out like tempered shining knights. Eisenhower was the conqueror of Europe, the new emperor, and we were his personal guards.

It didn't take long to get used to the life of a garrison soldier. The work was in the preparation; guard duty itself was almost too easy. The only problem I had during this time was with the shift Captain Martin placed me on. I was Sergeant of the Guard from 11:00 p.m. to 7:00 a.m. the next morning.

One night, five or ten minutes after the midnight curfew, a couple of soldiers came in late. Anyone coming in late had to be written up for a formal review and probable reprimand. When they came in I asked why and what was going on. "Girls," they said. Of course, I should have known. I fully understood but chewed them out a little anyway. I explained the penalty and sent them on after receiving a promise they wouldn't let it happen again. No sooner had they left my sight when in walked Captain Martin. He wanted to know who was coming in late. I told him and then he made me fill out a report on them. He wasn't going to cut anyone any slack. These guys were not troublemakers, but they were in trouble now.

Overall, this was an enjoyable time and we were all proud to be serving right under the big general himself; but still, the thing foremost in our minds was when we would be going home. To be snatched up and drafted into the Army to fight for your country was one thing, but now that it was all over everyone felt anxious to be on their way back across the Atlantic. The ship ride back, however, was an experience I didn't really want to think about.

On February 10th, 1944, John McGee and I had loaded onto a ferryboat and taken a ride across the Hudson River to Staten Island to board our ship for overseas duty. As we drove onto the pier a band played, people waved to us, and the Red Cross was handing out coffee and donuts. Once on board we found our assigned bunks. It wasn't too uncomfortable but some of the bunks were stacked so high we thought we should be drawing flight pay. The real unfortunate stroke was that we were in the bow of the ship that, once at sea, moved up and down like an express elevator.

After a briefing where we learned there would only be two meals a day and that we had to shower with salt water, we tried to settle down for some sleep. Sometime during the wee hours of the morning I felt the bed and floors start to vibrate and I knew we were getting underway. At first light the breakfast line started forming. But by then seasickness had hit me so hard I had to swear off food. I didn't think I'd ever eat again, and for three days I remained laid up in bed. Just to die I would have to start feeling better.

When improvement finally came, I was only recovered enough to crawl out on deck. I mused that by throwing myself overboard my suffering would end. But just then the fresh ocean air filled my lungs, and by watching the horizon I was able to judge the ship's movements through the open seas. It was like riding a horse: first you rode down into a hollow, then you rode it up to the ridge, over and over and over. With a single look around I realized we were far from being alone in our ocean crossing. As far as the eye could see there were ships of all descriptions. I decided I could start eating again and privately took back all the nasty thoughts I had concocted about food. However, I was careful what I ate for the entire trip.

* * *

Privately I wondered why arrangements couldn't be made to fly me home in a C-47. There were lots of them around and our pilots had to get back to the States like everyone else. But if offered a troop boat I knew I'd take it right away because I'd be that much closer to home and Minerva. F Company was full of good guys and I'd never forget them; however, I longed to pick up my life where I had left it and start living it again.

JUMP
Fifteen

"I'm not a damn Yank, I'm from Texas!"

The 508th Parachute Infantry Regiment was born on October the 20th, 1942, which was one day before my 18th birthday, the one that made me eligible for the draft. I had long believed that maybe we were made for each other. Training for the regiment started at Camp Blanding, Florida under the command of Major Roy E. Lindquist.[liii] After parachute training in Georgia the unit took advance training in North Carolina, South Carolina and Tennessee. Then Lt. Colonel Lindquist and his Red Devils moved to Camp Shanks, New York, where pre-shipping processing began. They were alerted on Christmas Day, the same day I was walking the streets of Columbus longing for home.

On December 27th the unit loaded on board the USAT *James Parker*. Its debarkation point was Belfast, Ireland; the date was January 8, 1944. The Regiment made its home at Port Stewart where it could indoctrinate and train new troops until it came up to full strength. Thirty-three days later was when I boarded another ship to join them. Nearly eighteen months I had called the Regiment home. But it was a difficult home because it was a place where brothers were always suddenly leaving. Yet the pains from those constant separations were much, much slower to go away.

A letter came one day from England. It was from an old buddy of mine, someone who I hadn't seen in over a year—John McGee. He had been released from the POW camp and had quarters back on the English Isle. He wrote that he had been to see our English friend Sheila Bull and her mother; he planned to leave for the States in a few days and wanted me to know he was okay.

The letter made me envious, but that didn't stop me from reading it a second and third time. It was such a good letter to get.

I missed John, he was more brother than most and now I knew I could catch up with him in Fort Worth. Every other trooper around me felt the same as I did about going home. There was a real good chance anyone remaining could earn a fourth stripe but I don't think anyone was even tempted. I was high on the point system for going home, but I knew it would be a couple of months until my orders came.

For now I had to be content with a seven-day leave to either England or Switzerland. The choice came as a pleasant surprise. I took England, where I hoped to take care of some unfinished business.

Catching a flight on the 26th of August with a friend named Paul, I felt almost free. The Regiment and battlegrounds were behind me and I was headed for England again.

On this flight across the Channel, in yet another C-47, Paul and I didn't even have to wear a parachute. The trip was beautiful. The plane never rose more than 2,000 feet and I could watch the valleys of France below without fear or anxiety.

We landed at Biggin Hill Airfield, a fighter base near London. We stayed there for one night. On the next day Paul and I walked to the railroad station and bought tickets for Nottingham. We learned there would be a few hours to kill before our train departure, so we looked around London a bit. I'm sure others loved this place, but as far as Paul and I were concerned it was just another big city and we looked forward to getting on our train for what we considered home.

The Nottingham train pulled into its destination late, but we were able to get a bed at the Red Cross Club. On day three I went to Jean's house, but no one was there. That seemed most unusual, for Jean's mother should have been there. I told myself I would spend the day looking around, visiting some old haunts, and come back late in the afternoon. I couldn't resist a visit to the old camp.

* * *

At noon I ventured over to the Paris Café, had lunch and a nice visit with the owner. He remembered John and me coming by so much and he said John had also been by to visit just recently.

Around dinnertime I went back to Jean's home and knocked on the front door. There was still no answer. It looked like they must have been on a holiday or maybe had even moved. Dejected, I walked back to town. My good mood was beginning to sour.

I walked around for a while trying to decide how to spend my evening. It looked like unfinished business would remain that way. There was a pub across from the Red Cross Club, so I wandered in there. Taking a seat at the bar I ordered a beer. I still didn't care a lot for the stuff but I had to order something if I was going to sit there. I felt perplexed. I had seen Nottingham and didn't want to spend the rest of the day walking around. If I had wanted to sightsee I could have gone to Switzerland.

I sat there taking little sips from my beer when a girl came over and sat down on the stool next to me.

"Hi Yank," she said.

I looked her way. "Hello," I replied.

She wasn't my type, not like Jean at all. I started to think that maybe Jean being gone was for the best. After all, I only had a short week away from duty and only three nights to spend in Nottingham. *What am I going to do? Look her up and tell her I was going home?* She likely knew that. I believe I just wanted her to know I was alive, that I had survived. But it could be argued that it was best she didn't know.

The girl next to me said, "Pardon me, Yank, but do you know a trooper by the name of Joe Trubor?"

I smiled at her. "Has anyone ever told you that you shouldn't refer to a Texan as Yank?"

She laughed and shook her head. "Oh, that's funny. So you're from Texas—smashing."

"I'm just teasing. What was your friend's name?"

"Joe Trubor. Do you know him?"

"No, I don't think I do. Do you know what unit he's in?"

"No, I don't," she said. "Headquarters maybe, or someplace like that. He wears two Airborne A's on his shoulder like you do."

I nodded and explained that double A stood for "All American." I refrained from mentioning it was a divisional patch or sharing just how many thousand soldiers were in a division.

She continued, "I haven't heard from him since he left for Holland and I don't know if he's dead or alive."

Poor kid. But on the other hand I had the exact opposite problem. The paratrooper had returned but the English girl was missing. I pondered the question of which was best.

"Can I buy you another beer?" I asked.

"Sure, I guess so. I'll have the ale." As she answered she put out her hand to shake. "My name is Kathleen." It seemed like a very American gesture. She didn't extend me her hand gracefully, like I expected young English ladies to do. Her hand was put out there as if to seal a business deal.

"Hi Kathleen, I'm Dwayne. I'm here for a few days furlough."

We sat and small-talked for a while and drank the English brews. I told her I had a sister named Kathleen and we discussed family a bit. She was rough in a sporty kind of way, very frank and open. I liked talking to her well enough. She was a different kind of girl and of course I loved hearing the English accent again.

"It sure is dead in here tonight. I think I'll go over to the Nags Head. Would you like to come along, Dwayne?"

"Sure, why not. I'd love it." But I went only because it was better than sitting alone. I was still in a down mood.

It wasn't far away, and we took about ten minutes to walk there. We sure found out where all the people were. We could hardly get in the front door. She led the way like it was home, and we pushed and shoved our way to the bar. The crowd in there was really happy, everyone was singing at the top of their voices. We got two beers from the bar and slowly started working our way around the room, hopeful for a table, but pleased to find floor space next to five GIs from a different regiment. There was a British soldier with them.

Kathleen and I stood trying to talk over the noise while sipping our beers. I tried to be friendly but I wasn't nearly as jovial as the rest of the room and didn't pay much attention to what was going on, except that the Brit soldier next to us was being rather loud. I think he was trying to be funny, wanted to show off to the GIs he was with and kept hollering to be heard. At one point he turned to Kathleen and in his blowing voice said something about her shape.

That got my attention.

I looked at him and the GIs. The Americans took notice of my glance, as their English counterpart continued to say something about what he would do if he had Kathleen alone in bed. With my disposition being as it was, that was all I needed to hear. I went after him. I didn't know what kind of girl Kathleen was, but in Fort Worth we have much better manners towards our womenfolk.

I had to step past Kathleen to get at him and she grabbed me by one arm as I walked by, trying to stop me. It didn't slow me down and I instantly set her aside, but before getting my first swing a GI stepped up to hold back what she couldn't.

I started screaming with all my strength at the Brit, "Hey you damn English bastard; where'd you learn your manners? I'm gonna take your head off."

I shook free of the first soldier and took another step. The British soldier seemed to see me for the first time and started stepping back. I reared back to land a punch but by then the other GIs all stepped in to restrain me. All the fear, sadness, anger and grief I had held back for the last year came boiling out. My face went flush. I was steamin' under the collar and ready to explode.

"Let me go you jerks!" I fought to free myself again. I broke loose from one, but another three still held on.

"Easy, Yank!" the English soldier said.

"I'm not a damn Yank! I'm from Texas, you stinking limey!" I was shouting so loud you could've heard me from the street.

The Brit tried to justify himself, "Well look, I'm drinking with your buddies so I'm joking with your buddies."

His remark made me madder still and I broke the grip of another American soldier and howled back, "You're not drinking with my buddies, because all of my buddies are dead!" ✓

There was a brief moment of intense staring, and then I suddenly went limp in the arms of the other Americans and Kathleen. Tears began streaming down my cheeks. I tried to look away to hide them and realized the whole room had gone quiet. Everyone there was staring at us. I looked back at the English soldier again but nobody said a word. There wasn't anything to say. We just stood there glaring at each other.

I didn't know if these guys had lost friends in battle or not. For all

I knew I was the only one in the room with combat experience. But in retrospect one thing stood out: the unexpected silence, generated in a normally noisy pub, was a moment of respect for everyone who had paid for peace in Europe with their life.

Kathleen broke the atmosphere. "Come on love, let's get out of here." And she pulled me towards the door.

* * *

The next morning, as I was having breakfast at the Red Cross, a young soldier came over to me. I didn't recognize him.

He addressed me rather politely, "Sergeant, could I have just one moment of your time?"

"Sure, okay." His gesture confused me.

The soldier continued, "I just want to tell you I'm sorry about last night. I think all the other guys feel the same way."

"That's alright," I assured him when I realized who he was. "I was just in a foul mood and what that Brit said hit me the wrong way. Any other time I would have let it fly on by. I didn't even know the girl, only met her about a half hour before."

"Well, anyway, I'm sorry it happened."

Sensing that his voice was genuine, I told him, "I'm sorry too, thanks for dropping by."

We shook hands on it and he said, "I'll see you around, Sir."

Most of that day was spent around the club writing letters home. At about five, I hopped on a double-decker bus and went to see some other friends of John and mine, Sheila Bull and her mother. I got off at the corner and walked up the street, but wasn't sure which house it was. I wasn't even sure I was on the right street. It had been more than a year since my last visit to them.

I walked back to the corner and was standing there viewing the cross streets when another red bus pulled up and Sheila got off. She was so surprised to see me standing there she could hardly say a word. She just threw her arms around me and cried.

"I didn't even know if you were alive! You should write a girl sometime."

"Well didn't John say anything?" I asked.

"He didn't know; he was here just two weeks ago but he didn't know if you had gotten through."

I said, "Sheila, he just wrote to me."

"Yes, I told him to," she explained, "but he didn't know if you were alive or not." Then she gave me a soft punch in the arm as a reprimand. "Come along now, you're having dinner with Mummy and me tonight."

The three of us had a fine meal together. I hoped it wasn't more than they could spare. We talked about the year before and about John going home.

After dinner I built a small fire for us in the fireplace and we sat talking right up until the last bus was due. I told Mrs. Bull goodbye but Sheila walked me to the corner bus stop. We didn't talk now. This was the last I would see of her. When we reached the corner Sheila took my hand in hers.

"I guess this is goodbye," she said.

"Yes, I hope to rotate home in the next month or two. It's been very nice knowing you and your mother. I'll never forget you." I watched a tear roll down her cheek. I added, "Don't cry. You never can tell—we may meet again someday."

We both saw the bus coming. She came to my arms and we kissed lightly in a sweet moment. I boarded the bus and it pulled away immediately. I looked back and waved and watched until the bus took the next corner and then she was gone from sight. I never saw her again, and I never saw Jean. Somehow I felt word of my visit might reach Jean. Of course, I could have written and don't know why I didn't.

* * *

Back in Frankfurt we killed time seeing the sights, using the riding stable and swimming in the pool. Sports became a big part of our lives and in September came football. Sunday afternoon games were something we all looked forward to. The Red Devils had an organized team in a newly formed Army league. We cheered them on to victory as they beat every team the Army could send against them and finished with an undefeated season. I'm sure General Eisenhower had to claim he was neutral but I'm also sure he was damned proud of the guards he had chosen to place around himself.

October came and along with it the orders for several of our guys;

the rotation back to America had begun. On the 20th we had a big anniversary. The 508th Parachute Infantry "Red Devils" Regiment turned three years old. The next day I turned 21. I was now old enough to vote.

A few days later Woody shipped out for the States. Ohio was his home. I wished him well, but there was going to be a void in F Company without him. John Hurst was gone as well.

When the November posting went up I found my name on the list as expected. The list named those men who would be transferred out of the 508th and into another regiment. It didn't really mean a lot. The 508th was my outfit and of course I would have preferred to go home with it, but there was no word when the Regiment might return. I was looking to go home the fastest way possible.

Most of the married men had already left; all the guys from Ireland were gone or were going on this trip unless they were staying with the Regiment. There just weren't any guys left who had made the Normandy jump. Besides, I had someone special waiting for me. Never consistent about letter writing, I now had the news of my rotation to share, so I got a letter out in the next mail bundle.

The final day arrived and several of us loaded a truck and traveled to a major rail station. By train we were sent to Berlin and attached to the 504th PIR, a good move since the 504th was a sister regiment within the All-American 82nd. They had fought with the 508th in Holland and during the Bulge. They were Airborne and I wanted to travel as a paratrooper, not as part of a tank division or some other group. I'm sure the guys fighting in tanks would feel the same if the roles were reversed.

My stay in Berlin was just long enough to see a few sights—the ones left standing anyway. From Berlin I found a new way to look at life. It was a very large city that our Allied planes had bombed out well. The ruins had displaced a lot of people, but it was the children that got to me. They stood, by the half dozen, around all the garbage cans begging for any of our leftover food. I quickly learned from the 504th guys to take all the food the cooks would offer, even if it was something I didn't like. The troopers ate only what they needed and we had plenty left over to give to the children, each one of whom held out two containers, one for food and the other for coffee or tea. By this method we made sure most of the little ones in our area got something to eat every day.

As the first snows began to fall that winter, the entire 504th Regiment boarded a train for the coast. The USS *Frostburg* ferried us across the ocean.

Going home had a strange sound to it. All my war experiences seemed suddenly surrealistic. I had seen 151 days of actual combat fighting. I'd watched a lot of men come and go, had made some close friends, and went the distance without encountering any problem. Out of the 140 company men who made the Normandy jump all were killed, wounded or captured, save one—I was left physically untouched. I hadn't taken even a scratch. Minerva must have been very good at praying and believing.

The voyage home was long, cold and somewhat barren as we sailed through waters that just a year earlier had been infested by lethal U-boats. Finally we came within sight of the States.

Outside New York harbor everyone went topside. The buildings of New York stood cold and silent in a wrap of light snow, but it sure looked good to me. During our out-processing they said it would be three days before most of us could move on, but a promise was made that everyone would be home inside of two weeks. I wrote Minerva and Mom one last letter, saying I was home—on American soil—and would be arriving soon. Three days after landing, many of us took a train ride to Tyler, Texas.

Out-processing required a painfully slow week before we were given our discharge papers. Then, on a beautiful, warm Sunday morning, five of us bunched into a cab and told the driver to take us to Dallas. It cost us $40.00 apiece—a fortune at the time—but it was worth it. The cabby drove 80 miles per hour with us yelling for him not to spare the horses.

I reached the Dallas Greyhound Bus Station two minutes before the bus rolled out for Fort Worth. From Fort Worth I took another cab to Lake Worth. The cab pulled up in front of the lake house and I got out. Before I could pay the driver, Mom and Dad came running out of the house. I visited with them in the warmth of their kitchen no more than thirty minutes before I asked Dad the question I'd wanted to ask when I paid the cab driver.

"Dad, can I borrow the car? I'd like to go get Minerva and bring her back for dinner."

He smiled and asked, "What took you so long?" He worked the car keys out of his pocket.

As I drove to Minerva's I kept pinching myself and saying, "It's for real, Dwayne. Believe it, the war is over. You're home." I had a really big grin on my face the whole way and I drove like an idiot—two years without driving, I had forgotten how—but I didn't care. As I pulled into the driveway at Minerva's, everything looked just the way I remembered it, like I had never been gone. I bounded up the steps, hoping and praying she was home. It was Sunday so she wouldn't be at work.

I knocked on the door, maybe too hard, and stepped back a bit. Someone unlocked the door and then it swung open. It was she. She was there. She was beautiful.

"Oh!" she greeted me. Her voice soft, she could say no more. We were in each other's arms.

Two years, seven months and 27 days after Army induction, I could close the book on one life and begin a new one.

Epilogue

It may have something to do with the greater good.

I made the most of being home. I wanted to just lounge around and I wanted to be everywhere and to see everybody all at the same time. I was smiling ear to ear everywhere I went. A lot of folks wanted to hear about the war, and I was polite and shared many stories, but I didn't really care to talk too much about it. I wanted to move ahead, not relive the past. Minerva and I started to make wedding plans. Mostly I just help set the date and then Minerva and her sisters made out the plans. Ed Mize happened to be home on leave from the Pacific, and I enjoyed a reunion with him for several days. I also spent a great deal of time catching up with John McGee. Just six weeks after my homecoming Minerva and I were married. We had selected the 23rd of February as in the 23rd Psalms; this was almost spiritual. It was a big formal wedding with Minerva's three sisters as bride's maids. Her brother, the minister, performed our ceremony. Ed had to return overseas to his Naval duties and could not attend or I'd have made him my best man but since I was getting married in my army dress uniform it was real fitting that paratrooper buddy McGee take that role and wear his as well at my side.

We had a weeklong honeymoon in Monterrey, Mexico, and then we settled into a little two-story house on Lake Worth. I even bought a '41 Packard like I had dreamed about when swapping stories with the boys after the Bulge was won. Happiness alone cannot describe how Minerva and I felt. All that we talked about, dreamed about and had waited to have for almost three years was becoming ours. She had said to believe but I couldn't have believed in this much.

Indeed our fate would not let this happiness last. Just eight days

before our first wedding anniversary, we were on the lake with my
father in his big inboard speedboat. Tragedy struck almost instantly as
the boat overturned during a sharp turn within sight of the dock. We
all hit the cold February water wearing our heavy winter clothes. I
took a bump on the head when the boat flipped and I came up dazed.
I was foggy during the whole ordeal and I couldn't swim anyway.
From witnesses' accounts Minerva had been thrown a ways and was
separated from dad and me. A fast thinking Bill Gunter left his dock
and came to our aid. He called over to Minerva and she told him, "Get
them out, I'll be alright." Then Minerva slipped beneath the surface
and drowned. In my stupor I didn't even know what was happening.
My angel, who had believed in us and had prayed for my return, once
again made sure that the good Lord was there to reach out and save
me from the hands of death.

Some pains never heal and memories both good and bad will
always be with me. In time I met and married another young woman,
Mildred, and I stand amazed at the life I was granted with her. To
complete my dream I did return to the aircraft industry, putting in my
life's work as a draftsman engineer with Bell Helicopter. Mildred and
I raised two sons and two daughters, born in that order. During the
1960's I earned my pilot rating in both sailplanes and single engine aircraft. I don't know the reasons how such sadness can coexist with such
wonderful pleasure; it may have something to do with the greater
good. Not unlike a justified war where soldiers are sacrificed for the
betterment of the world. I have a strong belief God has a plan and if
my life has been a part of it then that's alright. I can bear it and I look
forward to one day learning any answers that there may be to gain.

THOSE WHO MUST NOT BE FORGOTTEN

F-Company soldiers who never returned from their jump into the Valley of The Shadow.

Alva, Fidel	Pvt	9/18/44	
Apodaca, Juan O	Pvt	10/19/44	
Baker, Sherman L.	Pvt	7/6/44	
Bennett, Frank A.	Pvt	6/8/44	
Billington, Orren W.	Pfc	6/6/44	
Brightman, Gerald	Pfc	9/19/44	
Cabic, James F.	Pvt	10/2/44	
Chipman, Roy	Pvt	7/6/44	
Clegg, Robert F.	Pfc	12/26/44	
Colaw, Richard P.	Sgt	9/17/44	
Cook, Mack G.	2/Lt	7/4/44	Silver Star
Dennison, Ross	Pvt	9/17/44	
Ensminger, Joseph D. Jr.	Pvt	1/27/45	
Everitt, Edward M.	Pvt	9/18/44	
Fabuz, Raymond F.	Pfc	6/6/44	
Flanders, Francis E.	Capt	6/6/44	
George, John W.	Pfc	11/14/44	
Gillespie, Fred E.	1/Lt	6/6/44	
Goodale, Hoyt T.	1/Lt	1/29/45	Silver Star
Hare, Gene T	Pvt	6/17/44	
Harrold, Joseph	Sgt	7/4/44	
Haste, William K.	Pvt	6/7/44	
Hernandez, Joe F.	Sgt	9/18/44	Silver Star
Hiner, Harold K.	T/5	1/2/45	
Jatros, George	1/Lt	9/29/44	
Kellogg, Rankin B.	T/5	9/21/44	
Kellum, Jessie M.	Cpl	6/6/44	
Kincaid, Glenn E	Pfc	6/13/44	
King, Edward	1/Lt	9/21/44	
King, Ernest J.	Cpl	6/9/44	
Kulwicki, Richard J.	Pvt	6/13/44	
Lapham, Orville W.	Pvt	6/9/44	

Lazzaro, Joseph C.	S/Sgt	6/15/44
Le Boeuf, Jean B.	T/5	12/31/44 (Co. F & A)
Lilly, Gordon M.	Sgt	6/6/44
Lockwood, William	Pvt	6/7/44
Miller, David P.	Pvt	7/3/44
Murray, James J	Pfc	6/16/44
Nash, Thomas W.	Pfc	6/6/44
Nelson, Lawrence V	Sgt	1/30/45
Niemiec, Francis. E	Pvt	6/12/44
Nulty, John W	Pvt	1/10/45
Piatt, William A.	Pvt	6/6/44
Polette, Lloyd L. Jr.	1/Lt	1/22/45 (Co. F & E; Distinguished Service Cross & Silver Star with Oak Leaf Cluster)
Prieto, Ramon V.	Pvt	6/6/44
Richey, George L.	Pvt	9/23/44
Rickard, Patrick J.	Pfc	9/19/44
Rogan, Charles J.	Pfc	9/20/44
Sedam, Wendell E.	Pvt	12/29/44
Siniari, Lambert C.	Pvt	9/23/44
Sobezyk, Adam F.	Pvt	6/17/44
Spivey, Rex W	Sgt	9/19/44
Sprague, Edgar P. Jr.	Pvt	9/18/44
Sprinkle, Jack L.	Pvt	7/5/44
Stauffer, James B.	Pvt	7/6/44
Thomas, Vernon	1/Lt	12/25/44 (Co. F & H)
Ward, Glenn H.	Pvt	1/30/45
Wilson, Donald A.	Pvt	9/20/44
Wolcott, Jack F.	Pvt	9/18/44
Yoon, Donald	Pfc	7/3/44

The authors deeply apologize for any errors or omissions.

Notes

[i] One day before, May 10, the 82nd "All Americans" landed at Casablanca and became the first American airborne division to land overseas.

[ii] The head of OVERLORD's air operation, codenamed NEPTUNE, was RAF Air Marshall Sir Trafford Mallory. After reviewing losses and problems of troop carrier and airborne actions in Crete and Sicily, Mallory grew very apprehensive about casualties and encouraged Eisenhower to cancel Neptune. He figured as many as 75% of the gliders and 50% of the transports would be shot down before reaching the landing points. Rather than slaughter two fine American divisions in the air, the troops could be delivered on the beaches as elite infantry. It was Omar Bradley, former commander of the 82nd All Americans, who insisted that without an assault by Airborne, the beaches would be lost.

[iii] Prior to the U.S. military buildup during WWI, Army divisions tended to be very regional in nature, the troops drawn from neighboring areas or states. The 82nd was built up with men from every state in the union, the first to do so, and in 1918 took the nickname "All American" division. After WWI the 82nd was disbanded. Reactivation occurred in March of 1942 and its commander was Brig. General Omar N. Bradley. When Bradley was ordered to the 28th Infantry in June of 1942, the 82nd was passed to his deputy, Brig. General Matthew B. Ridgeway. Two months later Ridgeway began turning the division into an airborne unit. Today the 82nd continues as America's only active division of paratroopers.

[iv] Failure to slow down was usually the result of aircrews having their hands full or just plain forgetting under the heat of battle. As aircrews became experienced the problem diminished greatly. The 82nd Airborne Division was carried into Normandy by six air groups of General Hal Clark's 52nd Air Wing. These were the 61st, 313th, 314th, 315th, 316th and the 442nd. Of the six groups, only the 313th and 314th had experience in combat. The

61st and 316th were green but were considered suitably trained. The 315th and the temporarily attached 442nd, however, were units so fresh they couldn't take part in earlier practice jumps because they had to concentrate on the basics: formations, night flying and navigation to overcome wind and poor visibility. Based on the number of inexperienced pilots flying, many historians grade the aircrews' mission as very favorable. 98% of the transports flying into Normandy returned safely, thus proving Mallory's predictions of 50% loss to be wrong.

[v] General Gavin was widely known by the nickname "Slim-Jim," which his peers and the press used. The name "Jumping Jim" was used by many of the enlisted troops under his command. It was a name of respect. Gavin had gone through jump school and made the required five training jumps. Later it was determined a single combat jump was worthy of the honor of donning the coveted silver wings. Several of the higher-ranking Airborne officers, who had skipped the rigorous training at Fort Benning, earned their wings with a single jump. Other untrained airborne officers rode into combat by glider.

[vi] Drop zone N, designated for all of the 508th, was located on the west side of the Merderet River about equal distance from the La Fiere and Chef-du-Pont bridges. From the DZ the regiment would fan out and hold the south-western sector of the 82nd Division's assigned area. The 508th's missions included the capture and securing of the La Fiere and Chef-du-Pont bridges that crossed over the Douve and Merderet Rivers.

[vii] There were nineteen planes of pathfinders for both the 101st and 82nd Divisions. The pathfinders were to land at 0015 hours. The 101st Airborne, scheduled to jump at 0045, used 433 planes carrying paratroopers and 52 planes towing gliders. Members of the 82nd Airborne, traveling by a slightly different route, jumped at 0115 and used 369 planes for the paratroopers and another 52 as glider tows. At 0415 another 37 towed gliders were planned for landing in the 82nd area. Overall, the pathfinder missions were not very successful.

[viii] Of the 2,056 regimental members, only 124 Red Devils, seven plane-loads of paratroopers, made it to drop zone N.

[ix] Some history accounts depict only the 101st Airborne with toy crickets while the 82nd paratroopers used the password "Flash" and countersign "Thunder." While most of the 82nd may have been limited to word identification, the 508th at least was issued snappers.

[x] Unknown to Allied Intelligence, Picauville was the new command post of

General Wilhelm Falley, commander of the 91st German Infantry, a division of first-class troops. While rushing back to Picauville on D-day, General Falley's staff car was ambushed and the general was killed by members of the 508th's 3rd Battalion.

xi In his autobiography General Gavin gives extremely high praise to all paratroopers who fought west of the Merderet River.

xii The reporter was most likely William Welton who reported for TIME magazine. Mr. Welton had been traveling in the shadow of General Gavin and made combat jumps into southern Europe and Normandy. A photographer for LIFE was also in the 82nd Airborne area. Robert Landry had gone in with American troops over the beaches and stationed himself at Ste. Mere-Eglise.

xiii General Ridgeway's rules of combat for paratrooper divisions implied the 82nd should have been withdrawn to England by this time to refit and train for the next airborne mission. Heavy power strikes across the ground were the business of conventional divisions, which carried heavy armor and artillery. The light packing, fast moving paratroopers had none. But seeing an effectiveness in the Airborne, General J. Lawton Collins, Commander of the VII Corps, prevailed on General Omar Bradley to let him keep the 82nd. Bradley agreed and Ridgeway did not argue the order. Collins also retained the 101st Airborne, which served occupational duties on the Cherbourg Peninsula.

xiv From the pages of TIME magazine; June 26, 1944:

"Battle weary but still pushing on, the 82nd made a daring crossing of the Douve River. By nightfall Thursday, its general had his command post at a turreted chateau overlooking St. Sauveur-le-Vicomte. In the morning the general personally reconnoitered the frail sagging bridge leading into the crumbling, burning village and decided it would do. The 82nd marched in."

xv Before the Hill 95 attack, Lindquist, commander of the 508th, and Lt. Colonel Edwin Raff, promoted during Normandy to commander of the 507th, protested another offensive. They felt further action would decimate their regiments to the point they could not be reconstituted. They complained first to General Gavin. Gavin may have considered Lindquist a little green, not quite battle-proven, but they were friends from jump school. Raff however had led the 509th brigade, which won many honors in North Africa. Raff's comment was, "If we attack any more we won't have a cadre to make a regiment when we get back to England." These protests reached General Matt Ridgeway, Commander of the 82nd, who later wrote that the arguments made within the division had merit. However Ridgeway's final decision was to make Hill 95 the final attack despite the disapproval of some senior officers.

xvi Polette had also landed and fought west of the Merident River on D-Day and was one of the 200 plus men who held out with Shantley. His injury occurred there, as did the start of his reputation with the men in the 508th.

xvii The attacks on the hill confirmed Lindquist and Raff's fears that another battle was one more too many. Two of the 508th's best officers fell wounded in the battle. On the first day 2nd Battalion commander Shanley tripped over a booby trap and took several pieces of shrapnel. The regiment's Exec, Major Mark Alexander took charge but was hit by a German mortar the next day. Graham's command was short lived. The battalion was building up large losses in its current position and Graham believed there was a better way up the hill. He started pulling men back. Lindquist did not agree with giving up position and Graham was replaced with Otho E. Holmes who commanded the 2nd Battalion thereafter. Shanley rejoined the regiment in England and became the executive officer. Alexander never fully recovered but did hold down staff duties with the 82nd later in the war. Losses to the 507th on Hill 95 were even greater.

xviii Clay Blair wrote in *Ridgeway's Paratroopers*, "The 82nd Airborne Division, officially relieved of combat duties on July 8 after thirty-three days in action, became the stuff of instant legend. Its record in Normandy may well have been the most remarkable of any division in Army history." General Ridgeway summarized the Division's actions after the campaign in a brief statement to his superiors. "No ground gained was ever relinquished and no advance ever halted except on the orders of Corps or Army." This statement is now famous as the 82nd Airborne slogan.

xix Major Bill Lee later became a general and the first commanding officer of the 101 Airborne Division. Today he is remembered and recognized as the "Father of the U.S. Airborne Forces."

xx Ridgeway deemed practice jumps vital. Before Normandy the 505th had not jumped in six months, the 508th had not jumped in eight. The troop carriers needed the experience but the practice times were difficult to work out. The planes and pilots were carrying supplies into the European mainland to support ground troops. Daylight hours were short and the usual foul weather prevented safe close-flying formations.

xxi General Omar Bradley thought his ground soldiers were having such good luck in battle that he wanted to continue using the transport aircraft to bring in fuel and supplies. When the planes were withdrawn to support the airdrop, Bradley ordered Patton to charge ahead and take the planned objective first.

xxii After Normandy and before Market-Garden the top generals had considered no less than eighteen separate airborne plans. Several were in support of Patton. Only Choker progressed to the point of "sealing in" the 82nd. Military historian Charles B. MacDonald claims that "the paratroopers in England had become like coins burning holes in SHAEF's pocket. But SHAEF was refusing to use them just anywhere, they were looking around. . . . a sweet reward was wanted in return."

xxiii Martin was wounded in Normandy on D-day.

xxiv By this point in the war, little of the German Air Force remained to fight, but there was still enough to do terrible damage had the troop carriers been unescorted. A number of B-17 bombers with escorts had preceded the sky train of C-47s to bomb the flak installations. The minimal resulting hits were attributed to the bomber crews being unaccustomed to flying at the predesignated one thousand feet using a low air speed. General Ridgeway also rode in a B-17. Not directly involved in the Market-Garden mission, the former 82nd Commander watched the division drop from two thousand feet above.

xxv Roughly timed to start at the same moment as the parachute jumps were the British ground forces pushing in from Neerpelt. These forces were spearheaded by General Brian Horrocks' XXX Corp.

xxvi The 504th P.I.R. had been a major part of the 82nd Division throughout the southern European campaigns. It served occupation duties in Italy while the rest of the division transferred to England. Its delayed transfer came too late for the Regiment to partake in D-day. During the creation of the First Airborne Army, Gavin made room for the 504th within the 82nd Division by convincing Ridgeway to shift the 507th P.I.R. to the newly forming 17th Airborne Division, thus giving it a battle proven regiment.

xxvii The 82nd's prime objectives were the two main bridges (one railroad) over the Waal, but Gavin and General Roy Browning agreed to accomplish all secondary objectives first: the smaller canal bridges in the southern end of the sector. As the operation started Gavin deemed it favorable to seize the main bridges concurrently with the secondary bridges. The 508th's 1st Battalion got the call to give it a try.

xxviii The 1st Battalion was led into town by someone thought to be a member of the Dutch underground. The action of this person is often viewed as the work of a double agent. He left only moments before the battalion began to battle the 10th SS Panzer troops in a house-to-house fight. Most Red Devils there believed the underground member was killed while scouting ahead. The mission failed. It has been widely reported a platoon did reach and blow up the post office suspected of housing the detonator for the bridge. Eyewitnesses mentioned in Zig Boroughs' *The Devil's Tale* claim the detonator was in the Belvedere Tower where they planted charges and lit a fire. In the following days it was questioned if there was a detonator. Regarding the failure to take the bridge, Gavin blamed himself because the 508th "had many assignments and too broad a front to cover." Joe Atkins is another trooper reported to have reached the bridge. He led a three man patrol there while still daylight, but left when too many Germans started showing up.

[xxix] Before dawn Lt. Polette led an F Company platoon on a divisional mission to take a railroad and highway bridge spanning the Maas-Waal canal. This set of side-by-side bridges, known as Bridge 10, stood well defended by many Germans supported with mortars and machine guns. Realizing during the fight that the Germans were setting explosive charges, Polette spurred the platoon on. The railroad bridge was blown but the men from F Company routed out the enemy and saved the highway bridge. For leadership and personal courage Lt. Lloyd Polette was awarded the Distinguished Service Cross.

[xxx] This was a nickname for American paratroopers based on the diary of a German officer. He wrote: "American parachutists—devils in baggy pants are less than 100 meters from my outpost line. I can't sleep . . . they pop up from nowhere and we never know when or how they will strike next. Seems like the black-hearted devils are everywhere." This officer, with his diary, was captured in the battle for Anzio by the 504 P.I.R.

[xxxi] In the official history of the 508th P.I.R., F Company receives credit as fighting the battle inside the town of Beek. Paratroopers of the 3rd Battalion will proudly insist it was their objective and it was a bloody one at that. Gavin recalls visiting Lindquist and the 3rd Battalion in Beek who were at the edge of being overrun by the enemy. Gavin recounts he could give them only encouragement. He had just sent his only reserves, 300 quickly organized glider pilots, to the 505th in the south. Since Captain Martin was not with F Company at this time, it could be surmised the captain was with Lindquist in Beek and perhaps even had a F Company platoon or squad with him to help do battle. Unknown at the time, the Holland-German border ran between Beek and Wyler, making men of the 508th the first Allied soldiers to fight on German soil. This fact could

account for why the Germans kept counterattacking after losing the towns. They were trying to hold on to their country.

xxxii The 508th retained chaplains but they were usually busy dealing with the wounded and assisting the medics. In turn, when the chaplains had a chance to hold a worship or mass, the medics would assist them. It wasn't unusual for a religious service to include prisoners of war.

xxxiii Over dinner in a Paris restaurant, one staff officer from SHAEF mentioned to another that those 82nd Division paratroopers were the smartest, most alert looking soldiers he had ever seen. The other replied, "Hell man, they ought to be, you're looking at the survivors."

xxxiv On July 9, Col. James Gavin, commander of the 505th Parachute Infantry Regiment led his unit and certain support groups of the 504th P.I.R. into jumps over Sicily.

xxxv One week before Col. James Gavin was promoted to the rank of general and made the Assistant Division Commander to General Ridgeway within the 82nd Airborne.

xxxvi A design project of Lt. Yarborough was the two-piece jump uniform that is best noted for the two extra large pockets on the trouser legs. A parachute harness made the pockets of normal fatigues unusable. The creative Yarborough was also the designer of the paratrooper wings. In later years this jump-qualified officer became the creator and commander of the Green Berets, now known as Special Forces, where he used several of his Airborne ideas when he personally designed the Berets' uniforms. All Special Forces members are jump-qualified. Yarborough rose to the rank of Major General.

xxxvii Major Lee took the concept of the thirty-four-foot towers right out of a German parachute-training handbook. Used with the tower were twenty-two-foot harnesses, which gave the students a considerable freefall before their harness went taunt against a steel cable allowing the jumper to slide at a slope the remaining twelve feet. This training device caused more dropouts than anything else in paratrooper school. By comparison, dropouts on the two-hundred-fifty-foot towers were hardly accountable, due in part to the fact that once a trainee reached the top there was no walking down. Another jump and slide tower in use today has the same dropout reputation of its original thirty-four-foot predecessor.

xxxviii This was also taken from the German handbook. It was considered a conditioning tool. American cadre questioned the value of the training device, of which only one was built, and it was disassembled after only a few months of use. Yet within those months passed the bulk of airborne troopers serving in WWII.

[xxxix] In November lead elements of the 82nd Airborne began transferring to Great Britain.

[xl] Despite knowing that the Germans used the Ardennes and Eifel mountain routes to conquer France in 1940, the Allies agreed it was very unlikely any attack would come that way again. In fact the area was so tranquil and quiet it was used as a "break-in" ground for green troops from the U.S. and a rest area for both sides.

[xli] Gavin also had grown concerned that the luck of his division had been used up. The soldiers who landed in North Africa had four combat jumps, which Gavin decided was enough to rotate home. Eisenhower himself ordered the 82nd and 101st Airborne Divisions to move in the direction of Bastogne. General Gavin was called by the XVIII Airborne Corps' Chief of Staff Colonel Ralph "Doc" Eaton just prior to dinner. General Ridgeway was in England and the second ranking officer in the corps, General Taylor of the 101st, was in Washington. Gavin was told he was in temporary command of the XVIII Airborne and to have the two American divisions ready by first light on the 19th. About 8:00 p.m. on the 17th Gavin had his staff pulled together for a briefing and planning session.

During the briefing Colonel Eaton called a second time. The divisions were needed as soon as possible and Gavin was to report immediately to General Courtney Hodges at First Army Headquarters. Gavin then moved the 82nd's deployment up by a full day. He ordered the 101st to come when they were ready.

[xlii] The 101st was closer to Werbomont, but since the 82nd was first on the road Gavin ordered them there instead. Following six to eight hours behind, the 101st took the 82nd's original destination of Bastogne.

[xliii] There is evidence many German soldiers who fought in the drive for Antwerp had beforehand been reminded of the countless German victims, many of them women and children, who had died in terror during one of the many Allied bombing raids, thus raising them to an emotional state where they were more likely to murder. While few German officers actually ordered prisoners shot, they did admit their orders implied that "prisoners of war must be shot where the local conditions of combat should require it." One company commander went on record saying to his men, "I am not giving you orders to shoot prisoners of war, but you are all well trained SS soldiers." Other well documented cases include Honsfeld, where Americans pulled from their bedrolls in a 4:30 a.m. attack were lined up in a street and

shot in their underwear; and also Baugnez where approximately 130 sur-⎫
rendering soldiers were marched to a field south of town and then fired ⎪
upon from the machine guns of two tanks for 15 minutes until all moving ⎬
and crying ended. In the latter case 43 men played dead and lived to tell the ⎪
story.

xliv When the demolition team first hit the detonator, the bridge didn't blow
and Germans came across in limited numbers. Some armor also crossed but
the Germans were cautious because they expected the American paratroopers to blow the bridge. Faced with large numbers of tanks suddenly
pouring past the lines, a mixed group of 1st Battalion members counter-
attacked the bridge to reset new charges. It was suspected the fast moving
water under the low wooden structure had shorted out the wires leading to
the first explosive charge.

xlv Gavin had thought of withdrawing on the 23rd but feared that breaking
the "No ground gained was ever relinquished" motto might affect morale.
The orders finally came from the higher command, General Monty
Montgomery, who wanted to "tidy up the line." The move may have helped
stop the Germans because the defensive line was reduced by fifty percent
and thus paratroopers were now twice as thick. The 508th's withdrawal
march covered about eight miles.

xlvi This was probably an attack by the 19th Panzer Grenadier Regiment
and there ensued a hard three-hour firefight by several companies of the
508th on Christmas Day. There was another attack repelled by the 504th
predawn on the 27th, but Gavin recalls they were "a poor division, not well
trained."

xlvii Authors Booth and Spencer in the book *Paratroopers* give the 82nd
most of the credit for the Allied victory in the Ardennes with this explanation.

"When the two divisions, the 101st and the 82nd, had first deployed, a spur
of the moment decision had sent the 101st to Bastogne, and there, cut off
and encircled, the Screaming Eagles became immortalized by the press as
the "Battling Bastards of Bastogne." The surrounded 101st became
America's heroes.

"Yet many students of the battle conclude that it was the tough and
unglamorous action of units like the 82nd at the shoulders of the break that
destroyed the German plan. Maps of the battle which show the Bulge reaching to the south have caused many to forget the Germans were trying to
push north. It was their failure to crack the northern shoulder that caused

the Germans to fail in their thrust for the Meuse bridges and Antwerp, forcing them southward. The northern shoulder was where the weight of Sepp Dietrich's Panzers was supposed to break through, and that was where the 82nd had met them. The significance of the part played by the 82nd was that Gavin's force, in an emergency, was thrown into a role for which it was in no way trained and equipped, with no armor, no effective tank defenses except captured Panzerfausts, and little artillery. The 82nd had withstood the assault of four of von Rundstedt's best divisions and had wrecked the northernmost and quickest German route to Antwerp. Gavin's paratroopers enjoyed few advantages in battle and were at a severe disadvantage against enemy Panzer divisions, yet they were consistently effective."

[xlviii] The 82nd Airborne Division had engaged the push of four German divisions; the 1st SS, 9th SS, 2nd SS, and units of the 62nd Volksgenadier. The 508th P.I.R. had fought off the 9th SS Division. On December 31st General Gavin wrote in his diary, "at present these airborne troopers of this division are making monkeys out of the Germans opposing them."

In the January 3rd counterattacks, paratrooper forces overran the 62nd Volksgrenadier and 9th SS Division. 400 prisoners including five battalion commanders were captured. After this attack the green 517th P.I.R., an independent regiment, joined the 82nd to increase its ranks.

[xlix] On March 1, 1945 Ridgeway received approval to reorganize the American Airborne forces. It was his idea that airborne divisions were to consist of only three regiments; two parachute and one glider. Each of the regiments would contain four battalions with four infantry units and one of light artillery. An additional battalion of artillery glider riders would be assigned to the division for the divisional commander's control. The 82nd was sitting fat with five full regiments. General Gavin would soon release the 508th under Roy Lindquist. The 517th, just acquired in January, would come under the Command of Rupert D. Graves. The 508th became an independent unit within the First Airborne Army. The 517th was sent to the 13th Airborne Division, bringing the division up to Ridgeway's recommended level of strength.

[l] The normal opening shock was estimated at five Gs but could vary depending on the size chute one jumped with, the amount of extra equipment one carried, and at what speed the plane was traveling.

[li] She carried a great amount of guilt with her for years thinking the jump, made for her sake, had caused the death of six fine young paratroopers and a C-47 aircrew. In 1953 Red Devil Stanley Kass, who served in Regimental Headquarters, had a chance encounter with the actress and was able to end

her grief with the truth.

[lii] Troop carriers brought in two airborne divisions, the American 17th and the British 6th. In this lift one regiment, the 513th, rode in the new C-46s which had a jump door on each side of the aircraft for quicker deployment. Unfortunately the C-46 lacked self-sealing fuel tanks and several of them exploded in the air. They were never considered for paratrooper missions again.

[liii] Major Roy E. Lindquist was a transfer from the new Airborne Command. He formed the unit from volunteers and put the troops through Basic Training as a regiment at Camp Blanding. Following Basic the regiment was sent one battalion at a time to Fort Benning.

508